CRUISING

A MANUAL FOR SMALL CRUISER SAILING

FOURTH EDITION

J. D. Sleightholme

ADLARD COLES
8 Grafton Street, London W1

Adlard Coles
William Collins Sons & Co. Ltd
8 Grafton Street, London W1X 3LA

First published in Great Britain by
Adlard Coles 1963
Second edition 1970
Reprinted 1971, 1972, 1974
Third edition 1977
Fourth edition 1986
Reprinted 1988, 1989

Distributed in the United States of America
by Sheridan House, Inc.

Copyright © J. D. Sleightholme 1963, 1970, 1977, 1986

British Library Cataloguing in Publication Data

Sleightholme, J. D.
Cruising: a manual for small cruiser
sailing.—4th ed.
1. Yachts and yachting
I. Title
797.1′24   GV813

ISBN 0-229-11772-4

Printed and bound in Great Britain by
Mackays of Chatham plc, Chatham, Kent

Contents

Contents

Introduction

This book takes a broad look at the techniques involved in sailing small modern family cruisers of between 20 and 30 feet. Because the subject is so wide I have missed out a lot of the fine detail generally found in introductory cruising books, and nowhere will you learn how to make a sheepshank, nor will I attempt to explain lines of magnetic force or the difference between altocumulus and stratus. Instead I have tried for an overall approach to cruising, the practicalities and the problems which arise from the fact that, whereas small sailing cruisers have become sturdier and much more efficient, we poor old human beings remain just as bumbling and fallible as we ever were.

I have assumed that the reader has sailed a dinghy and knows the rudiments of chartwork and boat handling. Practical common sense is the root of sailing and seamanship and I believe that provided a total beginner is practical, sensible and interested, he could be stuck aboard a boat and left to fathom it out for himself. I wouldn't advise it, but he'd get there, albeit via a few costly bumps – learning by trial and error. But then, sensible people rarely get into bad trouble; it is the impractical big-heads with a superficial smattering of knowledge – theory rather than practice – who fill the lifeboats.

The hallmark of a good seaman is the worry-free cruise, which doesn't mean that it is a dull one, but that judgements and decisions made have been sound ones. Inevitably there will have been alarms and stresses, but a wise skipper balances his own stamina and that of his crew against the performance of his boat, and reaches a fair compromise.

The sea is like a heavyweight boxer; weight-for-weight you can't hope to win, but weave a little, duck a bit, and you can survive. To be strictly accurate though, the *sea* is not the enemy; the *wind* is the enemy, for without wind the sea is asleep.

An apology. Through this book I have used 'he, him and his' unstintingly, but I do so only because I find it easier, and I hope women readers will bear with me. Nowadays 'people' sail boats and nobody knows better than I that navigation and boat handling are not male prerogatives . . . but please don't ask me to write about *seapersonship*.

JDS

v

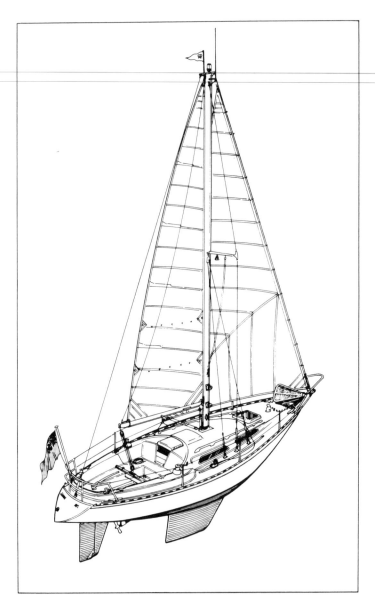

Fig. 1 The modern family cruiser with her moderate draft and fin and skeg rudder is designed for easy, positive handling under sail or power. She is roomy below without sacrificing a good hull shape and her cockpit, fully self-draining, is spacious enough to accommodate the whole crew without interfering with steering or the working of sheet winches. In many cases all halyards and even slab reefing lines are led aft and this arrangement combined with a roller headsail allows ninety per cent of sail handling to be carried out from the cockpit.

The relatively small mainsail with the deep second reef tied in is reduced in area to gale force proportions, although a separately rigged storm jib, independent of the roller headsail, is necessary to achieve a strong, efficient and well balanced sail plan for extremes of weather.

The anchor stows in a well forward leaving the foredeck quite uncluttered and at least one very large cockpit locker takes bulky gear such as warps, fenders and in some cases sail bags, thus leaving the forecabin clear of them. Such boats are well able to take bad weather in their stride, provided their crews are equal to the demands upon their experience and stamina.

CHAPTER ONE
The Small Cruiser

The Miniature Cruiser

There are some very mixed ideas about what constitutes a seagoing craft and for the newcomer it is all rather confusing. On the one hand there are boats of 20 feet and less making ocean passages and on the other these same boats may be labelled estuary cruisers. Because a few intrepid people do make such passages doesn't mean that a tiny boat is the ideal craft any more than a tightrope is necessarily the best way to cross Niagara Falls. It is wise to accept right from the beginning that cruises are made by boats and people – neither is any use without the other.

Ocean passages also are largely made with the aid of fair winds and in open waters, and while there are dangers in plenty from severe weather, the small yacht of around 20 feet meeting bad weather in the tide-wracked and turbulent waters of narrow seas, where a lee shore lies in wait a couple of hours' drifting time away, is usually in much more trouble. The strain on crew may also be greater, for they cannot afford to stop fighting. While a brilliant seaman can sail almost anything to almost anywhere, the weakness in a very small cruiser is that there is a great deal less reserve of strength, sail power and crew stamina.

Once at sea, and in general terms, bigger boats are easier on their crews than small ones. While a 40-footer in force 4–5 on the wind will be loping along at peak performance without much discomfort, a 30-footer is beginning to stagger, needing a sail reduction and making chartwork a bit difficult. A 20-footer, even well reefed, will be very bouncy going indeed, wet and exhausting, with chartwork becoming rudimentary. And this is only force 4–5, a good sailing breeze; how long can a 20-footer be kept going to windward in force 5–6? The problem of getting to windward in open water conditions of sea dominates much of the planning for her crew and even with the help of her engine, the incessant slamming and pounding, the wetness and the difficulty of trying to rest below, or navigate, or cook, make it a test of endurance.

Perhaps 50 per cent of the time in waters around the UK the wind will be forward of the beam simply because wind direction and strength are varying constantly; the American designer Dick Carter, when still unknown to the sailing world, came to compete in British offshore racing simply to get experience of windward sailing – which he did, in abundance. It is not so much the *boat* which is on trial, but her crew. If a small but sturdy and well rigged 20-footer could be radio controlled on a dead beat to windward she could probably be kept at it for days on end before some small thing went wrong and needed human attention. With a human crew driving her though, ten hours, maybe much less, of this punishment would reduce them to near exhaustion.

With a very small cruiser, then, it is not the distances covered in a rigid cruising plan that matter but the lure of leisurely wandering under sail, and there is as much fun to be found within a 50-mile radius of home as a bigger boat might provide in 500. For a beginner a thorough exploration of home waters within a 10-mile radius can be testing enough for the first season.

Having said all that – and maybe laboured the point a bit – the well designed miniature cruiser wisely sailed is safe enough on an open sea passage in all ordinary weather including the typical summer blow (the force 6–7 of short duration) and even the occasional gale, provided she is not caught in a situation where she will have to be beaten to windward for survival or where shallows or fast tides have raised seas of extreme roughness.

Oddly enough, the belief that such small boats are only suitable for estuary sailing and coasting is a bit misleading. Sea conditions can be much wilder in the mouth of a tidal estuary than they are further out to sea, and the safety implied by sailing close to land is often illusory. Coasts are as often as not fringed by offshore banks and reefs, currents run more strongly inshore and the rounding of headlands can be a major problem for a small boat crew. Neither is the presence of rivers and small harbours near at hand such a comfort as it might be, because in bad weather, attempts to seek shelter, maybe in driving rain and low visibility, can invite risks that would otherwise not exist. A boat is either *at sea* or *not at sea* and it is better to be right out in deep water than groping in and out of the rocks and sandbanks.

Passage time is another problem for the miniature cruiser; it usually takes her longer to get there than it would her bigger sisters, and I use the word 'usually' advisedly because some of these small craft are very fast indeed in moderate conditions. It is *average* speed that counts, though. If a 24–30-footer averages four knots on a passage she is going very nicely, but it still takes most of a day and a night to make an 80-mile passage, usually with more crew to keep watch and more comfort. A much smaller boat may average only three knots.

Plate 1 The Sadler 29, a typical fast yet comfortable modern cruiser. All cavities between outer hull and inner moulding are foam-filled to make the hull buoyant even if holed.

Hull and keel

The endless permutations in the basic boat shape produce a bewildering variety of hulls: beamy boats, narrow boats, round bilge, hard chine, straight stem, spoon bow, straight or raked transom stern, reverse raked transom, counter and canoe stern and so on – and on. It would be beyond the scope of this book to sort out the pros and cons of each, so let it suffice to say that the ultimate aim is for a stiff yet comfortable cruising boat which is handy yet not flighty, fast yet not wet in a seaway. Like all ultimate aims, however, most shots go well astray.

The choice of keel design alone is wide. The traditional long keel could run for half or three-quarters of the total hull length, as exemplified in the fishing smacks which needed to be steady working and sailing platforms. The long keeled yachts had a well raked back sternpost and a smooth upward sweep from keel to stem making them quicker on the helm for racing and manoeuvring. In time, keels became shorter until finally keel and rudder parted company and a fin and skeg form emerged.

Every keel type, from fixed to swing or lifting keel or twin keel, has a purpose and it is important to know what sort of sailing you plan to do when considering this keel design – out-and-out racing, long-distance passage making or shoal water cruising. The deep, narrow blade of the extreme fin keel with all its cruising disadvantages in terms of drying out and nosing into shallow waters should be weighed against the stout twin keels which are as much at home on land as on water.

A deep, narrow fin keel projects down into denser water and its ballast acts as a powerful righting lever, less weight being needed to do the same job as a stubbier ballast keel would achieve on the same hull, albeit a heavier keel. In times past the racing rating rules produced narrow slim-hipped hulls with very deep keels to make them stable and from this extreme there developed the classic curves of later breeds, with beamier and more powerful hull shapes removing the need for such veritable lead-mines deep below. These were still heavy displacement boats though, and perhaps it took the arrival of the budget, mass-produced boat to alter this tradition.

A substantial penny dropped. To make a boat stiff and to give her the keel area she needed for sailing she needed beam and keel depth, but you didn't need a vast area of immersed hull to achieve this. You could have a lightweight hull with a keel simply bolted to the bottom of it and the rudder could be carried on a separate mini-keel or skeg and also bolted on – or you could do without the skeg as well and let the rudder stick straight down on a powerful stainless steel tube.

This concept is the root of almost all popular modern designs and was made even more practicable by the advent of glass fibre. Resulting from this saving in weight (and costly materials), hulls became flatter

Plate 2 Pioneer, a 26-footer in either fin keel, drop keel or twin keel versions, a breed of cruiser aimed at self-contained comfort and convenience rather than speed.

floored, which meant that standing headroom below was also reduced and so designers simply increased the height of the topsides and cabin top. The sheer or dip in the deckline also vanished and today's boats are often downright ugly in the eyes of traditionally-minded people, but they are practical and they are efficient. This height of topsides, which would ordinarily suggest a boat impossible to handle under engine in windy harbour conditions because of the way she blew around like a paper bag, is offset by depth of rudder and keel. It is the high topsided, shallow draught boats which one must watch in this respect and it is only the current tendency to over-engine boats, to give them far more power than an auxiliary engine ever had in the past, that makes them practicable.

The development of the small diesel auxiliary engine is the second part of the modern metamorphosis in design and it has made possible another dramatic change – the coming of the yacht marina: a chicken-and-egg situation perhaps, since one isn't much use without the other. Once upon a time cruising yachts only entered harbour to berth against a dock or quay wall or to enter a dock, but these were unusual occasions which occurred only during a cruise. This being something of an event, the crews were very much on their toes; engines were less reliable and less powerful and things could go wrong.

Nowadays it is taken for granted that a skipper needs only to be told the berth number allocated and he (or she) will take the boat straight in without much fuss. Modern yachts under power are nimble and yet easily stopped by a powerful burst astern and most, being of the fin and skeg keel form, can be spun round in almost their own length. Only the remaining long keel boats, with their wider turning circle, present much of a problem. How easily a boat can be taken in and out of a marina under engine is of prime importance to a newcomer to cruising and if the boat is to be doing this often it is unwise for a beginner to buy a boat which is a problem to handle in tight spaces.

What sort of sailing?

The average busy sailing family may spend an average of 50–60 days aboard their boat in a season, including a two-week cruise and about three weekends out of every four. By far the greatest time will be spent at anchor or berthed; perhaps 80 per cent of the time spent under way will be cruising in local home waters, with the minimum of time at sea on passage and the least of all spent sailing at night. There are plenty of exceptions, of course. It depends upon other demands and interests; gardens and houses demand time, as do other hobbies. The exceptions are those who live in town flats and take off every Friday evening bound for the boat, returning late on Sunday.

It sounds dull, this gentle cruising, but it is far from it. There are adventures and problems enough in just deciding whether to sail or stay in harbour (a consequence of our erratic climate), and with children to consider and perhaps a less enthusiastic wife, a family skipper who forces the pace runs the risk of turning a pleasant and shared activity into a weekly ordeal.

All this affects the choice of a first boat. There may be pipe dreams of ocean cruising some day and it may seem sensible to look for the sort of boat that could be used for long-distance cruising in the first place, but this, in the case of a first boat, is usually a mistake. As experience is gained, ideas change, and the ultimate boat may be totally different from the original conception, not only in size but also in rig and type. You have to allow sailing to shape your ideas as you go along. It is better to graduate through a series of boats, beginning with a small but comfortable one which sails adequately and doesn't cripple her owners financially. If she is of a popular class there shouldn't be much problem in selling her in due course and moving up after a few years. The important thing is to buy a boat and learn all she has to teach you through modest voyaging within your capabilities. That many people plunge right in with a bigger boat than they can cope with and aspire to voyages that they are not yet ready for, perhaps all on the basis of boat-show euphoria and a crash course of instruction, is a pity because they miss so much of the real fun.

Shoal draught

In general terms a fixed or fin keel hull of around 4 ft draught allows good access to the upper reaches of most creeks and although it still excludes a boat from the very shallow reaches and the benefits of getting away from crowded deep water anchorages, it is a fair compromise between true shoal draught and offshore windward efficiency. The truth is, though, that with any form of fixed keel or keels we tend to navigate with a bit in hand – we don't take a draught of 4 ft into water which is only a fraction more than that, we regard 6 ft as the least depth necessary for staying properly afloat.

Beating hard to windward in a smart breeze and the sort of sea that goes with it will see a boat with a 4 ft draught holding up well, but making a great deal more leeway than a deeper draught would allow. You have to accept this in the light of the sort of sailing you want to do – if it is club racing and cruising in deeper water there is little advantage in going for shoal draught.

If all-out windward efficiency is not a target, though, deeper draught has less to commend it for general cruising than has moderate or shoal draught because even in deep water regions a shoal draught boat can be snugged further into the shelter of a bay, further up the shallow reaches

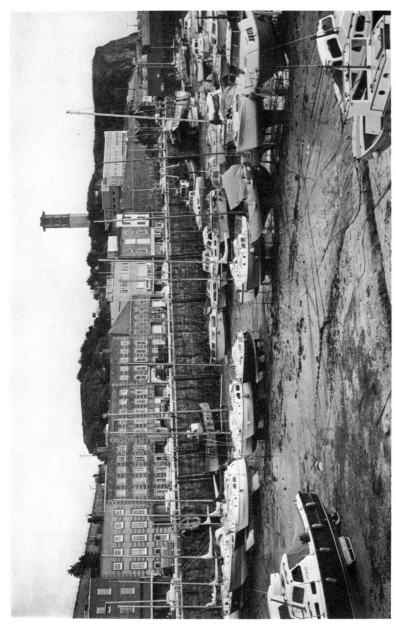

Plate 3 Drying out in Jersey Harbour. A mixture of twin keelers and conventional craft fitted with legs. All are moored fore and aft to a heavy ground chain.

of rivers, and if she can be dried out on twin keels, the many small and drying harbours can be used as well.

Twin keels

Very few owners of boats with twin keels seem to exploit the advantages fully. In today's crowded anchorages a twin-keeler can often be anchored on the shallow fringes shunned by deeper boats and if she touches at low water her crew are often not even aware of it. Provided the bottom is fairly level and not a miniature mud cliff, or bisected with gullies, or littered with rocks or stones, a boat will sit upright in fair comfort. There is the slight disadvantage that in muddy areas her crew may not be able to get ashore or aboard around low tide and the loo cannot be pumped to flush it, but one learns to plan around these things, limiting shore trips to the tide and hauling a bucket of water aboard in advance of the tide leaving the boat.

Ideally, keels should be well splayed out like a man standing with legs slightly apart and at least a proportion of ballast should be carried on each. They may even be very slightly set outwards to give a modicum of lift when heeled and sailing to windward, but I doubt if this really works. The splaying out is important in two ways. The boat is much more stable when dried out on her keels, particularly if she is beam-on to a sloping creek bed (Fig. 2), and also when heeling, one keel is almost vertical while the other is lifted to the maximum advantage as a righting lever. Conversely, narrowly spaced vertical keels make a boat unstable when dried out and lose efficiency when heeled under sail.

Fig. 2

Although twin keels are undoubtedly ideal for drying a boat out or for laying her up ashore, beaching for a scrub, etc., they are liable to be a problem when running aground by accident. If the boat is upright when she grounds and if she grounds hard there is then no way of reducing draught to get her off because unlike a conventional single keel boat, which can be heeled over further to reduce draught, heeling a twin keeler merely digs in one keel. If she is well heeled when she grounds, taking down sail to bring her upright and then motoring or kedging her off usually works – provided the skipper remembers that he has to do the opposite thing to his deep single keel peers.

Swing and lifting keels

The conventional, indeed traditional centreboard or centreplate is slotted through the ballast stub keel and hinged or rather pivoted at its forward bottom corner so that when fully raised it is contained in a watertight case within the hull. Simple systems of rope or wire tackle raise or lower the plate, which may be made of steel plate galvanised or wood, perhaps ballasted sufficiently to overcome its natural buoyancy. The case may either stick up bang in the middle of the saloon with the cabin table hiding it, or it may be of an 'L' shape with the vertical arm of the L moving in a box which is built into the side of a fore and aft bulkhead, acting as a lever for raising and lowering the horizontal part of the L. This arrangement is fairly unobtrusive down below. These plates don't have much effect as ballast, which is contained in the shallow stub keel, and unless the ballast in this keel is generous its lack of depth and therefore leverage makes for a tender rather than a stiff boat which in turn demands a hull form which has beam and firm bilges to provide initial stability. A narrow gutted centreboarder is likely to sail on her ear; she will be self-righting but not much of a sail carrier in stronger winds.

The modern 'swing-keel', however, is a ballast keel hinged like a centreplate or board and operated by hydraulics or low power gearing. Either way it is a fairly slow job to lift such a keel plate whereas the conventional centreplate can be yanked up within seconds – unless, that is, it has been refined by the fitting of a geared windlass which can be slow and dangerous if it runs amok. Hinged plates of any kind have the advantage of lifting themselves should the boat run aground while going ahead, a feature which was widely used as a warning of shallowing water before the advent of echo sounders. The ability to twitch a plate up or partly up is valuable in shoal waters since it means that upon running aground, just enough can be raised to allow the boat to be backed off or sailed off, perhaps without even losing headway.

The lifting keel on the other hand is what used to be called a dagger board, that is to say it lifts vertically instead of pivoting. It won't lift itself when running aground but the same advantage of being able to lift just enough to get off still remains. Its real asset is that the boat can (like the other lifting keel types) be anchored in very shallow water, and hauled onto a road trailer with little fuss. In all cases a lifting or pivoting rudder must be fitted.

Certainly the ballasted swing or lifting keels are more efficient to windward, but well designed traditional centreboard boats can also be efficient provided the ballast ratio is good. Twin keels are marginally less efficient on the wind than the fixed fin or the swing or lifting keel, perhaps pointing 5 degrees less close to the wind, perhaps overall to windward 10 per cent less efficient, and in rough following sea conditions liable to be harder on the helmsman. These figures are based upon trials between identical hulls fitted with various keel options. At other times and on other points of sailing it is often impossible for a casual observer to know what kind of keels are down below him as he sits at the helm.

Multihulls

The unfair publicity which has stuck to the multihull image, concerning the fact that it is possible to capsize them, has grown much out of proportion. A multi, especially a catamaran, is an ideal family cruiser offering space, an absence of heeling and the undoubted advantage of being able to put small children to bed early in one hull while the adults can relax in a roomy saloon on deck.

There is no good reason why a cruising multi should capsize. Racing craft which are finer, lighter and driven harder have been capsized and so have record-beating multis in extreme ocean sea conditions, but the cruising versions are built for great stability, at the expense of speed. In fact most of them are not particularly fast except on an occasional broad reach and they are often slower to windward than comparable sizes of keel yacht. Racing multis can be rendered unstable by overloading but the cruising designs can carry a vast amount of extra weight and remain absolutely safe. In fact the favourite argument in favour of multis, that they are unsinkable since they don't carry a huge iron ballast keel on their bottoms like conventional displacement yachts, remains valid even when fully loaded with stores and crew. Catamarans and trimarans can be beached on any smooth stretch of sandy shore for the benefit of bathing parties and they can be anchored in a few feet of water, or dried out on a mud bank in complete comfort. They sound, in fact, like the ideal family boat.

There are a few disadvantages. Handling under power in the confined waters of a marina can be a problem in windy weather; also, they are more difficult to manoeuvre into a marina berth – and costlier in marina charges too, since they occupy double the space of a conventional boat. Some cruising multis are slow in tacking and may well miss stays altogether especially in a short and choppy sea. Although they heel very little they tend to have a jerky motion which can be equally tiring at sea, and when at anchor in windy weather they have a greater tendency to sail around their anchors. Additionally there is the undoubted fact that although capsizing a cruising multi is improbable, it is not absolutely impossible, which means that leaving a novice in charge of the deck is risky in bad weather – but then, it would be unwise in any boat.

One thing, though, is very evident: while there are a great many people who simply don't fancy owning a multi, those who do become owners seem to become utterly and sometimes almost fanatically committed and thereafter want no other type of boat.

Moving up

A couple of feet of increase in overall length above 20–22 feet may not seem much but the effect on the general capacity of a boat is striking. A modern 24-footer will have standing headroom for an average man in at least one part of the accommodation, a fair measure of privacy, and of course a far greater passage-making potential. She will have a proper galley area and there is room for a small chart table. She will be able to sleep four adults in reasonable comfort which means that there is a safer reserve of crew strength and her motion at sea will be correspondingly easier. She is still quite a small boat though, and with four aboard plus their baggage and provisions life is still very cramped, which is perhaps why the popular modern family cruiser is closer to 30 ft overall.

The extra length means a roomier cockpit where crew can sit comfortably without crowding and work the sheets without falling all over the helmsman. Locker space, deck space and below-deck comfort increase spectacularly. The fore cabin becomes a cabin in its own right, providing the privacy for two couples, or a retreat where teenage kids can mutter rebellion against tyrannical parents, and there can be a toilet compartment with a separate door.

However, for a couple of people or a couple with small children, the 20-footer offers every bit as much fun on a more limited scale as her bigger sisters; berthing is much less expensive and if she is trailer-stored costs are even lower, although the advantages of trailing are not as exciting as they may seem.

Accommodation

There is a vast difference between room to sleep four and space in which four adults can live, particularly if there are people aboard who have

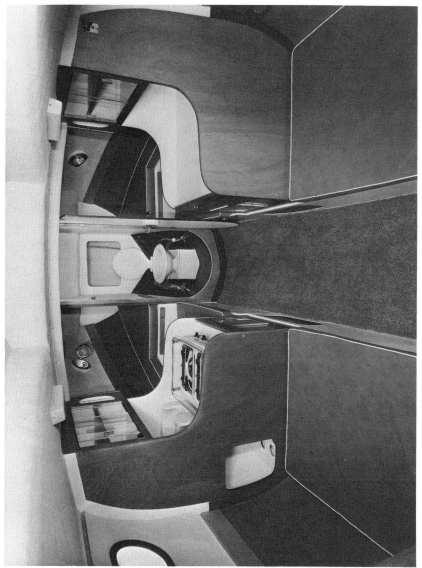

Plate 4 The interior of this Westerly Windrush typifies the open plan approach to design which had its vogue, but many prefer a two cabin layout at the expense of slight restriction of movement. (*Photo: J. A. Hewes AIIP, ARPS*)

13

never cruised before. Experienced crew have a knack of dodging and weaving around one another when all are below at the same time and hence there are fewer buttocks obstructing the access below. Unless all are young and impervious to close contact with others it is always safer to leave one berth empty if the cruise is going to extend longer than a weekend. This is even more vital if the boat has limited headroom because the human form bent double takes up one hell of a lot more space than when standing erect.

If everybody came aboard stark naked or at least with only the clothes they stood up in, living in cramped conditions would be no problem. But each person has a necessary bag filled with spare clothing and toiletries and each must have oilskins and maybe boots, all of which individually are relatively unobtrusive – until it is time for all hands to turn in for the night; the boat then becomes a jungle of possessions which have been turned out of the bunks to make way for the sleepers. Consequently, accessible stowage is a key part of good accommodation.

Few boats can offer this. Most have enough cubic footage of stowage space, but much of it is under the berths or in awkward lockers and so people tend to tire of rummaging about, and leave their belongings strewn around. Ideally, strict discipline would be imposed and a tidy ship would result, but this can be regarded as tyranny and be resented by newcomers to cruising and it is one of a skipper's duties to try to hit a fair compromise between chaos and naval orderliness.

Sleeping and sleeping comfort are often given scant attention by builders. In a family cruising boat which spends most of her time at anchor with short day sails in between, many hours will be spent sitting below, especially early and late in the sailing season, and settees which are slightly too high (to make room for tanks beneath them, perhaps), or which won't allow you to lean back without your head banging on a locker, can become a misery. Cost-conscious builders can also make the mattresses too thin (four inches for comfort) and this affects sleep as well. A hard bed may be good for you but it is murder on somebody who is used to a soft one.

A berth cannot afford to be shorter than 6 feet and 6 ft 2 in is the minimum for comfort – longer for a tall person. Width is usually around 22–23 inches although a narrow berth is better for use at sea as it limits hip-rolling. Most brochures make great play of the fact that one berth is convertible to a double, but these doubles are often far too chummy to permit much sleep. Berths up forr'd are often too narrow at the foot end to permit two adults much rest and it is one of these which is usually left vacant for loose gear. All berths must have some sort of side canvas or lee-board which can be set up really taut; not only is this essential for sleepers at sea, but the berths are the only safe places to stow loose gear when the boat is heeling and jumping around.

The accommodation tells much about the market which a builder is trying to attract and there are many small cruisers in which the boat is clearly designed around the accommodation, hull shape taking second place, and conversely others in which the accommodation is fitted into a hull designed for sailing efficiency, and creature comfort below is an afterthought. Once again it depends on the sort of sailing you want to go in for: if a portly little cruiser can waddle comfortably from port to port in safety there isn't much wrong with that, but her owner must not get impatient when other boats overtake him. Every vessel afloat has its purpose, from destroyer to river barge, from offshore racing yacht to family weekender, and the more we can stick with the purpose for which the boat was intended the more enjoyable, and the safer, the boat will be.

The general layout below, within a given size of boat, doesn't vary much and galley, chart table, toilet and so on can't be moved around very much within the confines of a small hull. It is no accident either that galley and chart table are close to the main companionway where fresh air is constant.

The amount of cooking that will be done while under way or at sea is usually minimal and the profusion of instant soups and foods makes galley work even less essential. At sea people need digestible, nourishing food and hot drinks of one sort or another at regular intervals, and unless the cook happens to have a cast-iron stomach, trying to cook more elaborate meals merely writes off one member of the crew from seasickness. It is not so much the heating of food that constitutes the problem at sea, as trying to prepare it when there is no safe place to put anything down for longer than a few seconds. The cooker can be the simplest of two-burners, but the putting-down arrangements need to be well thought out. They very seldom are, though.

A good sink is the first essential because mugs can be lodged in it while they are being filled (half-filled if you are wise) and there must be a safe place to put a hot pan when it is taken off the stove. A ladle is a curiously useful piece of equipment for serving hot soup in a seaway because it obviates the risk of trying to pour, and many people prefer a pressure cooker for similar safety reasons.

A fully gimballed cooker is perhaps the ultimate aim, but again very few are *fully* gimballed in production boats. If the boat gives an extra-violent lurch most of these semi-gimballed cookers come up against their stops with a bang and shoot any pans straight off the hotplate and the dangers won't need elaboration. Unless a cooker can be gimballed to at least 90 degrees it is better to leave them fixed and fit good high fiddles or pan clamps. High-sided pans must be provided so that they need only be half filled to allow for the angle of heel at sea.

A gash bin, a refuse container, is another essential on even the smallest boat for this is the age of packaging, tea-bags and general detritus, all of which the acting cook is lumbered with and being thus lumbered, will fast become exasperated. Nowadays too, people are concerned about litter thrown at random overboard.

A cutting board is an essential in a boat with glossy expanses of GRP galley – any scrap of plain wood will do – and ready-use lockers or fiddled shelves within arm's reach of the cook, but *not* behind the cooker, forcing him or her to reach over hot pans. Ideally there will be a crash-bar across the front of the cooker and a cook's belt at waist height, although these may not be practical in a very small boat.

A chart table of some kind is really mandatory in all boats whatever the size because the same rocks, shoals and complexities have to be dealt with by all navigators. It can be a plain board to be used on a settee or a proper fixed table, but it should not be smaller than a half-folded Admiralty chart. Navigation is taxing enough in choppy conditions without making it even more so and if a new boat is poorly equipped with a flimsy chart table her new owner must certainly do something about it.

People living in cramped conditions must learn to relax a few conventions and abandon a good many of their shore-side standards of creature comfort, but there are limits beyond which many of us are reluctant to go and the toilet arrangements in a small boat can at times be so primitive that they can cause real distress to shyer people.

The smaller boats often have a chemical toilet which has to be emptied regularly, in theory at a special place provided in yacht marinas, in fact, and more often than not, straight overboard when nobody is looking. The 'bucket-and-chuckit' system has been in force with miniature cruisers for generations but it is no more palatable for that. There may be no alternative and people sailing these smaller boats have to make the best of it, but while there are those of us frank enough to be able to sit on the can with only a plastic curtain separating us (but not our feet) from the rest of the cabin, there are others for whom it is a great and painful embarrassment. For a shy child it can be an agony.

The proliferation of yacht marinas with their toilet facilities does much to overcome the morning problem, but it remains with us when no marinas are to be found.

In blunt terms we are up against sound and odour and whether we have a bucket or a pump lavatory a plastic curtain remains a derisory form of privacy. If anything can be done to fit even a light plywood door it is usually worthwhile – unless of course the crew are all equally open about things. In slightly larger cruisers which have a proper built-in compartment the usual problem is bad ventilation, which can at least be improved by fitting a more efficient type, or indeed an extractor fan with the switch connected to the inside door bolt. Sound is another matter and because the hull of a boat is like the sounding box of a violin, acute embarrassment can arise.

Perhaps I am making rather a fuss about the subject, but if an assortment of people of all ages are to be able to live in a minute space without strain, it has to be considered. There are two strategies for overcoming the sound problem: one is to keep the ship's radio on continually for the first hour after rising and the second is for the skipper to make a regular practice of running the engine to charge the battery at a fixed time every morning when at anchor. The background racket of either alternative will be received with secret gratitude by the shyer members of the crew.

Buying

Boat hunting is fine fun and it is not until you are down to a short list of three boats that the agony of indecision begins; there is no chill of doubt so frosty as the moment of handing over your cheque. Buying a cruiser is for most people the biggest financial step of their lives, after buying a house, and for a beginner it can be a worrying time.

Assuming that he knows the sort of sailing he wants to do, and his financial restraints in terms of running a boat, and that he has therefore a pretty fair idea of the sort of boat needed, the actual choice of a particular boat, new or second-hand, calls for extra information not always readily available. An experienced yachtsman will have past experience of boats and perhaps some knowledge of the one he has decided to buy, or at least an eye for building quality. The beginner is strictly virginal in this respect.

If the chosen boat is new to the market the only guidance available will be the builder's brochure and the boat test reviews published in yachting magazines, since there will not yet be a field of existing owners to turn to for information. The builder's reputation with earlier designs offers some help but even reputable designers and builders can produce the occasional maverick. Yachting magazines try to publish honest and objective reports, but their editors are under severe pressure from their companies, via their advertisement departments, to publish flattering reports, or at least, not downright damning ones. One magazine of my experience does indeed put candour before all and it has teetered on the doorstep of the libel courts repeatedly. Usually, though, the policy is to say nothing or merely hint at a fault, unless it is a catastrophic one, in which case the policy is not to review the boat at all.

Quite often a brand new design will appear at a boat show without ever having been in the water, let alone thoroughly tested, and such prototypes can have design faults which will be remedied in later models; therefore it is always safer to wait until a trial sail can be arranged. Salesmen at shows may well argue that waiting for a trial sail may mean losing a few places in the queue of keen buyers and perhaps not taking delivery of a boat until the summer is half over. Buying at boat shows is entirely different from buying at other times because there is a sense of urgency and tension at shows. It is also very easy to go way over the price ceiling hitherto fixed, especially when buying on a mortgage loan – the extra thousand pounds for this or that becomes chicken feed.

Well established designs are easier to find out about. In any good cruising club there will be other members who have either owned or sailed in the boat being considered, or people who can at least offer shrewd judgements. *Yachting Monthly* magazine runs a readers' service called Second Opinion which puts would-be buyers of particular classes in touch with existing owners who have volunteered to talk about their boats.

Whether to buy new or second-hand is a prime decision to be made. Broadly speaking a second-hand boat will be completely ready for sea although inventories do vary, some having the bare essentials while others may be complete down to the first aid chest and the lifejackets. With a new boat, on the other hand, the inventory may be very sparse. With some boats sails may not be included, anchor sizes and length of cable will be the minimum that the builder can get away with, and warps and fenders likewise. A buyer has to do some very careful costing to see how much extra will have to be spent to bring a new boat up to scratch. He may, for instance, have to buy an inflatable dinghy, a VHF radio and perhaps a liferaft which will cost the better part of another two thousand pounds – and that is only the beginning. But the boat will be new, her engine will have no dark secrets and the equipment will also be new, whereas the second-hand boat with a dazzling inventory may sound better in the advertisement than she really is in fact.

Never buy a second-hand boat without a full survey. There are plenty of cases where a surveyor has failed to spot a vital fault, but there are far more cases in which a buyer has been saved from making the costliest mistake of his life. Neither does it always mean that the seller is dishonest; the owner may be shattered to find out that his boat has a serious fault. Any fault, of course, makes the asking price negotiable if these faults have to be rectified.

Financing the buying of a boat is another thorny path and the only general advice I can give is to shop around among the marine finance houses for quotations and then try your bank and any other finance house. Unless you are at home with finance you should then take the whole lot to a good accountant for advice. Very often it is the bank that can put the most attractive deal together.

CHAPTER TWO
Sail and Engine Power

I lump together sails and engine under one heading because nowadays the auxiliary engine is no longer regarded as a poor relation and people feel no shame attached to its use. Our boat may be a sailing craft, but in the busy shipping lanes and crowded harbours of today a reliable engine is perhaps the greatest saviour from maritime mistakes. Today it is the *passage* that matters; many owners will lay out a passage plan which is based upon being able to make good a particular average speed and when the wind falls light they use a touch of engine as a matter of course. This may rob the passage of much of its charm for some, but for others it is a professional way of looking at things.

The calculated use of an engine to manoeuvre out of tricky marine berths, to cross shipping channels and to counter a foul tide, or to enter an unknown harbour or river, is part and parcel of cruising in busy waters. Those lucky enough to be based in areas not much used by commercial shipping, where there are few harbours and many natural anchorages, can get untold pleasure from doing everything under sail, but to drift around at a knot and a half with fifty thousand tons of rushing steel breathing down your neck verges on the irresponsible. The happy compromise is to plan your passages as *sailing* passages, using the engine when necessary – but it is all too easy to become a slave to your engine. A typical instance would be the catching of a fair tide at some headland when a touch of engine for an hour is all it needs to round it on the last of the fair stream, then perhaps the wind comes fair and firm and the yacht makes excellent time along the coast with the next headland looming ahead. The temptation is to motor hard for it, and get round it on the first of the next fair stream, so that by going hell-for-leather you can just catch the *third* headland as well. Once into this attitude you motor, motor, motor. Your passages become races against the clock. The wind has only to falter a little and you reach for the button and drop the headsail, only to set it again five minutes later when the new breeze comes in.

This is one reason why a first boat which is a sluggish sailer in light airs can dictate your whole sailing ethos. Some of the tubby little cruisers that score so heavily in terms of accommodation below are disheartening to sail in gentle conditions and constant motoring becomes the normal practice.

Sails

The sails you buy as part of the package may be strong and adequate but far from perfect in terms of cut and shape. If they are set properly, though, it is more than half the battle – and conversely, even the best cut sails will be poor if set without care. Sail setting is a big subject and worth studying at length. The basics, though, are these: get the mast set up straight and tensioned so that any bend in it while sailing will be beneficial to the shape of the sail, adjust luff and foot tension according to wind strength but never tolerate a sloppy luff.

Setting up the rigging

More damage can be done by slack rigging than one realises, not only to the performance of the boat but also to the mast and its fixtures by constant movement and consequent metal fatigue. It is nearly impossible to over-tighten stays and shrouds by hand. Gripping the upper part of the bottlescrew with a mole wrench, the bottle can be turned using an 18-inch screwdriver as a lever.

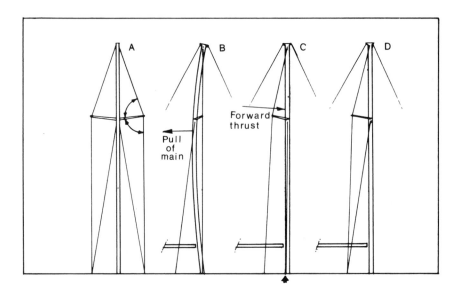

Fig. 3 A: lower shrouds brace the mast laterally while cap shrouds and spreaders brace the head. B: the mainsail pulls the middle of the mast aft. C: the spreaders, if swept aft, apply a forward thrust to counteract this. The lower shrouds in the sketch are positioned in line with the mast. D: shrouds and cap shrouds may in some cases be connected to the same shroud plate, but while this is simple it also places a severe load on a single fitting.

A deck-stepped mast is positioned roughly with rigging just tight enough to hold it, then the main halyard is used as a plumb bob to get the spar quite vertical athwartships – a bucket of water can be stood on the coachroof to reduce the oscillations of the plumb bob, but of course a very calm day is needed. A more common trick is to take the tip of the halyard down to the toerail so that it just touches, then swing it over to the opposite side of the boat at the equivalent position. If the mast is straight it will also just touch the toerail.

Having established a slight rake of the mast aft, tighten the fore and backstay firmly but not fully. The lower shrouds come next and by sighting up the mast track straightness can be judged and fore-and-aft line attended to. It is often beneficial to set a slight forward bend in the middle of the mast by tightening the forward pair of shrouds, or the babystay if so rigged. The cap shrouds which pass over the ends of the spreaders must be marginally tighter than the lowers.

The mainsail

In broad terms luff tension controls the fullness of the sail in its forward part and foot tension controls the lower half, with leech tension controlling the after area of the sail; the fullest part of the curve should normally be just forward of the middle of the sail. Increasing luff tension flattens it and draws the draught (camber) forward. Tension is increased for fresher wind forces, eased for lighter airs, but foot and leech must also be adjusted in harmony and because wind force is greater higher up the sail, a little twist, slight sagging away at the head, is also important. This is regulated by the position and tension of the mainsheet and by the use of the kicking strop.

The headsail

A tight forestay is the first essential and halyard tension dictates the position of maximum camber as with the mainsail. Initially the luff is set up very hard, to be eased just a little as the wind eases, not forgetting the vital leech line tension. The angle of sheet lead is very important and roughly speaking it should bisect the sail from about half-way up the luff to the clew.

The foregoing barely begins to touch the subject of sail setting and it is intended to serve as an indication of how important it is to set sails correctly and as the sailmaker designed them to be set. Sail setting and trimming should be studied in greater depth than the scope of this book allows.

In a family cruiser where adult crew shortage may be a problem it can be important that sails can be hoisted, lowered and handled easily, and to this end mainsails which run in a mast groove rather than attachment by slides or toggles, are not recommended. The problem is that should a mainsail have to be lowered in a bit of a hurry and then set again almost immediately it will not only have to be secured meanwhile, or it will blow around, but feeding the sail luff into the mast groove one-handed while trying to hoist at the same time is a slow and difficult task. Being able to drop the sail without such complication is an essential part of handling a sailing boat. Easy sail handling also means increased crew safety.

No cockpit is completely safe when a boat is heeled hard down and rolling, but the less the need to leave its comparative safety in order to go forward the better, and one of the main reasons for needing to do so is to change headsails or reef the mainsail. These jobs have to be done promptly if the boat is to be kept under the right amount of sail for the conditions and at times it can be difficult and even dangerous.

Foredeck work in rough weather may mean calling a partner up from below, perhaps half-asleep, struggling into oilskins and harness and then clambering forward to the end of a very wet see-saw, and hence the job is apt to be postponed, perhaps in the hope of getting under the lee of some

Fig. 4 In smooth water a small cruiser can carry more sail in strong winds than she can bear in rough water and the violent lurches of a beam sea.

Plate 5 Slab reef pendants – the lower reef line is not rove, but this boat has an extra deep line for really hard weather. (*Photo: courtesy Yachting Monthly*)

headland. However, reefing must never be postponed, and if it is then the job only becomes nastier. The old saying that the time to reef is when you first think about it, is a sound maxim.

Slab reefing

The redevelopment of two old ideas has made shortening sail very much easier and safer. Slab reefing a mainsail, which is a modern version of old fashioned points reefing, is faster and more effective than roller reefing, especially when the sail has to be reduced very drastically. If a mainsail is rolled down to the equivalent of three or four slabs it becomes shapeless and the boom end drops often to the extent that it cannot be sheeted hard in without pulling it down on the cabin top, but with a slab reef the sail remains a properly shaped sail retaining drive even though it has been snugged down to a third of its size.

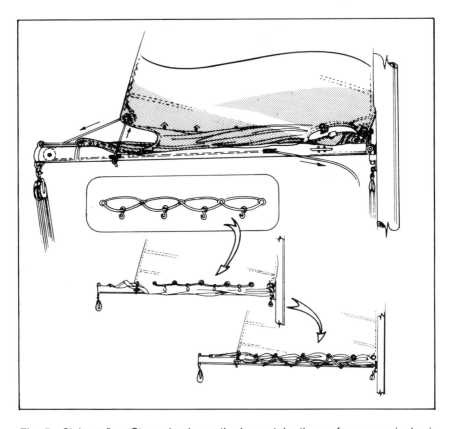

Fig. 5 Slab reefing. Strong hooks on the boom take the reef eyes or cringles in the luff of the sail. Reef pendants at the outer end of the boom are used to haul the leech cringles down – the positioning of these is critical. With the sail snugged down to the boom at its ends a rubber cord hook-and-eye system, or an equivalent, takes care of the loose folds of sail between them.

Plate 6 Rubber cord and hooks are used to secure the loose bunt of the sail.
(Photo: courtesy Yachting Monthly)

Usually with slab, a sail is equipped with the means to pull down two sections, but it is worth having a third for really heavy weather, especially if the boat tends to be a shade tender. It is very simple: heavy eyelets equidistant above the boom and parallel to it have permanent reefing pendants rove through the outer ones (in the leech) and there are two strong hooks on either side of the boom close to the mast. The sail is lowered far enough for one eyelet to be dropped over a hook and the appropriate pendant is hauled taut to pull the opposite eyelet down to the boom, then the halyard is set up again and the job is done and in an emergency nothing more is needed (see Fig. 5). For the complete reef there are smaller eyelets along the line of the slab to permit rubber cord to be pulled down and nibbed over small metal hooks along the boom, thus tidying up the slack fold of sail. In many boats the halyards are led aft to the cockpit allowing one person there to control the lowering and raising of the sail during reefing, and a few also have the slab reefing pendant (a single one) led aft. Incidentally, there is one snag about aft-led halyards in that it is difficult for a single-hander to let go a halyard and then go forward to gather in a sail because any jam-up due to a kink in the halyard means that an extra trip aft to the cockpit is needed to free it.

Aft-led halyards can greatly add to safety. I was once caught in a Mediterranean storm that came upon us with horrifying speed from astern. Within seconds our 30-footer was running at uncontrollable speed, I tried rounding up to get the full mainsail and jib off her, but we were blown flat and it was only being able to cast off the halyards from the cockpit and just let the sails fall halfway down as the boat rolled that saved the day for us. The development of the mast-furling and reefing mainsail, although expensive, has further improved control.

Roller jibs

The other development is the roller headsail, an old idea which has benefited from modern design, materials and engineering. There are valid criticisms of the roller headsail in terms of sail shape and the control of shape and while it is also true that you cannot roll a headsail down to storm jib size because it becomes a shapeless triangle which is too high and lacks the necessary weight of sailcloth, it is still effective in winds of from zephyr to force 6 or possibly more. It means that the boat need never be overpowered by her headsail and in a sudden squall the sail can be rolled away altogether while the boat is motorsailed under her mainsail or laid-to under it.

If a boat is to be properly equipped to face really heavy weather under sail a storm jib is essential and the roller headsail is rolled up completely. The best and most frequently recommended arrangement is to have a dummy stay from the mast to a suitable strongpoint bolted to the foredeck and set up by means of a hook and bottlescrew; to this stay a small heavy jib can be hanked in the normal way. The strongpoint may itself be braced down to the keel by means of a strut or wire beneath the deck. An arrangement such as this may, just *may* be vital some day – or it may never be used at all.

There are simple roller arrangements and more sophisticated ones which allow a variety of different jibs to be used on the same roller gear. While this means that a smaller and heavier sail can be used for heavier conditions, the change-over from a lighter sail can be a problem since by the time an increasing wind makes it seem advisable this lighter sail may have been rolled down to half its size. It must then be unrolled in order to lower it before replacing it by a heavier one, and unrolling a big, light sail in a rising wind and perhaps at night can tax a single hand on the foredeck to the limit. There are also roller headsails which have been cut and built to provide a heavier cloth at the leech when rolled down, but there is still no real substitute for a proper and separate storm jib, whether set on the roller or on its own stay. Storm conditions could conceivably damage the roller gear, which could put the boat in real trouble.

Whether working on the foredeck or reefing the mainsail the operation must be a partnership between those forward and the person who is steering. In racing the helmsman is only concerned with keeping the boat sailing as fast as possible while work is going on, but in a cruiser there is no point whatsoever in deluging the foredeck workers with water and throwing them around when a careful helmsman, or woman, can slow the boat to a crawl. If sheets are eased out to the point at which the boat retains just enough speed to give steerageway, bearing off a few degrees if she is on the wind, the decks will be kept dry and the boat will lurch lazily over the advancing waves. In a bit of a breeze this isn't always easy to achieve, and an inexperienced helmsman may allow the boat to stop completely, which means that she will bear away of her own accord, fill her sails and begin to travel too fast. It takes practice, but it is worth it because the job can be finished more quickly and in greater safety.

Chinese lugsails

We can't consider labour-saving rigs without including the Chinese lugsail pioneered and developed by those stalwarts of the North Atlantic, Col. 'Blondie' Hasler and Jock Macloud. I have only two personal experiences of the rig but the first of these, sailing with Col. Hasler, was impressive enough.

The boat was engineless, the day was filthy and it finished up with a blinding gale-force squall against which we were forced to beat back into the Hamble river. The rig consists of a single fully battened lugsail set on an unstayed mast. The sail is reefed from the cockpit by means of a complicated system of lines which allow the panels of sail between the battens to be dropped one on top of the other. It means that there is a great deal of rope to handle, but once understood, the system is extremely simple. The harder it blew the more panels of sail were dropped until we were threshing along under a minimum of sail and surrounded by a maximum of rope.

I had nothing to do, having no jib sheets to handle, and while the boat did not lie quite as close to the wind as she might under a conventional rig, she looked light and easy to handle. Finally came the little matter of laying the boat alongside the pontoons which, because we had no engine, meant a head-to-wind approach and the instant control of sail. 'Blondie' Hasler went at the pontoon full bore and it was not until we were a matter of feet away that he dropped the remaining panels of sail and rounded up neatly at a standstill alongside.

Plate 7 The Coromandel at under 21 feet in length is junk-rigged and usually powered by outboard motor. A very simple rig.

Undoubtedly this rig has a great deal to offer the short-handed crew. The absence of stays to the mast, which includes the shrouds, means that by freeing the sheets the sail can always be spilled of wind on any point of sailing and therefore it can always be dropped. Admittedly the system of cordage looks complicated but it has stood the test of time and numerous ocean crossings and the unstayed keel-stepped mast in its specially designed socket bends like a giant fishing rod if over-pressed. The only real disadvantage of the rig is in light airs when the conventionally rigged boat can carry vast lightweight headsails or a spinnaker. In very light airs the unstayed mast can still bear the load of a very light genoa set flying (not on a stay), but it isn't efficient if the boat is trying to get to windward.

The cruiser chute

Perhaps it was the cruising owner's traditional dislike of the spinnaker which caused the cruiser or cruising chute to be developed. A spinnaker, with its complexity of poles, guys, lifts and downhauls, and its potential for trouble if the breeze should freshen and the crew is both thin on the ground and inexperienced, is nonetheless a valuable sail for down-wind work. The cruiser chute was intended to replace the spinnaker with something simpler and easier to tame. Like the spinnaker it is set flying, attached only by its three corners, but in effect it is a cross between a spinnaker and a huge, lightweight genoa. In its original form it was a poleless sail, but getting it to fill when running dead down wind, wing-and-wing with the mainsail fully out on one side and the chute on the other, is by no means easy unless the sea is very quiet and the boat is running straight and smooth.

Usually the aim is to ease out on halyard and tack downhaul until the sail is floating high and far in front of the bows, but more often than not users have found that the sail still needs a light pole to keep the clew open. The sail is at its best on a quartering reach which means that both mainsail and chute are getting an uninterrupted flow of wind. It can also be used on a broad beam reach, but once the wind freshens and the apparent wind – a component of true wind direction and the yacht's forward motion – draws ahead of the beam the sail tends to lose efficiency fast and a big ghoster genoa set on the forestay works better.

The cruiser chute can still give trouble when a rising wind makes it necessary to take it down. Much the same procedure as for handing a spinnaker is followed, with the tack being let go so that the sail can be hauled in by its sheet under the lee of the mainsail, but unless the halyard is lowered at just the right speed and the billowing mass of sail can be smothered and hauled in fast, it can get out of control. The use of a special tube, a sort of sock which rides up the sail as it opens out when being set, has proved highly successful in this respect. All that is necessary when the time comes to douse the sail is to ease the sheet under control while hauling down on a line that pulls this sock downwards, swallowing the sail and forming it into a sausage which can then be lowered to the deck without fuss.

Sail plan and rig

Small mainsails and very large headsails are a fact of life in efficient modern racing design, offering an aerodynamically effective combination aimed at getting the maximum amount of drive from the airflow over both sides of both sails. The aerodynamics of sailing is a weighty subject in its own right which I will hardly touch upon here. The large genoa spilling its blast of accelerated airflow along the lee side of the mainsail provides most of the lift and drive that gets a boat to windward at a competitive speed.

For the short-handed cruising family, handling these big headsails in fresh breezes is another matter and even roller headsails of maximum size can constitute a problem and call for far more powerful sheet winches than the boat may have when she is bought.

Plate 8 Headsail and Chinese gybe. Several turns can accumulate making it difficult and sometimes impossible to clear, especially with a roller headsail which cannot be lowered in this condition.

There is another aspect to consider in the matter of sail sizes: it is often easier to handle a boat under mainsail only when carrying out some manoeuvre such as sailing into an anchorage and a very small mainsail may leave the boat too under-canvased to be handled properly. The opposite holds true for using the headsail alone. Most modern yachts can be handled under headsail alone provided the headsail is not of maxi proportions; when lacking a mainsail the boat may be slow to tack and the effort of hauling a mass of sail across the deck for a short tack can foul up the operation. A boat buyer on a trial sail may find it very instructive to test the boat under single sails.

Most cruisers are sloop-rigged to the masthead, but as boats increase in size other options may be offered such as the yawl and ketch rigs. The basic advantages are that the total sail plan is then split up into smaller areas which are easier to handle. Most modern yawls have a mizzen so small that quite often it isn't used much, but on a broad reach the mast allows a big between-mast reaching sail to be set and in very strong winds a quick emergency reduction of sail can be made by dropping the mainsail and sailing under mizzen and rolled down or storm jib. Ketch rig, usually only found in boats of about 40 feet and above, offers much the same advantage except that the mizzen, being much larger, gets as much use as the mainsail in normal conditions.

Cutter rig (in which there are two headsails), although not fashionable nowadays because of the loss of efficiency caused by the interrupted airflow, still has much to offer the cruising owner. The headsails consist of a staysail of relatively small area which has a short boom or 'club' on its foot sheeted to a track across the deck forward of the mainmast. Although the sheet tail leads back to the cockpit the sail is also self-tacking and under staysail and mainsail the boat can be put about by the helmsman without the need to handle jib sheets. The jib proper in a cutter is usually set on a short bowsprit which is often a plank type enclosed by a pulpit and if it is a roller jib the combination of self-tacking staysail and roller makes for a very easily handled rig.

Cutter rig is very often the headsail arrangement when the cruiser has a gaff mainsail and gaff rig. Whether in an old boat or in a modern GRP counterpart, this rig has a number of real advantages. A gaff mainsail involves a second (peak) halyard, but it is an easy sail to handle and has the added plus that a gaff mainsail can be lowered when the wind is following, which a Bermudian mainsail cannot. There is some loss of efficiency to windward in that a gaff rigged boat cannot be pointed quite as high as a Bermudian rigged one, but it is less than many people think. A clean-hulled and well rigged gaffer with well cut sails may point a shade lower but she may be making better ground than just any Bermudian rigged boat pinched up hard. Gaff rig varies between the gunter form which has a gaff that stands almost vertical, and gaff proper with this spar setting at a lower angle and thus leaving a space above it for a topsail. Gaff topsails, however, are usually difficult to set efficiently on the wind, although they are great fun to play with.

CHAPTER THREE
Basic Equipment

Boats are often sold new in what the trade calls 'sail-away' condition. This can vary from an inventory which includes such commonplace items as fenders, a few warps and a cooker and toilet, to the starker realities of sails, anchor and engine. A second-hand buy is more likely to have a full sailing inventory although more sophisticated equipment such as a life raft, VHF radio and position-finding electronics are usually a matter for price negotiation.

Just what is and what is not an essential is a matter for some debate, but the absolute basics are aimed at personal safety, boat safety and plain navigation. In short, you must be able to survive ordinary bad weather at sea or at anchor, know where you are, be seen by other vessels, and be personally protected against wet, cold and the risk of falling overboard – or be able to remain afloat if you do.

Clothing

Personal equipment applies to everybody aboard, including small children. Protective clothing must be the best you can afford because no oilskins ever keep you completely dry in prolonged wet, but good ones come closest to it and keeping dry and warm is vital to conserving stamina; a miserable crew is working at half-cock. Non-slip shoes and boots are a safety essential. Non-slip decks can't be relied upon because there are always coamings, hatches and other areas which are shiny and slippery. Life-jackets must be distinguished from swimming aids, too; a life-jacket will float an unconscious person face upwards, which an aid may not. The safety harness is the first line of defence, worn and hooked on.

It is possible to buy waterproof smocks which have a harness built into them and these are a guarantee that the harness is there ready to use whenever the weather is bad enough to merit wearing a smock. Conversely, though, when the weather is warm a smock is not worn, although the risk of falling overboard remains. Arguably one should buy an ordinary harness as well, but in the case of a typical family of four this is going to be very expensive. Perhaps it is better to economise elsewhere and put the safety and comfort of crew into top priority. In passing, and on the subject of harnesses, there is a risk that the mere fact of putting one on makes you feel safer, but a harness not hooked on does about as much for your safety as a Beefeater's halberd does for the defence of the Realm.

Instruments

The basic instruments of coastal and narrow seas navigation are compass, log and depth-finder and if these are accurate and reliable, coupled with up-to-date charts and pilot books, tidal data and so on, you can manage to find your way around in safety. You need good binoculars of course, and a hand-bearing compass, chart tools and a chart table, but your accuracy then depends on your care and skill. Beyond these basics come the electronics, the radar, the automatic position finders, radio direction finders, Decca or Sat-Nav. Radar has a foot in both the navigational and the safety fields and so of course do the position-finders because knowing exactly where you are when your mind is dulled by tiredness or maybe seasickness is a huge contribution to safety.

Initially, though, it is the quality of the instruments that is most important, assuming that their user has the basic skills to plot a position. A log, for instance, can be quite basic but highly accurate, or it can be elaborate and offer a variety of passage-measuring functions. It is better to buy a very simple instrument made by a highly reputable company than an elaborate multi-function type at an attractively low price. Reliability in all weathers is essential and the clever bargains often don't live up to this aim.

All-weather extras

Assuming that the boat, sails, spars, rigging and engine are all sound and adequately strong – and it is quite a big assumption – the all-weather extras might include a roller headsail, storm jib and the means of setting it, an extra reef line added to the mainsail permitting it to be shortened down still further than the customary two-reef standard, jackstay wires to take safety harness hooks, side screens carrying the name of the boat and offering protection to the cockpit, and a spray hood over the companionway. Bigger or extra sheet winches may be needed if the usual crew are a bit weak in the arm, and other odds and ends around the deck. It is wise to lay off buying too many of these until their value is really understood because a modern chandler's shelves are an Aladdin's cave of 'essential' gear, most of which you can manage without.

The boat may have a basic bow pulpit navigation light, a white steaming light on the mast and the usual stern light which are legal and adequate, but an owner may decide that the masthead tricolour is more likely to be seen (which it is), and opt for it as essential. He may also wish to have fitted a pair of spreader lights to illuminate the deck and there are two schools of thought about this. In terms of working on deck at night it is rare to find a night so black that they are really necessary and when it is then these lights effectively destroy the night vision of helmsman and lookout. On the other hand, in a last-minute collision situation there is no doubt that illuminating the whole boat briefly ensures that she is seen.

Radar reflectors are a basic essential. A reflector should be the best you can get hold of and although the simple octahedral form is efficient when properly displayed it is still a lot less efficient than some of the well-proved and more sophisticated reflectors available, particularly for a sailing boat, because it is the heeling angle of a reflector which is important. There is an optimum angle where the return signal is at its most efficient; thereafter, and as the boat heels to more than about thirty degrees, efficiency drops sharply to 50 per cent and less of its maximum.

Anchor and cable

One of the most important of all pieces of equipment, and one most often skimped on, is the anchor and cable. It is the ultimate hope when all else fails, yet many owners regard it as a means of stopping for lunch or over-nighting in some sheltered creek, without ever considering that with a rope round his propeller and a jammed main halyard the anchor may be all that can save the ship. Boats bought new and with a basic inventory never have an anchor which is a fraction heavier than the boatbuilder can get away with, nor a foot of anchor cable more than the bare minimum (usually fifteen fathoms or its metric equivalent). Yet new owners never question either size of anchor or length of scope.

Plate 9 (*Left to right*.) Small and large CQRs, fisherman anchor, Meon or Danforth and two sizes of Bruce anchor.

The old rule of thumb was one pound weight for every foot length of the boat, and while this tends to be a bit generous with the modern high-efficiency burying anchors used by the vast majority of weekend and holiday sailors, it does offer peace of mind. A survey carried out among ocean cruising yachts, which have to be able to anchor in a great variety of seabeds and ride out serious storms in tropical waters, showed that every boat carried anchors which, whatever the type used, were approaching double the weight carried by the average yacht. Most boats had at least three big anchors and all had a vast range of cable, either rope or chain.

Our typical family cruiser needs a minimum of two anchors, a best bower for ordinary use and a kedge. Usually this means that if an owner bought a new and heavier anchor he could use the one which was provided with the boat as a kedge. Admittedly it would be a heavy kedge, but the majority of kedge anchors carried are far too light in the first place, and the disadvantage of extra weight to manhandle into the dinghy is largely offset by its increased effectiveness and the fact that in extreme conditions of wind and sea it is an excellent back-up anchor. As for scope of cable, the minimum fifteen fathoms provided should be at least doubled.

Life buoys, VHF, life raft

The boat will need at least two life buoys of horseshoe type on deck, one with an automatic light and a heaving line or throwing quoit. She will need distress signals, fire extinguishers, additional mooring warps and fenders, a boarding ladder, boathook, a radio for receiving weather forecasts, a good barometer, plus all the galley equipment, spare gas bottle, sleeping bags and so forth – a long list. She will need a powerful hand torch, ideally a dan-buoy with its staff coated with light-reflective material, a fog horn, signal code flags and many more items.

The real crunch, though, may be whether her owner can afford, or thinks he needs, VHF radio and a life raft. Any coastguard will answer a firm yes to a VHF radio. In an emergency help can be asked for over the radio early enough for the rescue services to reach the scene in time, which is not always the case when everything hangs on whether rockets and flares have been seen and acted upon. At sea and out of sight of a well populated coast there seems to be at best a fifty-fifty chance of distress signals being seen, let alone acted upon. Even close to a well-used shipping lane distress signals can be missed, or only half-seen by the watch of a big ship – and a junior officer will think twice before starting a wild-goose chase about something he *thought* he saw.

The question of a life raft and its advantages is a little less clear cut. Won't an inflatable dinghy do just as well? I have discussed this question

Plate 10 The 3-M retro-reflective tape applied to lifesaving equipment (and on oilskins) can be picked up at great distances with an ordinary but powerful hand torch.

in a later chapter, but it is something which an owner must consider very carefully. While a dinghy may serve well enough in an emergency where time is not pressing and protection from the elements of minimal importance, such as might be the case if a boat was holed on a rock in reasonable weather and with rescue close at hand, there is always the very scary thought that somewhere out there, while you are racing through the night, a huge baulk of half-submerged timber lies in wait.

These extras still depend very largely on the sort of use a boat is going to get, whether it will be ninety per cent quiet creek-crawling or ambitious passage-making. Every owner has to decide for himself – or his chequebook must decide for him. He has to decide between what is vital and essential and what merely makes the job easier. One final possible extra: if much in the way of electronics is going to be fitted, a much bigger battery, or better still a pair of batteries, will be needed and with a pair of batteries one can be kept for the sole purpose of starting the engine.

CHAPTER FOUR
Family Cruising

Before we can consider how a family sail a boat we must take a look at individual attitudes to cruising. Usually it is the man who introduces the family to this sport and only very occasionally is it the other way round, although nowadays more and more couples come into the game as beginners together. To buy a cruiser means setting aside a very large sum of family money, devoting a great deal of leisure time to sailing (which may mean having to abandon other hobbies and interests) and being prepared to put up with a great deal of discomfort in order to enjoy the pleasures of sailing. The pleasures are not always obvious. Most of them come from the satisfaction of handling the boat and exhilaration of sailing and if you neither take part in the seamanship and navigation nor feel the thrill of a boat snoring along in bursts of spray, there isn't a hell of a lot left. While one partner may start off being less than keen, enthusiasm can grow with time – but only if the other partner helps it to grow.

In well over 80 per cent of boats the husband is the undisputed skipper, usually by mutual agreement because he has more experience of sailing, but there is also the tacit agreement that skippering is a male prerogative. He may also drive the family car although his wife may be the better driver, but it is also he who fiddles with the motor lawnmower, unblocks drains and repairs the garden gate. Nowadays there is no practical nor physical reason why this should be, and women are equally capable of skippering should they wish it.

In recent years a totally new idea has developed: the joint skippers. More and more couples take up sailing together from scratch, attending sailing schools and evening classes together, taking the same tests and winning the same certificates and eventually choosing and buying a boat as a joint venture and afterwards sailing on equal terms. Some just up and buy a boat and learn together by getting on with it, reading a lot and taking very cautious steps – and provided they really are cautious they usually manage quite happily.

In some joint-run boats they don't even recognise the need for a nominated skipper, while others do so (in which case it's usually the man) purely for convenience in harbour form-filling. I'm not too sure about this no-skipper philosophy though, because the role of a skipper is that of an orchestrator, a giver of the executive command, a conductor, and you don't have to wear a cocked hat and sword for that. Both partners can be equals in knowledge and skill but only one (either of them) can give the executive order.

The real benefit of both husband and wife learning together lies in the added safety which naturally results and in the sense of accord it brings. When decisions have to be made they are joint ones, discussed and arrived at with both knowing the full odds involved. From the moment you go aboard a boat you begin making decisions, great and small; some turn out to be right ones, some wrong ones, and occasionally there's a nautical howler that curls your toes up. The luckless skipper who makes one of these blunders, treating his family to a night of wet misery and worry, may be given a lot of stick by an anxious and uncomprehending wife. Next time he is faced with an uncomfortable decision he may try to take the easy way out rather than risk carrying the blame, although the easy way isn't always the seamanlike safer way.

He might, for instance, be faced with risking a river entrance he doesn't know and in poor conditions rather than condemn his crew to a nasty night at sea, simply because the anchorage promises comfort and shelter. If both partners are equals in training and experience the decision made will be the safe one and whatever it leads to, both will be responsible and neither will blame the other.

Job-sharing in a family cruiser is a very individual matter. Many women don't want to be involved with the complexities of navigation and boat-handling, they confine themselves to running the domestic side of things efficiently and they can steer, reef, handle sails, ropes and fenders with expert dispatch when needed. They sail watch-and-watch with their husbands on a passage and do a score of other sailing jobs cheerfully, but when it comes to sailing decisions they leave them to him from choice. Others go to work subtly and influence his decisions. As a man once said to me, 'I make all decisions, except for where we go, when we go and when it's time to stop'.

Sometimes a husband and wife share the skippering rather cleverly and whoever happens to be on watch is the skipper, but when both are on watch and an emergency occurs *he* takes charge. This is quite sensible when both are equally skilled because when the person off watch has been asleep below he or she cannot be relied upon to make an instant snap decision if woken suddenly and roused out on deck to take charge. In many boats the wife is the navigator, perhaps because she has a special aptitude for it; in others it is she who takes the helm and carries out any tricky manoeuvres that may be needed while her husband rushes around handling ropes or sails – or jumping ashore with a line when berthing in a marina.

Sadly, there are quite a lot of wives who in their heart-of-hearts would much rather be somewhere else than rocking around in a boat, but they go along with it for their husband's sake and milk what pleasure they can get out of it. It is a fact too that they are often more seasick and more prone to feeling chilly than women who are genuinely interested in sailing for *its* own sake. In such cases a wise male will do all he can to make sailing more pleasant by avoiding unnecessary rough stuff and keeping stern-jawed determination in the face of fiendish odds for when he's sailing with the lads – sailing is supposed to be fun for all.

Children

Sailing with small children is a different matter altogether. It has to be fun for them too and fun usually means a sandy beach at the end of the day's sail. The smaller they are the shorter the passage should be and one hour's duration per year of age is a general rule for toddlers because sailing can be deadly boring for a small child no matter how many diversions, I-spy games or surprise packets are produced. Babies are very little trouble apart from the domestic demands of feeds and 'changes' conflicting with sailing requirements.

With older children, from perhaps seven years old or even younger, the aim should be towards making them a genuine part of the crew but without forcing the issue, and there are many little jobs which can be their own special contributions. Children are never happier than when rowing the dinghy and ferrying people ashore and back – a slow process perhaps, but worth a bit of patience.

Many couples, after one or two gentle seasons, resume their normal passage-making with no further concessions to having children aboard. Night passages are especially easy and the longer legs of the cruise are deliberately made at night while the children are soundly asleep. However, much depends upon the expertise of parents and how smoothly things go, because a boat which is sailed from one crisis to the next with all the yelling and head-clutching that may go on is a disturbing place for kids.

Child obedience is the crux of the whole thing. In a boat a disobedient child is a child at risk and disobedience can be a product of fear and uncertainty brought about by a sense of insecurity. Children are shrewd little people and when they see father bounding around in panic they are likely to react. You have to keep things very low-key. Children have a wonderful knack of standing on the very rope you need to use and getting in the way generally during hectic moments, but you have to be very patient yet firm. The classic procedure is to batten them below the moment things begin getting active, but a child locked below and listening to the din of wind, wave, and father, can be terrified.

With the very young, mothers naturally give children first priority and this must be allowed for by the father. Either it becomes a rule to take another adult or older child along to crew, or the husband must take pains to ensure that he can, when necessary, sail the boat single-handed. There should be no problem in doing this in a modern boat apart from berthing or perhaps picking up the mooring. A woman must be free to choose when to help on deck and when to look after her children – or, for that matter, take over the boat and let *him* cope with the kids.

Freedom to move around is the very breath of life to a three-year-old and that includes climbing as well. The fewer times one has to say 'don't, no, do-as-I-say', the happier all aboard will be and this applies to children generally. Life jackets at all times of course, harnesses when the boat is in motion, and a few firm but not unreasonable rules are all that is needed. For the very small, netting can be rigged right round the guardrails. Children who grow up to the sailing life come to accept the rules laid down and to *understand* them, which is very important. The boat becomes 'our boat' and they take a lot of pride in their little skills as the years go by.

It is the children who are plunged into the sailing world when they are already old enough to have other hobbies and interests who sometimes constitute a problem. At first it is utterly novel and fascinating, but if they find that going aboard the boat means that they are going to be shouted at, forbidden to this and that, made to do things that scare them and denied their pony-riding, or other well-loved shoreside hobbies, the boat soon becomes an ordeal. Worse still is the implication that sailing is in some way 'good for them' and will 'make men of them' – a fat lot of comfort for a fluffy little girl! How parents handle this problem will depend upon the sort of rapport they enjoy with their children, but it usually helps if their kids are encouraged to bring their friends along. There is a shameless tendency in most kids to brag and to show off the superiority which having *our boat* fosters, and the child who refuses flatly to help wash down the decks at other times will demonstrate this ancient skill with boot-faced satisfaction before an audience of his or her peers.

Teenagers can either be a tremendous help as crew or a thorough pain, which is part of the process of being a teenager. A boat which has a forecabin where a teenager can retreat from the unfair persecution of parents is the ideal because a child must be able to escape and sulk now and then. At that age too the apparent listlessness and lack of interest can be due to things other than boredom; it can be a fear of doing things wrong or of giving in, capitulating, but it can also be a reluctance to admit to feeling a bit queasy (a younger child tells everybody) or just to feeling tired. Young people have enormous flash-energy but like a sky rocket they soar, fizzle and sink. In my days as an instructor of seamanship in youth training I saw it again and again. In middle and later age we develop a sort of enduring stamina and provided no violent effort needs to be made we can go on and on, day and night, long after a fourteen-

year-old has gone into a dormouse act. It helps to remember this when it
seems that youngsters are slacking.

For small children, then, a safe rule is an hour's sailing for an hour
on the beach, for growing children active share in the working of the boat
with other children aboard when possible, and for teenagers endless
patience and a good deal of praise. For parents, self control, which means
making sure that you take the heat out of things, knowing what you are
doing, and not trying to do things that are likely to end in chaos.

Living small

It is a curious fact of life that three diminutive beginners down below in a
small cruiser take up more space than four large but experienced people.
The human form standing erect doesn't occupy much floor space, but as
soon as it stoops or bends it trebles its air space, and bending and
stooping below is the norm. A wet weekend afloat spent mainly at anchor
can trigger off a lot of aggravation just by the constant manoeuvring,
bumping and side-stepping that goes on as people move around. The
over-crowding of chickens in a pen results in much pecking and general
mayhem, for much the same reason.

An experienced hand below in a crowded boat instinctively jigsaws
movements into the movements of others. He or she never blocks a main
route; the beginner will stand in the main companionway at ease with
elbows on the coamings admiring the view – to the great exasperation of
others trying to get past. His vast buttocks will half block the saloon as he
rummages eternally in his locker and the moment the cook stands at the
cooker he finds it necessary to push past. The old hand, reading the signs,
nips quietly up through the forehatch.

It is very much a matter of give and take. If half the crew are
struggling to get into oilskins the other half wait for them to finish, if the
sink is full of dirty mugs the first person to pass by with a moment to
spare washes them, and when everybody is ready to turn in the thoughtful
ones stay on deck for a quiet pipe until the tumult dies down. Tidiness
and order, though, are the key to harmony; not rigid naval discipline so
much as automatically putting things back, rounding up mugs, folding
clothing, hanging up oilskins. It is not only a more civilised way to live, a
boat is a working thing which must be ready for any emergency. If the
navigator has to chuck a mass of discarded sweaters off his table in a
hurry, he loses his pencil, which distracts concentration and a mistake
may follow.

It is at sea in rough weather that the interior of a small boat is most
in need of orderliness. Wet sails bundled below and the comings and
goings of people in wet oilskins quickly combine with the battened down
accommodation to produce a damp fug, cushions shoot off settees,

lockers fly open and disgorge their contents, and crew, not wishing to spend a second longer below than they have to (unless they can lie out prone), hurl their belongings around at random. The lee saloon berth becomes a junk heap of clothing, cameras, packets of biscuits and a dozen other objects.

You cannot fit too many open, deep fiddled shelves, bits of netting or open bins in a small cruiser. Similarly, the more items of regularly used equipment you can mount to the bulkheads with plastic spring clips, slots and webbing or rubber cord the better, provided things are always replaced immediately after use. Bearing compass, fog horn, duty torch, distress flares and so on can all be stowed this way.

Finally, the FFs. I once sailed with a racing skipper who had gone through his boat meticulously noting what he called 'fatigue factors', or FFs, and removing them. His theory was that when people are tired and tense, as they often are during the latter stages of a race, little annoyances trigger off frustrated anger and lower morale to the detriment of efficiency. He listed bolts which were stiff. corners that could catch on a pocket or an elbow, lockers in which things slid to the back out of reach on one tack, a head-banging beam in need of padding and many, many others, all of which were eliminated. You didn't realise that he had done so, only that life was much calmer and less irritability showed in the crew.

Another racing yacht I cannot forget was owned by a manufacturer of beds, and whether in harbour or at sea the bunks were superbly comfortable, each having a mattress adjustable for tension and width, quilts which were just warm enough for a fully dressed sleeper or doubling up if the sleeper had undressed; each also had a proper pillow rather than the usual makeshift saloon cushion which is as hard as a prize marrow. The saloon berths were pilot-type, behind the settees and shut off by curtains should a sleeper be troubled by the light, and each berth had carefully thought-out hand grips enabling users to get in or out easily, and quickly, at whatever angle the boat might be heeling.

I mention the above in some detail because it illustrates two things, first that the boatbuilder's idea of how to arrange things is not always either the best or the only way to go about it, and second the reminder that boats down below should be designed for *people* and people should not have to adapt themselves to uncomfortable and unreal conditions – well, not too much anyway.

In very small cruisers of 18–22 feet in length a good cockpit awning is important. A wet day in an anchorage can be a misery without one. Not only does it permit more freedom of movement, but it also stops dampness from spreading below. Oilies can be left in the cockpit, and driving rain is kept out. Its size depends on the size and shape of the cockpit, but ideally it should extend forward over the open companion hatch, secure to the mast, and give standing room under it. The usual cockpit cover, used to close up the boat when she is left on the mooring, is only suitable to rig as a fly-sheet over the boom and cannot be expected to keep out much weather if there is wind with it. A cockpit tent, on the lines of the Norfolk Broads cruiser tent, which has walling and windows, would be the ideal, of course, and many small cruisers have had them specially made. It need only be of lightweight canvas, since it is only in use occasionally, and press-fasteners can form the attachment to the coamings and coachroof. On a really windy night, though, it is unsafe to leave it rigged – and the billowing noise doesn't make for peaceful sleep.

CHAPTER FIVE
Handling

Handling under power

In early editions of this book the emphasis in boat handling was on handling under sail, but changes have taken place. Then, cruisers tended to be smaller and a great many were powered by outboard motors and being lighter boats a good deal of manoeuvring in harbour was done more by dint of boathook and a well placed seaboot than by clever seamanship. Nowadays the marine diesel engine, more powerful than auxiliaries in the past, and the development of yacht marinas everywhere, have meant that for many owners the first skill they need to practise is handling under power.

Yacht harbours and marinas are all fairly similar in general design. There is an approach channel with berths and perhaps finger piers on either side at right angles to it, or there can be a number of approach channels each of which is wide enough to allow a boat to be turned ninety degrees into or out of her berth, but not always wide enough for her to be turned through one hundred and eighty degrees should her skipper have mistaken his approach and have to get out again. Many modern fin and skeg rudder hulls can be turned almost in their own length, provided the skipper is a person of great resolution, or bravado – or knows exactly what the boat is capable of doing under engine.

Wind strength and direction, and in some cases tidal stream, are extra ingredients which can turn the best of manoeuvres into a free circus for bystanders and it is the sorry lot of many beginners that, having got out of their berth and had an encouraging first sail in their new boat, the return to the berth is a traumatic experience not easily lived down.

Suppose a 30-foot modern cruiser is in her marina berth, stern to a moderate breeze, no tidal factors to consider, but needing to be hauled out astern under engine, then put ahead turning ninety degrees to port to head out down the approach channel. It is quite a simple manoeuvre but it has one or two hidden gremlins waiting to foul it up (see Fig. 6(A)).

Plate 11 The turning circle of many small modern cruisers under power can be little more than their own length.

Windage

Before a boat is fully under way with full rudder control she is partly, and sometimes strongly, influenced by windage. Her natural tendency is to point her bows downwind, stern upwind and half-way through the manoeuvre she's going to be stationary, almost beam-on to the breeze. Although her engine may be going ahead as her skipper tries to turn her down the channel, the rudder is full over to port and the thrust of the propeller is pushing her stern round; she is hardly moving ahead at all. If at this moment a fresh gust of wind hits her the bows will try to bear off and even if it is a very brief gust she may end up so close to the line of moored boats which she has just left that she has no room for her stern to swing as she begins turning to port (Fig. 6(B)).

This is a little classic. There may be several contributory factors. For instance, there may be crew standing on the foredeck hanking on a jib and creating windage right in the bows where leverage is most powerfully placed to turn the bows downwind. Or the skipper in backing out may not have gone far enough across the approach channel before going ahead, or having got this right he may have been slow in banging the rudder hard over so that he wastes half the width of the channel before the boat begins to turn. We'll start the whole manoeuvre from the beginning.

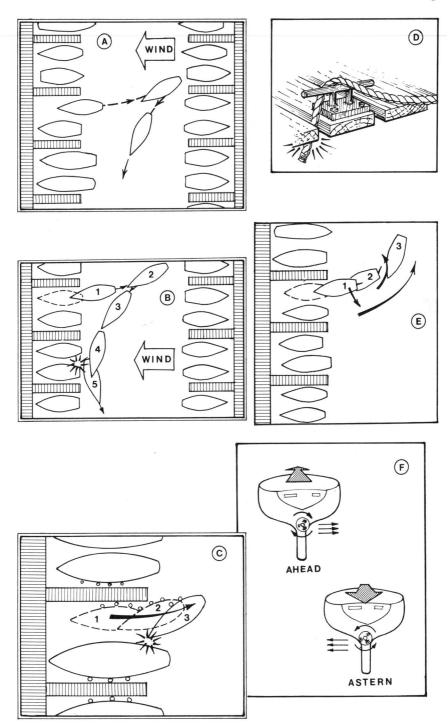

Fig. 6

Pivot points

The first thing to accept is that a boat turns by pivoting her stern round and the pivot point in a sailing cruiser is roughly below the mast. When she is going *astern*, though, she is pivoting on a point more or less below the helmsman's feet and it is the bows which swing round. This means that when we begin moving astern out of the narrow slot of the berth any movement of the rudder will start her bows swinging and if excessively done her bows will hit either the finger pier or the neighbouring yacht in the next berth (Fig. 6(C)). So she has to be drawn straight out of her berth until her bows are clear to swing.

The stern will follow the direction in which the rudder *blade* is pointed, slowly and reluctantly at first, then quite violently as the pressure builds up against the rudder blade, and you have to be ready for this with a firm wrist. The whole aim is to ensure that the stern swings the way we want it to go, taking the boat cleanly out of her berth in a smooth but increasing curve astern (Fig. 6(E)).

So the engine is running to warm up, crew have singled up the lines, holding on by one bowrope while the skipper aft at the tiller holds the stern in with the sternrope. Both of these lines are cast off from their cleats and are held clear above the rails so that when they are thrown onto the finger pier they won't foul anything aboard and they will be left behind in fairly orderly coils to be picked up on the return. If the berth is being left for good and the mooring lines are to be taken with us they may be slipped, the short end of each passed round the mooring bollards on the pier and led back aboard to be let go and pulled back aboard. In passing, the slipping of lines in this way can go wrong if for instance the rope has a spliced eye or a knot or a clumsy whipping on its end which can snarl up as it is pulled (Fig. 6(D)). The slatted planking of a finger pier can jam a rope's end in this way, or even a vigorous tug can cause the end to whip round and take a half-hitch around some small projection. The safe way is to haul the lazy end of the line gently and smoothly.

Propeller effect

We have not even left the berth yet. The skipper puts the engine slow astern, *really* slow that means, because a firm burst astern may produce a propeller side-kick (about which more in a while) which deflects the stern and starts the boat moving aslant her chosen line of exit. Slowly she begins to slide astern, the skipper waits a few seconds watching ahead and astern to see how she is lined up, then orders lines to be let go. A crew stands by with a boathook but does nothing with it unless told to, or, being experienced, sees that the bows need a gentle straightening nudge away from the pier or from the neighbour boat. At this stage too an eye is kept on the fenders which are still hanging down the topsides because one of these snarling momentarily against something can also deflect the straight astern course of the boat.

The skipper gauges that the boat is now far enough out of her berth – maybe half-way out – for him to use some rudder. She is far enough out for it not to matter that her bows will swing towards the neighbour boat or the pier end, according to which way the turn astern is to be made. He can increase engine revs a little, but that will depend somewhat on how she is beginning to turn and on the paddle-wheel effect of the propeller in this particular boat; if she is turning nicely on low revs there is no point in using more revs.

This paddle-wheel effect is negligible in some boats and so marked in others that it is made use of in the whole business of short space turning, so a little digression is in order. When going ahead the propellers in most boats spin in a clockwise direction, shooting a jet of water astern which drives the boat forward; when she goes astern the propeller spins anticlockwise and shoots the jet forward, but in spinning the propeller blades also have a side-kick effect. If we substituted a paddle wheel for the propeller this side-kick would be the total effort and it is easy to imagine what would happen the moment you engaged the gear lever. Spinning clockwise the stern would be swung to the right and spinning anticlockwise it would swing to the left, so when going ahead with a normal propeller there is a ghost of this kick-to-the-right effect and a ghost of a left kick when going astern; as you can see when the boat is running dead straight under engine and you take your hand off the tiller (Fig. 6(F)).

In our case we'll assume a right-handed turning propeller – which is now turning left-handed because we are going astern out of the berth. In Fig. 7(A) we see that the aim is to turn her stern to the right, to starboard, but the ghost side-kick will be trying to turn the stern to the left and if our boat had a long straight keel to restrict tight turns and a big diameter slow-turning propeller kicking her stern strongly to port we might find that even on full starboard rudder blade all we'd manage would be a straight line dead astern with no starboard curve at all. On the other hand if we'd *wanted* her stern to go to port she'd have gone that way like a lamb.

Our boat has only a modest side-kick to port when astern, which the rudder easily overcomes, but a hard burst of power could still, momentarily at least, result in a smart kick of her stern to port, so we keep the revs down. Remember, too, that possible windage effect which *could* be trying to turn our bows downwind to starboard. If the propeller were also trying to turn the stern to port we would have a nice couple operating, both aimed at fouling up the whole works.

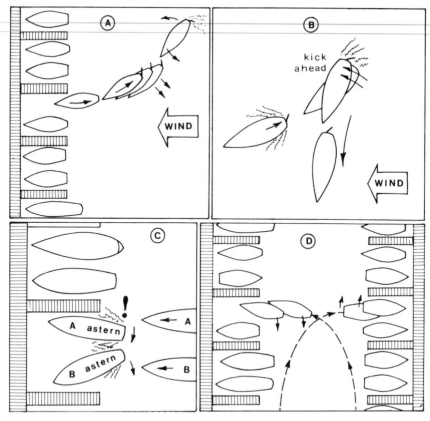

Fig. 7

I may seem to be labouring this rather and by now a total beginner reading this may have had the fear of God injected into him and be terrified of ever leaving the marina berth. It is all a question of taking things quietly and weighing things up a little before we start. So, to proceed.

The boat is now fully out of her berth and her stern is beginning to swing nicely to starboard as she backs out across the approach channel, and at this stage the line of moored boats on the other side of the channel will suddenly begin to look awfully close. It is easy to panic a little, to slam the engine ahead and bang the rudder over in a premature attempt to make the forward turn, but as mentioned earlier this can leave us scraping the line of berths we have just left. Let her trickle quietly astern until you could touch the opposite boats with an arm and a long boathook, then gear to neutral, through to ahead, and put the tiller right over and hold it so that the propeller stream is striking the rudder blade now pointing to port (Fig. 7(B)). Hold the tiller there and 60 per cent or more of the power will be directed at turning, swinging the stern before

Plate 12 Berthing in a marina in a gale force wind can be a highly exacting operation, best not attempted unless you are confident in your handling of that particular yacht – better to take an easy hang-on berth and move later.

headway begins to build up. Admittedly if the wind had been blowing us out of the berth and towards that opposite line of boats across the approach channel we wouldn't have backed out so close to them; we wouldn't have needed to, because our turn astern would have been sharper due to the windage on our bows as we began to swing. The bows would have blown to port, down-wind, assisting the turn. Having got out of the berth and had a nice day out we now have to get back again.

If new to the boat it is wise to find a quiet patch of clear water and make a few turns and manoeuvres (see Chapter 17 on Test Sailing). This will teach you how tightly the boat can be turned at various revs and what her propeller effect is ahead and astern, and also what her stopping power is with the wind ahead or astern. All this will inspire a lot of confidence and be of great help in future close-quarter situations. Now back to the marina.

Return to the marina

If you are cruising and have never visited the marina before you may have a diagram of it in the pilot book or on the chart, but usually there will be a visitor's berth somewhere easy of access to which you go prior to

Plate 13 Approaching a marina berth. This yacht is hugging the starboard side in readiness for a swing to port, where a crew member waits ready to take a line.

being allotted a berth if one is vacant. This is the civilised way. On the other hand, the marina berthing master may hail you as you draw closer and tell you which berth to go for. 'Number 18 to starboard', he might call, and thereafter you begin to plan.

Number 18 may mean berthing with a following breeze, or a stiff breeze on the beam, berthing into the wind or in some cases with a knot or so of tidal current with, against, or across your approach. There is also the matter of which side to hang out your fenders. Again, it may be windless, tideless and perfectly simple, or the berth may be one in which a buoy has to be picked up and taken in over the stern or bow, depending upon whether you go in bows or stern first. In short, you have to keep your options and eyes well open and go in slowly but with proper steerageway.

It is tempting to go in too slowly and then find that when you begin to make your turn towards the vacant berth the boat is so sluggish from lack of steerageway that it doesn't seem as though she's going to make it. With the tiller hard over her bows still seem to be pointing obdurately at the stern of the next-door boat, which appears to be getting uncomfortably close. At this point there seems to be a choice between increasing engine revs to jink your stern round or doing the opposite, going hard astern. This may be when the side-paddle effect of the propeller going astern may either rescue or ruin things, for with our clockwise or right-handed propeller (when ahead, that is) turning anticlockwise and nudging the stern to port this could help if you are turning to starboard into a berth, and blow the whole thing if you are trying to turn to port into a berth (Fig. 7(C)). The latter situation can lead to what I call the 'fatal zigzags', to be explained shortly.

With the majority of modern boats though, and in ordinary conditions, provided you use the full width of the approach channel and make the turn with adequate steerageway, there are no problems (Fig. 7(D)). It will have become plain to see which side of the boat to put the fenders out, warps will be ready and crew will be keeping their heads out of the helmsman's (or woman's, because in a lot of boats the men do the rope-jumping and bully work while she steers) line of sight during the final run-in.

. Once the boat is three-quarters of the way into her berth and by now with the engine out of gear and aiming straight, the engine can be put astern to slow and stop her while one of the crew, with a rope which is attached to the point on the boat forward of the mast, is standing outside the guardrails holding onto the shrouds and ready to jump lightly ashore. If the yacht is being berthed port-side-to, the engine astern (right-handed propeller) will kick her stern neatly alongside, but if she is being put *starboard*-side-to it will do just the opposite, pushing her stern away from the finger pier (Fig. 7(C)). If the boat has fenders out on both sides and if she is moving slowly this doesn't much matter because no damage will be done. On a day of wild wind squalls it may be rather more alarming of course, especially with a beam or stern wind, but no amount of my explanations, diagrams and dotted lines can offer the sovereign solution to this problem, it is something you develop a gut-reaction to – and *still* get it wrong on occasion.

This largely goes for the difficult approaches mentioned earlier. A stiff beam wind may mean a crab-wise approach and a following wind into the berth will cause her to sail in under bare mast and far less engine is needed initially, but one hell of a lot of astern-power may be needed to stop her once she's in. More difficult is a following tidal current. It may be no more than a knot in strength, but the boat may still need to motor at two knots in order to retain good steerageway through the water, resulting in a total speed of three knots into the berth. If there happens to be a following wind as well, then either you need to be expert or you need to go somewhere else and wait until the tide or the wind eases.

It will be apparent from the foregoing that it is very handy to know two things: which way the propeller throws the stern ahead and astern and how much it does so, and how abruptly the boat can be stopped with a burst astern. Once again, the aim is to carry out these harbour manoeuvres as slowly as is consistent with having proper steerage way.

The fatal zigzags

Finally the 'fatal zigzags'. This is the situation which can develop when trying to turn a boat through 180 degrees by repeatedly going ahead and then astern as if reversing a car in a one-way street. In a car we turn the wheels one way to go ahead and the opposite way when backing and in a boat we do much the same with the rudder, but the outcome can be very different. Cars don't drift sideways.

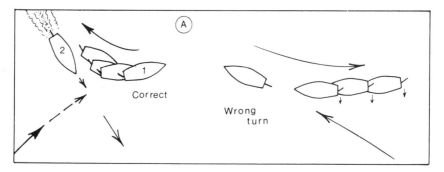

Correct

Wrong turn

Fig. 8

This backing and filling manoeuvre *can* work satisfactorily in windless conditions, in a handy boat or if there is room enough, but then if there is plenty of room the boat can be turned while going ahead in any case. Likewise when a boat has a heavy side-kick from her propeller this can be used to good ends – or as seen earlier it can make the manoeuvre impossible, depending upon which way we are trying to turn. In Fig. 8 a boat which kicks strongly to port when going astern (right-handed propeller) is shown turning successfully to port first, then unsuccessfully to starboard. In both instances she completes the forward turn without trouble but whereas putting the engine astern nudges the stern favourably to port in one case, it does the very opposite in the other.

This is how the fatal zigzag can begin; a forward zig takes the boat halfway through the turn only for the astern zag to cancel the swing just made good. The same thing can occur even with a boat which normally responds well to her helm under power, as shown in Fig. 9. Here she has come into the confined space with a following wind, her first turn to starboard ahead takes her half-way, but as soon as she is put astern, and in spite of the fact that the propeller kick should have aided by nudging her stern to port, the wind on her beam starts her bows swinging to leeward and she crabs back across the space without gaining any more

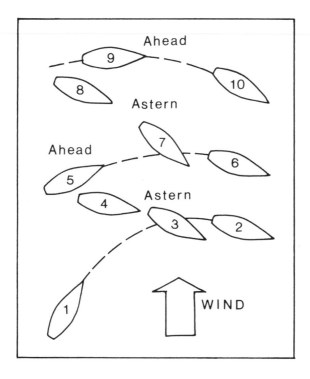

Fig. 9 The fatal zigzags. With a fresh breeze on the beam each attempt to back her stern to port during the turning manoeuvre is frustrated. The boat gradually zigzags her way to leeward.

turn. After that the fatal zigzag continues with each attempt but gradually drifting the boat to leeward as well.

In a case such as this there are several possible options. The anchor could be let go in the middle of the space and on just enough scope of cable for it to bite and swing the boat head-to-wind; she then motors ahead for the open sea and freedom with the anchor being hauled in as she passes over it. Or, since the boat seems keen to turn her stern into the wind, help her to do just that, then motor out stern first, provided of course that the skipper knows that the boat can be controlled in a straight line astern. The third option is apt to be a touch messy and only to be resorted to if it promises to do less damage than any other method, and this is to let the bows collide very gently with the other moored craft or the quay wall or whatever constitutes the boundary. If crew are ready with a line to secure the bows for the brief while it takes for the boat to swing – and there will be considerably more strain than holding on by hand can take – once head-to-wind the bows can be pushed off again and the boat can be motored ahead. However, almost certainly *some* damage will be done to one boat or another, but it is likely to be far less than a full-blooded thump can cause after a botched turning attempt.

Perhaps we should mention a possible fourth option, the kick-turn. This method is particularly suitable for long keeled boats which have a wide turning circle and the aim is to keep forward way to a minimum. With a kick-turn the rudder is put hard over while the boat is barely moving ahead and the engine throttle is opened full out in a three- or four-second burst, the aim being to deliver a side kick. The moment the boat begins to pick up headway the engine is cut back and with the rudder remaining where it is the engine is given a touch astern to check the headway, then full blast again, and so on. If the boat's stern naturally kicks to port in reverse engine then plainly this method is more likely to succeed if the turn is being made to starboard (Fig. 10). This kick-turn technique is useful even for ordinary tight right angle turns such as when entering a berth; it can also go spectacularly wrong if the boat is allowed to make headway or sternway to any extent, and nothing generates blind panic so successfully as a boat plunging and bounding from one side of a marina approach channel to the other.

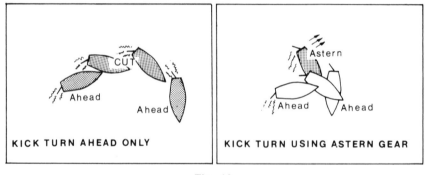

Fig. 10

Handling under engine, then, is a matter of anticipation and foreknowledge. Remember the windage and the propeller side-kick, know about stopping distance and how far a boat will continue to hold steerageway after the engine is cut back to neutral, know how tight a circle she'll turn at various revs ahead, how straight she steers dead astern, and above all, don't go any faster than you need for firm handling.

CHAPTER SIX
Handling, Sail and Power

There is a difference between the ability to sail a boat and the ability to handle one. A slick gybe or a neatly executed tack is good sailing. The barge-master who furls his sails and lets his barge blow down to leeward beam-on until she falls into a berth is handling her.

I have seen a successful offshore racing man, with a stack of cups to his name and a fine reputation in bad weather, who went to pieces when faced with having to sail into a berth alongside – she had to be towed in. To handle a boat means that you must be able to gauge just what she is likely to do when she is drifting, as well as knowing how she'll respond to her rudder under varying combinations of sail, wind and current. The cruiser motoring back to her moorings against wind and tide may suddenly be put into a tricky position by the engine stopping (they do it on you sooner or later). The handler takes a look at the forces and assesses the situation. He will try to judge whether his craft, without the aid of sails, is going to drift into trouble or whether she is safe to leave while he tinkers with the engine. This is the fisherman's way. All too often the yachtsman is sparked into frenzied and often unnecessary activity with anchor or sail.

Handling is another way of enjoying a boat, particularly one so small that long-distance passages and marine touring of the more-days-more-ports sort is out of the question. It takes the panic out of congested rivers, and it is something to take pride in.

A boat sails into trouble far faster than she is likely to drift into it. Pressed hard in a squall an owner tends to hang on like grim death and sail into all kinds of nasty situations when, quite often, the boat with her sails down would probably fare far better and lose less ground. Remember, too, that unless you are on a dead run a boat can always be slowed down by easing sheets, while still remaining under your full control.

When the wind's against the tide they rarely balance each other so well that a boat will stay in one spot if she breaks down when under power. Her probable direction of drift will be somewhere between the direction in which the current is bearing her and a point either side of the wind's eye. It is usually far better, if no sail is set at the moment when things go wrong, to turn her a hundred and eighty degrees with the last of the steerageway (if she was going in on the flood) and stem the tide with a following wind.

When wind and tide are together you must either anchor in the first clear space or get a sail set – whichever is the quickest – or there'll be a chance of damage done. On a flood, never discount the idea of running hard ashore at the first sign of trouble – this is in smooth water, of course. Be sure too that it is mud and not a rocky lee shore. It sounds drastic but it can save money.

Handling sails

In a boat which has a roller headsail of the multi-purpose kind, e.g. the same sail rolled or unrolled according to prevailing wind strength, there is no real sail handling to be done because both mainsail and headsail are under control by virtue of being attached to stay or spars. To handle a sail which is attached only by its three corners, like a spinnaker or cruiser chute, is a very different matter, and so is changing headsails on a breezy day. A sail which is full of wind and under load is impossible to handle with bare hands alone and a sail which is flogging, perhaps in the process of hauling it down or getting it out of a bag preparatory to hanking it on, is also out of control.

Always keep to windward of a loose and flogging sail. A case in point might be when stowing the mainsail while the boat is under engine and with the wind from abeam: the sail will be ballooning and threshing around, and to be standing on the coachroof trying to muzzle it could be very risky if you get to leeward of it. The aim must be to spill wind by reaching over the boom, grasping a long fold of sailcloth low down and pulling it up to form a trough into which the loose upper area of sail can be flaked down; the whole bundle can then be rolled up in a long sausage and a sail tier crisscrossed around it. In a situation like this with the wind from astern the boat may well be rolling badly, and working on the coachroof is precarious. It also means leaning against the boom while working and it should be a rule that the helmsman automatically secures the mainsheet permanently so that it cannot be tripped free of its jam-cleat allowing the boom to swing outboard and perhaps dropping somebody overboard.

A headsail must be treated with the same caution if there is a smart breeze blowing, keeping to windward of it and keeping it low on deck. A bagged sail should come out tack first and the aim is to feed it from the bag and onto the stay, remembering to grab the bag before the last of the sail is pulled out, otherwise the bag will be lost. When handing and unhanking a headsail the usual practice is to unhank from the head, kneeling on the loose sail until it can be stuffed below via the forehatch.

Synthetic sailcloth is slippery stuff and one has to be careful not to stand on a sail. Lightweight cloth also seems to have a life of its own on a breezy day and those who wear spectacles must be especially wary.

In a headsail change the usual order of operations is either to lower, unhank and pass one sail below before getting the replacement sail on deck, or to overlap the two stages. This is the faster and smarter way of changing sails and the boat is left under mainsail only for about half the time she would be on the two-stage change. The procedure is as follows: take the new sail forward and in the space below the lowest hank of the sail already set, and to windward of it, hank on the new sail, being careful not to get any twisted hanks. The existing sail is then lowered and the tack hook and halyard are transferred to the new one. Then the sheets are transferred, or at any rate one of them, and the working lee one is attached to the new clew. The new sail is now ready to be hoisted and sheeted, and finally the old sail can be unhanked and bagged or shoved below.

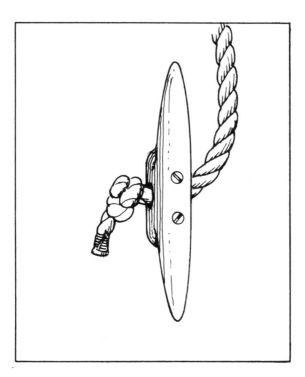

Fig. 11 The bitter end of a halyard should always be made fast so that it cannot blow loose and out of reach up the mast. The stopper knot through a hole in the cleat is a common practice, but many new owners mistakenly haul the whole halyard through the cleat each time the sail is hoisted – this can be a source of trouble if the sail needs to be lowered in haste.

It is very easy to let go of the halyard when changing headsails, and when releasing it from the head of the sail it must either be transferred at once to the new sail or snapped onto the guardrail or pulpit, even if only for a few seconds, because a halyard whips viciously when a boat is pitching or rolling. It is also sensible to have a permanent sail lashing or rubber cord attached to the bow pulpit with which to hold a sail down when it is lowered. A headsail left to its own devices tends to climb the forestay and flog madly, and apart from the harm to the sail and the annoyance, a sail half-set could ruin a manoeuvre under power by creating sudden forward windage.

It is difficult to imagine the brute power of even the smallest sail in a gale of wind until it has been experienced and it makes good sense to treat sails with respect even from the gentlest beginnings.

Leaving the mooring

Without much doubt the simplest and safest way to leave and to pick up a mooring is under engine, but doing things under sail is more fun, more gratifying and the expertise learned is an insurance against the time when the engine refuses to cooperate. There is also another advantage. A good deal of our sailing is day sailing, the Sunday sail down the river and back which more often than not is carried out entirely under sail. The modern diesel auxiliary doesn't much like short, half throttle runs which are cut off before it can warm up properly, and also, starting a cold engine can take a big sock out of the battery which a run of a few hundred yards doesn't really put back by charging. The same problem faces the owner of a boat in a marina of course, but with the boat on a mooring which can sail off and on again, it can be avoided.

Nonetheless there are a few points to look out for when using the engine to leave a mooring and to pick it up again. It is wise to warm the engine for a while prior to letting go and if it is at all temperamental, a headsail ready to hoist and a single tier on the mainsail will mean that the boat will not be helpless should it stop prematurely. When the boat is lying head to wind and current, the obvious manoeuvre is to motor straight ahead until the boat can be turned out into the channel, but beware the buoy rope if there is one because it can foul the propeller, the rudder, or in some cases the keel or keels should the boat motor over it.

With wind and current opposing each other and the boat lying across the wind, or sheering around, it pays to stand for a while and note her behaviour, judging any down-tide obstructions and assessing the odds. Often it may pay to transfer the buoy rope to the stern briefly in order to cant the boat towards open water, but usually the problem will be to get clear of the buoy once it is let go and a short burst astern may be the safest plan. It is usually best to turn into the current with wind astern rather than the opposite.

Picking up a mooring under engine looks easy but it still calls for forethought and it is always better to approach head-to-current even with a stiff following wind and bare mast. In these circumstances hardly any revs will be needed because the boat will be sailing under the windage of hull and mast and the difficulty will lie in stopping her because the side kick of the propeller can slew her off-line during the last vital few yards. The job of the crew forward will be to pick up the buoy rope or to pass a line through the ring on the buoy and then take a turn on the mooring cleat and wait until the way is off the boat before hauling in and making fast properly, and it is the helmsman's job to make this task as easy as possible. If he sees that his approach (or hers, because in many boats it is the wife who takes over the helm) is a bad one, the attempt must be aborted and the crew forward must be told not to make a grab because it will either lead to a dangerous attempt to hang on or to the loss of the boathook.

With wind and current from the same direction it is much easier and the boat can be kept under full control at the slowest revs and the only problem will be to know when the buoy is within boathook reach. The crew forward usually signals by raising one hand, but it is worth carrying out a simple pre-check. If the usual helmsman, standing, notes when the buoy ahead just disappears from view as the boat approaches and the actual distance is noted by someone else, the helmsman can then know that when the buoy just dips out of sight there is still, say, half a boat's length to go.

Leaving the mooring under sail

Getting away from the mooring is just basic sailing practice. One must decide in advance which is the most favourable tack and, depending upon tide, of course, be prepared to haul her head off by taking the mooring aft along the weather side and/or backing the jib (Fig. 12). It is important to see that the cruiser doesn't sail over her own moorings as the bilge keels, or even the rudder, can easily be snagged on under-water lines.

On a breezy day and with an inexperienced person as mate it is better to take the foredeck job and be sure that the mooring pick-up rope is going to be dropped clear, that the buoy isn't going to get hung up around a stanchion and that it is let go at the precise moment when she is filling on the chosen tack. It's easy enough to yell helm orders from forward, but hard to explain how to avert a mooring mix-up when you are aft.

In breezy weather a small cruiser will go away like a greyhound and if the headsail is aback to turn her it may force her over hard before you can reach the tiller. There is always a critical fifty yards or so after leaving a mooring. The yacht is not in trim, she has steerageway, but perhaps not in the direction of the open water, and with a novice at the helm things

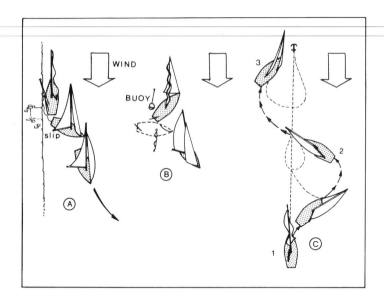

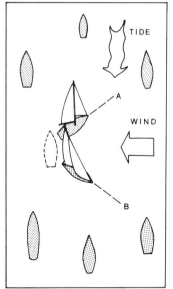

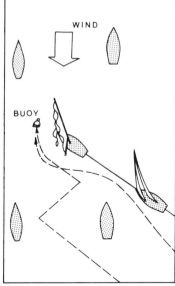

Fig. 12 A: leaving a quay wall under sail. Care is needed or the corner of the stern will grind hard against the wall. B: if the mooring buoy is taken aft along the weather side while the headsail is backed and the main sheet is freed right off, the boat will turn down-wind in her own length. C: sailing out the anchor. A useful trick in fresh winds when the engine is out of action, the boat is tacked (don't pin the sheets in too hard) and cable is hauled in as she sails over it, finally snubbing out the anchor. (Bottom left) A choice of A or B upon leaving the mooring, B could be hazardous due to the tidal current, A will take us safely to leeward of the moored yacht. (Bottom right) It is better to approach the mooring to be picked up on a close reach so that speed can be regulated by playing the mainsheet.

can go wrong fast. Aim to have the mainsheet either slack or made fast with one single turn, thus if it is necessary to bear away hard the mainsheet can be allowed to run in an instant – which it certainly can't if the sheet is made up with half a dozen turns. Decide on the plan before letting go the mooring and see that the crew knows what to expect. Remember too that the runaway cruiser, hot from her mooring and aimed at a neighbouring moored craft, will do less damage all round if, when it is a question of either bearing off or luffing up, she is put head to wind. Bearing away in a confined space depends upon three things, getting the mainsheet to run right out at once, having room to move the tiller, and possibly getting the jib a-weather. A sharp luff needs only a movement of the tiller. Bearing away means picking up speed, but luffing means losing speed, and the fact that she may not have way enough to go about is less serious.

Most small cruisers respond instantly to the helm as soon as they begin to fall astern. By reversing the tiller (pointing the tiller in the direction that you would like the bows to pay off) the abortive attempt at an emergency tack can more often than not be saved, but the action must be quick or she may pause, fall astern, and then carry on sailing on the same trouble-hunting tack which all the fuss was about.

With wind against tide the cruiser will be lying half wind-rode and half tide-rode and probably rolling like mad. It is inadvisable ever to try setting the mainsail until clear of the mooring or the cruiser will begin to sail wildly to and fro. Set the jib, back it to cast her head in the desired direction, and then let go the mooring. If it is important to turn down-wind immediately, hang onto the mooring and walk it back aft on the windward side, during which time she will be rapidly spinning her bows down-wind. Let it go as soon as it leads right astern, and then sail clear of the moorings before rounding up to set the main.

Picking up a mooring under sail

Picking up a mooring is the beginner's first nightmare, and it's not as simple as the diagrams make it out to be. Success depends upon planning and knowing just what the yacht will do. The small cruiser carries very little way and a long shot at the buoy rarely comes off. The weight of the wind will affect the issue as will a popple or a tide to be contended with.

Practice is the only answer, though many owners shirk it and start the motor as a matter of habit; this is crazy and bad policy. The yacht is primarily a sailing craft and handles best under sail. On the other hand, for a beginner to go at a mooring bald-headed from the first is bad seamanship; let him use his engine (in neutral) and regard it as an insurance. To become really competent, practise somewhere else in clear water. Buy some toy balloons, anchor them with string to half-bricks, and keep on practising.

Plate 14 Wind against tide effect. In an anchorage or mooring area where strong tidal currents prevail yachts will sheer around dangerously at times and if swinging circles are tight they can collide. (*Photo: courtesy Yachting Monthly*)

You can approach from leeward and then luff head to wind to take her up to the buoy; or you can come in on a close reach, easing the sheets to slow her as the buoy comes closer (Fig. 12(c)). Then if she appears to be under-shooting, the sheets can be hardened a shade to give her more way. Getting onto the buoy against a fierce tide can be made simple by this trick for the cruiser can be 'crabbed' across the current.

Although a smart luff for the buoy which brings the cruiser up quietly head to wind with the buoy just under her bow is the dream of every yacht-handler, the small light-displacement cruiser carries so little way that this manoeuvre often comes unstuck. Hitting the least popple will stop her almost dead in her tracks, and with way off her there will be some moments of uncertainty when the helmsman is trying to get her to cast off onto a safe tack and gather headway again. The over-estimated luff is less likely to go wrong provided the buoy is brought smartly aboard and the foredeckhand gets a quick turn on a cleat to check headway. It need hardly be pointed out that not only is it unwise to try grabbing the buoy from the cockpit, but having grabbed it, the antics of a boat moored by her tail with all sail set will be more rewarding for the watchers ashore than for the yachtsman on board. If the luff for the buoy looks like failing, pay off at once and sail past with dignity.

It is a good plan to make use of shore marks when making for a mooring across the tide. With both wind and tide together it is easy to misjudge the last few hundred yards to the moorings and end up to leeward and down-tide of it, sometimes within a yard or two of the buoy but fated to miss it despite a last-minute frenzy of short tacking. Take a sight on your own mooring buoy, and watch the shore behind it. As long as your buoy stays fixed against the background you can be sure of making it, but if it begins to cover the shore as though it was under way, then it is time to harden up a bit. In any case sail for your buoy as if aiming to get to windward of it; you can always fall off a bit when you get nearer.

With the wind against the tide there is only one rule. Sail up wind, lower the main (or both in a strong breeze) and run down against the tide. The only time this rule can be disregarded is when the wind is strong and the tide weak, or the other way round.

Handling and anchoring

Getting away from an anchorage calls for dexterity in handling under various combinations of circumstances. It may be that the shore is close astern, and very little time is left for manoeuvring once the anchor is off the bottom. A jib is a handicap to the man on the foredeck, and if it is possible to leave it lashed up clear of the deck, so much the better.

Once the mainsail is set and the jib hanked on and lashed up clear of the deck by one tier, the anchor should be hauled up fairly smartly to give the helmsman a chance to cast the cruiser's head in the direction of the best tack. This must not be done too soon or the chain or warp will be leading at a wide angle to the weather bow, thus making life harder for the anchor man and probably hauling the bows around onto the wrong tack just as she breaks out. If this should happen and if there is precious little room to sail clear on that tack, it is far safer to let go the chain again at once, anchoring once more and snubbing her around onto the proper tack.

The man forward is going to be busy getting the anchor aboard, clearing it of mud, lashing it and setting the jib. This should never be a two-man job with a three-man crew if the cruiser is so small that weight forward affects steering. The helmsman, as soon as the anchor is off the bottom, must concentrate on getting proper steerageway even at the cost of easing the mainsheet and running a little inshore. Under main alone it is unlikely that a tight windward course can be laid, and if it is vital that the boat is brought hard on the wind from the very start, then, of course, the jib will have to be set before the anchor is broken out. In this case you must control the jib just enough to save the anchor man from being slapped about and snatch it in hard the moment the anchor comes clear of the bottom. Then get her moving and jog her along as slowly as possible until the anchor is on deck otherwise it will be streamed aft under the hull and may damage the skin or foul the twin keels.

With more sea room astern there is no need to worry about any particular drill, the main is set, the anchor is hauled in and, with the cruiser dropping astern, it is only a matter of putting the helm over to cause her to fall aslant the wind and begin to sail. The helm must then be reversed at once, of course. It sometimes happens that the yacht is lying head to wind and tide with very little room at either side for turning. The usual solution to this problem is to start the motor – the best thing for the beginner to do, perhaps, but not for the man who takes pride in his seamanship. Depending upon the strength of the wind and the behaviour of the cruiser – whether she'll turn fast enough, that is – it may be feasible to haul up and down, set the jib, back it, break out, and, by putting the tiller across *opposite* to the jib as she begins falling astern, pin-wheel on her heel until she is running before the wind. This is something to practise, as it is pretty to watch.

Most small cruisers can be handled reasonably well under mainsail alone – though not sailed to windward, nor too well on a reach until they have full steerageway, but all owners should try sailing under main to get some idea of behaviour. The same goes for handling under the jib.

Heaving to

One of the simplest of all manoeuvres in a sailing craft, and one of the most useful, is heaving to. Most people associate this with bad weather and critical situations. Whether you want breathing space for chart-work or quieter going for a while to prepare food, it is handy to know how to heave to. Basically you have merely to come on the wind with the headsail sheeted to windward. It may be necessary to ease the mainsheet a shade, and in a few cases to lash the tiller slightly a-lee. It is also possible to heave to in some craft under mainsail alone or foresail alone, lashing the tiller in each case to oppose the thrust of the sail from turning the yacht (Fig. 13). In fact, heaving to in a small cruiser through force of bad weather isn't entirely advisable unless the sail areas are very small and only then if you have experimented beforehand to get some idea of how she'll behave. Lying close-hauled and without appreciable headway, small, light craft are knocked over easily by sudden heavy squalls and with a sea running they cannot be prevented from alternately paying off and luffing up. Bad-weather handling is dealt with more fully in another chapter.

Perhaps lying-to by simply easing out both sheets to their fullest extent and then, when the boat has almost stopped going ahead, lashing the tiller slightly to leeward, is the most useful trick because it provides breathing space to study a chart or to clear away the anchor ready for letting go. Beam-on and with sails shaking, most boats will lie quietly and with the barest forward movement.

Fig. 13 Heaving to is not a manoeuvre restricted to bad weather and it is a valuable way of slowing or stopping a boat, perhaps to allow the skipper to study the chart more thoroughly. A balance is found between the turning force of the mainsail and the backed headsail, the right position and angle varies according to each boat and to the strength of the wind. Many boats will lie quietly under backed headsail with the tiller lashed to leeward.

Working to windward

Getting a boat to windward under sail is a technique which has improved over the centuries from the lumbering crawl of square sailed ships which at best could lie no nearer than sixty degrees to the wind, to the modern yacht capable of eating up at almost half that angle and still making ground. This is the crux of the matter – a boat with her sails strapped hard in may be *pointed* tightly into the wind but she may not be making much real ground to windward; 'she looks but she don't go' was the way the fishermen used to put it, meaning that while her sails were holding wind the boat was heaving up and down and making as much leeway as headway.

How efficiently a boat can be taken to windward depends upon a number of things. It depends on her hull form, stiffness, the cut and set of her sails, the helmsman and the sea conditions relative to wind strength. Plainly a boat designed expressly for racing and sailed by a racing crew will out-foot a boat of similar length designed for cruising accommodation and all-round cruising purposes but it doesn't follow that cruising boats are necessarily slow and with sails that are poorly cut and trimmed, or that the crew will be indifferent to performance, particularly to windward.

The wind is never constant, it varies from minute to minute both in strength and direction, shifting a few degrees from close ahead to further aft. In practice this means that a boat hard on the wind can either be put on a course which is ruler straight and averaging these shifts of direction, or she can be *sailed* to windward with the helmsman bearing off fractionally as the wind heads and luffing as it draws aft, making good a sinuous course which takes advantage of every freeing puff.

On an offshore passage and out of sight of land, where the wind is usually steadier, the navigator may order a course that can be steered 'full-and-bye', this being the best angle to the wind found by experience of a particular boat, which keeps her sails full and which creates the least amount of leeway for the conditions. Thus a boat might be able to hold a good course closer to the wind in a firm force three and on a calm sea than she would when reefed well down and crashing along steeply heeled in a tumble of sea. This straight course (in fact, no course is ever absolutely straight) also allows the navigator to plot more accurately, calculating the course actually made good as against the course being steered.

Or the case might alter. There may be a vital headland to round before the tide turns foul and then the helmsman ignores the compass and concentrates on getting every foot to windward that careful helmsmanship can yield. This is the mark of a good helmsman; after a few minutes at the helm a sort of rhythm develops when the speed of the boat, the angle of heel and the pressure of the tiller merge together and the helmsman knows that he is 'in the groove'. Even when a compass course is being sailed a good helmsman will make better speed and ground than a poor one. The average course made good will be nearer to the navigator's expectations, but the helmsman will have juggled the boat through the waves avoiding the steeper ones which would have slowed the boat, luffing into the freeing puffs of wind, keeping the boat swinging along smoothly and thereby minimising leeway.

Tacking in crowded waters is a slightly different technique because there are moored boats, river bends, navigation buoys and other traffic to be avoided and the helmsman is very much in charge, scheming ahead and planning the tacks. There may also be a strong tidal current to cope with which can mean that tacking up-tide of a moored boat is to be avoided due to the risk of being set down on it while going about and temporarily slowed down. On a windy day, with the mast heeled steeply, there is also a risk of fouling it by sailing too close to another moored boat. As the river bends some tacks will be *making* ones which take the boat almost straight along the channel, while the opposite tacks will be short ones, perhaps across tide and *losing* tacks, which still have to be sailed at the best angle to the wind although losing ground while doing so.

The helmsman must also put the boat about at a speed which the rest of the crew who are handling the headsail sheets can cope with. A racing helmsman's job is to tack fast and without losing a split second, but in a lightly manned cruiser and on a breezy day this is pointless if the crew are still struggling to flatten in the sheets minutes later.

Windward passages at sea are very exhausting due to the constant pounding and the angle of heel (unless the yacht is a multihull) and according to the strength and stamina of a crew the skipper should either keep them short, avoid them in any wind strength above force three to four, or be prepared for a hard time. It is certainly foolish to take a weak crew straight out of a quiet river or harbour and into a hard thresh which is expected to continue for many hours – perhaps a day and a night on passage. Not only does it inflict a good deal of needless misery on the less committed of them, but it weakens the yacht's potential to cope with anything worse.

Usually it is the classic story of a holiday drawing to an end and the need to be home in time for work. The weather pattern may not be serious, but winds are fresh and on the nose and it is natural enough for a skipper to want to go out and have a look at it. If the crew is really weak it should be a very careful look and his decision to go on or go back should not be made in the first ten minutes because the initial exhilaration of bursting spray and sunlit waves fades quickly with seasickness and quicker still when the sun disappears.

Too many family cruisers come to grief because all aboard are seasick, cold and, having neglected the chart table, lost. A boat sails by virtue of the stamina and skill of her crew and these erode quickly once members begin to fall by the wayside. Often too it is all quite easily avoidable if the boat can be set on a course which is a little off the wind and therefore a drier, faster and easier course. It may not be taking her in quite the intended direction but it is far better to make for a port forty miles to leeward of the intended destination and reach it in comfort than to slam and crash day and night long with all aboard wet and miserable. This is when we have to ask ourselves just what the hell we're there for in the first place.

Play with your boat

It always strikes me as curious that most people sail their boats straight here or there and straight back when they go for an afternoon sail and you very seldom see them manoeuvring for the sheer fun of it, handling their boats just to see what they can do with them. Partly this is because a crew is divided into two camps, the helmsman who merely sits there sailing the boat and the others who have the more active role of working the sheet winches, and a skipper feels reluctant to inflict unnecessary work on the rest of the crew.

It makes a change, during a short afternoon sail, to take turns on the helm, perhaps circling and zigzagging round a mooring buoy in some quiet patch of water, or perhaps throwing overboard a fender or lifebuoy. The aim may be to bring the boat to a standstill as close as possible to it or to circle it as tightly as possible, which necessitates very fast tacking and gybing. The aim of these exercises is to give everybody a feel of the boat in varying strengths of wind, acquiring dexterity and judgement. The more the boat is turned and twisted in circles, figures-of-eight or in a square box pattern, the more confused the helmsman becomes regarding wind direction, and it is in order to develop a sense of rapid wind orientation that these exercises are carried out.

The point of it all may come home dramatically if an emergency change of course is needed in fog or at night, or for that matter when out of sight of land due to distance or haze. A case in point might be when a big ship suddenly looms up ahead and the yacht, which has been hard on the wind for some hours, has to bear off to a broad reach or even a quartering run. Suddenly the wind strength as felt by the helmsman drops right away and shifts from bow to beam or quarter, the boat comes upright and begins to roll and the helm becomes light. With the compass card spinning as well the boat may take charge and before he knows it the helmsman has gybed her and become totally disorientated.

Of any regular crew who cruise as a team every member should have a chance to throw the boat around in these fun exercises and it should be a regular feature during these afternoon outings, otherwise they only learn to steer in straight lines and perhaps only one person aboard is really competent to handle the boat. There is a particular point to all this. The ultimate test of boat-handling is also the ultimate sailing emergency – man overboard.

Man overboard

There are many theories concerning the best drill to follow and theories are revised constantly by different authorities, but the first essential is to recognise that the situation will be different for every boat and crew, therefore every crew, not just its skipper, must adopt and adapt the drill most likely to suit their case.

A crack racing crew, with plenty of experience in boat handling during mass race starts and plenty of brawny man-power, is very different from the man, wife and children crew of a small cruiser. A boat may be quick and easy to turn or slow and lumbering, she may have very high topsides or low ones. The man may be a portly or burly person and none too nimble and his wife may be small and physically weak, or both may be young and agile, or one may be very inexperienced, the other very competent. There is no rule of nature which says that the person left aboard to make the rescue is the best one to be able to cope. The vital thing is for this emergency to be thought about very thoroughly and, having made a plan, that it should be practised regularly. Very, very few do so.

This needs to be qualified a bit. The man-overboard crisis is a two-part one: first, the need to turn and bring the boat back and then to stop her exactly alongside the person in the water, and secondly, to get that person back on board. While crews will often carry out what they call 'man-overboard drill' by throwing a lifebuoy overboard and then sailing back to recover it with a boathook, this is so totally unlike the real thing as to be almost worthless. In fact it is almost harmful insofar as it engenders a sort of false confidence and a feeling of righteousness at having 'taken steps'.

When it happens it is either a shock so great that those left aboard are temporarily numbed into inaction or over-reaction, or at first it seems a great joke – until the truth dawns that the person in the water is struggling and looking terrified. Plainly it should never happen at all if strict use of safety harness and/or lifejackets is the rule aboard, but human fallibility and the feeling that it-can-never-happen-to-me are always present in the unguarded moment, which can happen as easily on a quiet sunny day as during a rough sail.

Drills, of whatever kind, have the great advantage of being automatic. The mind may go blank but the body slips into the familiar drill which, if it does nothing else, ensures that the correct first steps are

Plate 15 Rescue. A throwing quoit has been used to bring the victim alongside, the survivor aboard has dropped all sail to stop the boat, but the most difficult part, getting him aboard, may yet be still to come. (*Photo: courtesy of Yachting*

taken and triggers off conscious thought. The correct first step is to yell the alarm, release a lifebuoy and preferably a dan-buoy with a pole and flag and to detail one person to do nothing but watch and point to the person in the water. This is perhaps more important than anything at this stage because a head and shoulders in the water is lost to sight extraordinarily quickly among even small waves and if the boat is turned fast the disorientation which can follow may mean that nobody knows in what direction to look.

Crew panic must be controlled and one person must be in charge and stay in charge. It may not necessarily be the nominated skipper. Until such an emergency has been faced no person knows how he or she may react; they may become numb with shock and unable to give sensible orders. Speed is always essential, but here again the actual circumstances will dictate what sort of urgency exists. Early in the summer the water may be so cold that ten minutes in it may reduce a healthy person to a state of shock incapable of self-help. Or it may be a poor swimmer who is panicking, or he may be dazed from a blow on the head in falling. Conversely the person may be an excellent swimmer, cool-headed, or wearing a lifejacket, and the water may be quite warm.

These factors determine whether to concentrate first upon going back close enough to thrust a lifebuoy into the person's hands without trying to bring the boat to a standstill, or whether there is plenty of time to concentrate on the pick-up manoeuvre. The big risk is to rush in before the boat is properly under control and positioned for the final approach, then muff the shot and have to go round again – possibly several times. In simulated exercises against a stopwatch this happens repeatedly and even the best helmsman can fail to make a successful first shot.

There is a big division of opinion about whether it is better to drop all sails, lash them roughly and make the pick-up under engine, with the real risk of the propeller injuring the swimmer, or whether it should always be under sail. It *must* depend upon how well the surviving crew aboard can sail the boat and if the person who goes overboard happens to be the only person aboard who is expert enough to carry out a sailing pick-up then the engine is an obvious choice, but with the absolute rule that the engine is cut dead completely the instant the swimmer is grasped.

The pick-up manoeuvre must be aimed at bringing the boat back to the person in the water from leeward and placing him under the lee side, if under sail. The classic advice used to be that when under sail and a person fell overboard the boat should be gybed at once, but thinking has changed. There are two good arguments against gybing: if the helmsman reacts fast and gybes instantly, from being closehauled or reaching the boat will quite possibly make a circle that brings her back to the person in the water, but so fast that there is no time to do anything about it. If on the other hand the gybe is delayed, the boat will come back to windward of the person and have to be borne off hard in order to get downwind for

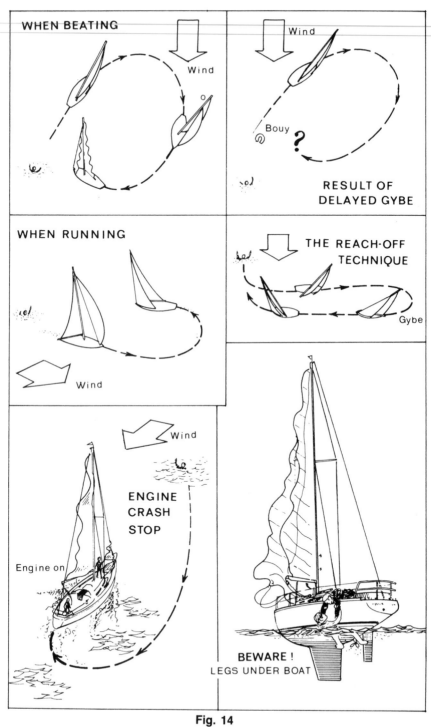

Fig. 14

another luffing approach. The sole virtue of the gybe-at-once theory is that it is simple and automatic. It should also be realised that the boat may not be ready for a gybe and a heavy gybe could mean damage, fouled-up sheets and frantic winch work as she comes up to the wind with her jib aback (Fig. 14).

The current Royal Yachting Association rule is that the boat should be put on a straight broad reach no matter what point of sailing she may be on, the helmsman should note the compass heading, then when the crew are ready he can turn, tack and sail back on a reciprocal compass heading. There may be a spinnaker to lower if the boat was running, or a guy on the boom to be got rid of, or the rest of the crew may be asleep below. The only weakness to the plan that I can see is that an experienced helmsman may not steer very straight initially and it is hard to judge a reach unless the person has a good wind-sense. Usually one tends to make up-wind a little rather than across it, then when the boat is tacked for the return and the real wind direction is felt as she slows a different course back is sailed. Could a novice be sure of noting the compass heading and then working out the reciprocal?

Having returned, got to leeward and either luffed up for the person in the water or, as I would prefer, approached him on a close reach while spilling wind from the sails to slow the boat, the person in the water will be lost from view by the helmsman and there is a risk of actually running him down unless other crew give directions. It now depends upon whether the person in the water is capable of grabbing a rope's end and helping himself. If that is so then a boarding ladder can be hooked onto the lee rail and with some help he can get aboard.

A boarding ladder must be secure or the climber may kick sideways and dislodge it. The rungs must stand out from the yacht's side in order to afford a good foothold (rope ladders are useless) and the bottom rungs must go right down well below the water otherwise a less than agile person will never be able to reach it with his foot. Permanent stern transom ladders are often hailed as the complete answer, but they are not. In fairly calm waters they work fairly well although the bottom steps are never low enough, but in a moderate to choppy sea the stationary boat will be pitching head to wind or pitching and rolling beam-on with this stern ladder rising and falling violently. If it doesn't actually injure the person its fast acceleration on the uprise will probably tear it from his grasp. It should be remembered that a fully dressed person weighs a great deal more than normal due to soaked clothing.

Another ruse often advised is simply to drop a bight of sheet over the side for him to stand on, then winch the rope in by degrees until he is high enough to be dragged in over the rail. This *can* work, but a rolling boat, scrambling crew and panic can make it impossible – certainly impossible for a lone survivor aboard unless the casualty can help himself. Neither will the boat always lie quietly with her tiller unmanned. Freeing

Plate 16 A boarding ladder must stand out clear of the topsides so that toes can get a safe hold. This one has two optional lengths, allowing it to hang below the surface of the water in its life-saving role.

sheets right off and lashing the tiller to leeward *should* work, but may not, and the boat may be luffing herself, may even tack herself and in so doing heel *away* from the person in the water, breaking his grasp. In any case she will be drifting to leeward and a little forward at perhaps a knot and a half, .which will tend to drag the person's lower limbs under the hull.

The pick-up

Various methods are suggested including dropping the mainsail out of its mast track completely, bundling the loose sail over the side to form a sort of sling into which the person can be laid, then haul-rolling him up to the rail by winching on the halyard. This is possible, but in windy weather the sail, now attached only to the boom and halyard, can become almost unmanageable. A similar use of the jib is also suggested, by bundling it overboard just as it is and winching in on the sheet. Others advocate swinging the boom outboard and using the sheet as a lifting tackle; this supposes the topping lift to be strong enough and the sheet tackle to be powerful enough, and few boats satisfy either requirement. A more practical idea is to keep the dinghy on deck half-inflated during any offshore passage and this when dropped overboard offers an easily entered horseshoe into which the person is pulled in order to buy precious time. Whatever the device used, the first vital need is to tie a rope round the casualty's armpits to keep his head above water and to prevent him drifting away.

The majority of people when asked how they'd lift a person aboard say instantly that they'd use the main halyard and winch him up, but they say this without ever having tried it. The extreme emergency would involve a lone woman having to lift a heavy and waterlogged husband who cannot help himself and unless she was a competent, cool and determined sailor he would be doomed. Before assuming that this method would work it should be tried out by attaching the halyard to the safety harness of a heavy person, standing on deck, and then getting a physically weaker member of the crew to attempt to winch him into the air. In the great majority of cases it is impossible because the average small halyard winch worked one-handed by the average woman just isn't powerful enough, moreover there is the added weight of soaked clothes to consider and a total lift of maybe four or five feet in a rolling boat to cope with.

All manner of ingenious ideas are suggested, leading the halyard back to the more powerful sheet winches and so forth, but anything which needs special setting up using equipment which has to be rummaged for in lockers means lost time, and time is short. Of the various devices offered for sale, one consists of a pole with a stiff open loop at the end and the idea is that the loop can be dropped down over the casualty's head and shoulders, then the halyard is attached to its inboard end ready for hauling up. This is a promising idea in that it means that rescuers on deck can *reach* the person in the water and reaching him can be otherwise impossible in modern high freeboard yachts; which raises another question.

Should a member of crew jump overboard to the assistance of the person? Some years ago a frightened woman, alone on a small cruiser, had a terrible tale to tell. Briefly, she, her husband and a man friend went sailing; the man fell overboard. After repeated attempts to reach him the husband jumped overboard with a rope's end. Both men were lost. However, it could just be that in certain circumstances a member of crew wearing a life-jacket and with a rope loop might be the only hope of saving a casualty who was already beginning to drown. It would mean that the boat would have to be safely under control and that there was adequate muscle still on board to effect a double rescue afterwards. This is the sort of split-second decision that can only be made at the time, but it is dangerous.

Returning to the question of lifting an inert person, there is one method involving equipment which would need to be always on deck at sea and crew trained in its use. It consists of a powerful rope tackle comprising a treble and a double block which reduces the weight of the load to one-fifth. The tackle is made up and fully extended (overhauled), then the triple block is hoisted aloft on the main halyard, which is then made fast. The other end of the tackle is snap-hooked to the lifting strop and if necessary the hauling end of the tackle can be taken to a mast winch – not always possible due to the angle of the lead. A tackle fully extended cannot be stowed away in a locker without it tangling, therefore it is single-plaited into a short bunch of loops which, when pulled sharply while hoisting, fall free and ready for use (Fig. 15).

A final comment on the man-overboard emergency at night. It is obviously far more dangerous, mainly due to losing the person from view but also because at night work on deck is more difficult in every way. The life buoy which is stowed right aft closely within the helmsman's reach should have an automatic water-activated or turn-over activated flashing light. All members of crew should have retro-reflective cloth patches bonded to the shoulders of their sailing smocks and more should be added to life buoys and to the whip staff of the dan-buoy. This retro-reflective cloth is probably more important than any battery-operated life buoy light which has a limited life of a few hours because the beam of a powerful torch scanning the water picks up on it at astonishing distances.

Every boat should have at least two life buoys on deck, one as above with its light and also a small parachute drogue of maybe a foot in diameter which will prevent the life buoy from being skimmed away downwind. Both buoys should be of horseshoe type which is easier for a

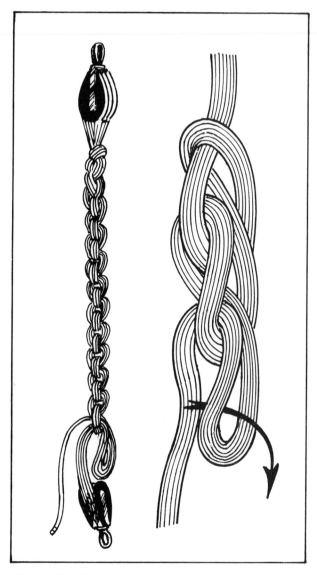

Fig. 15 A lifting tackle fully extended can be prevented from tangling by making it into a single plait as shown. It can then be stowed away somewhere easily accessible and unplaited simply by pulling.

person to get into in the water, and a second one might be stowed, plus a drogue, on the top of the sliding hatch, held by a single strip of rubber cord. A third buoy or buoyant cockpit cushions are also advised. The aim should be to avoid trying to throw these buoys unless it has been practised in advance because even a moderate wind tends to make accurate throwing impossible.

79

A great deal more can be said about this particular emergency but I have said enough, I hope, to stress the need for individual thought, crew discussion and practice because it probably constitutes the greatest test of helmsmanship, seamanship and cool decision-making that anyone is ever likely to face. I have only once in my life been present in a boat when a man has fallen overboard, but I have never forgotten the struggle which three strong, fit men had to pull one person back aboard.

The dinghy tender

Although the increasing numbers of yacht marinas everywhere now mean that it is possible to cruise for weeks on end without ever needing a dinghy as a tender for reaching the shore, it is essential to have one aboard otherwise the quiet places can't be visited. The lonely creeks and sheltered rivers and bays which are the real job of cruising – they can be visited of course, but having anchored, nobody can get ashore. A dinghy has other uses as well; kedge anchors may need laying, nearby boats can be visited, a dinghy half-inflated as mentioned earlier may save life, and not least of all a dinghy for kids in life-jackets provides endless hours of occupation.

In the past the choice was between conventionally built planked dinghies, plywood versions and folding canvas-sided boats. Today the inflatable has largely replaced these, being lighter and far safer, but one original requirement remains: no matter how small the cruiser, human beings remain the same size and weight and the dinghy must not be miniaturised.

A wooden, plywood or GRP 'hard' dinghy does have some qualities that the inflatable usually lacks; it is easier to row whereas an inflatable is an absolute pig and when loaded impossible to move by paddle-power in anything of a breeze and chop. Hard dinghies usually mean dry feet also, while inflatables if soft-bottomed mean a perpetual pool of water where your feet press downwards. Hard dinghies with proper buoyancy chambers or bags are unsinkable, too, even if damaged, whereas a gashed or punctured inflatable becomes useless.

The big argument against hard boats is that if the cruiser is too small to carry them on deck they have to be towed at sea, and in bad weather, particularly when running, they become unmanageable and a constant worry. An inflatable which can be stowed in a parcel or carried half-inflated on deck wins hands down, but if you have one it means that an outboard motor to drive it is practically essential if more than a couple of people are to be carried in all conditions of wind and tide, and this raises a warning. When the yacht is lying head to wind and the dinghy is moored alongside, any weight in her stern will raise the bows and it needs very little by way of a sudden puff to capsize her if the wind gets

Plate 17 A Tinker Tramp. This versatile inflatable can be rowed, motored or as shown here, sailed. Perhaps its most distinctive feature though is that it can be fitted with a canopy for use as a form of life raft. (*Photo: Henshaw Marine Ltd*)

underneath. This is particularly so when one person is crouching aft attaching or removing the outboard motor, and while a safety line on the motor may guarantee its safety, the person involved may be at risk. It is always safer to dump a weight of some sort in the dinghy bows while attending to the motor or when leaving the dinghy alongside with motor still attached.

One of the meatier bones of contention is the argument that a dinghy cannot be regarded as a form of life raft and many people insist that because a dinghy can be propelled and a life raft cannot it follows that a crew adrift after their boat has sunk may be able to reach land or a well-used shipping lane if they can row a few miles, while a life raft might mean that they drift out of reach of help. There are dinghies designed to fulfil a dual role, such as the British Tinker Tramp which has air-bottle inflation and a full protective canopy, and can be sailed as well as rowed. Boats of this type are not automatically inflated, though.

The real killer is not extremes of wind and sea, despite the fact that they are a threat, but death from exposure, from hypothermia. Thus a canopy is essential; also if at all possible crew taking to raft or dinghy should remain dry in the process and take with them warm clothing, food, fresh water, distress flares, a radio beacon and much more besides. Most of these are pre-packed with the life raft but would have to be contained in a grab-bag for a dinghy escape. Dinghies are in regular use and therefore crew are experienced in boarding them and handling them, while life rafts are a virtually unknown quantity. However, the life raft has one particular quality which the alternative may lack and that is that it is instantly ready at the jerking of a release lanyard, and should a boat become badly holed and be sinking fast, or have an explosion aboard and become a mass of flame, this quality would save life by a matter of precious seconds. Whether to drift with the tide in a life raft or have a chance of getting somewhere in a dinghy is for the individual to decide.

An ordinary inflatable dinghy, however, is *not* a substitute for a life raft because it offers no protection from the weather. Usually a yacht's tender is too small to take the full crew and at sea in even moderately choppy conditions it would quickly become half awash; at best it would support the crew provided help was quickly at hand. The grim truth is that for any person of late middle age or older a single night in soaked clothes in a dinghy would probably prove fatal – at least in these northern climates.

Trouble-free handling

Trouble-free sailing is largely achieved by thinking ahead as a matter of habit. Things rarely seem to go wrong singly: an accidental gybe, a jam in the mainsheet, a wild luff which loses a sail-bag overside – and in the ensuing fracas to pick it up the ship is run ashore. A chapter of accidents like that is no exaggeration, and yet most of it was due to bad management.

Embark upon no manoeuvre without first looking ahead for possible snags. Plan ahead the whole time. If the motor misses a beat and then resumes running smoothly, cast off a couple of sail-tyers, coil a heaving line up again, or check that the anchor is easy to clear away. It is a habit of mind, and one which eliminates half the scrambles of sailing. Orderliness, too, pays off handsomely: one warp always coiled, stopped with breaking stuff and easy to get at; the boathook ready to grab; at least one fender handy if not the rest – and so on.

Besides planning and order, cultivate calm. Most men on their own stay reasonably controlled in a spot of bother, but give them a wife or a crew and they feel that a performance is called for. The old saying, 'If in danger or in doubt, shout and scream and rush about', is too true to be really funny. No matter how small the vessel, a hysterical skipper is a crime. One order, repeated only if it hasn't been heard, no sarcasm and no heroics. The quiet of an anchorage broken by the yelps of a big man in a tiny boat makes one shudder. Keep the voice down and stay cool, then, if something really merits a bellow you have an unexpected shout in your locker. Don't try to do everything yourself, even if you could do it better and faster, or your crew will let you get on with it and stay half-trained. Explain what you plan to do and then do just that thing – if a change of plan is forced upon you, then say so at once. Make decisions and stick to them as closely as possible and then, if the hunch doesn't pay off, don't embark upon a course of humble apology – even a two-man crew must have trust in the skipper's judgement. Be distinct and logical. Don't say 'To starboard' meaning put the tiller to port, either point, or say 'Port your helm' if you want it that way, and finally, learn to trust the crew when they're in charge and you are below or else don't blame them if they do something wrong; ultimately it's the skipper's fault.

CHAPTER SEVEN

Anchoring, Mooring Up, Beaching and Reduction to Soundings

The anchor and cable is any vessel's last line of defence; when sails and engine are for various possible reasons out of action, or the crew too tired to cope, the anchor becomes what it has always been – the symbol of hope. Anchor design today is more efficient than it has ever been. Nowadays, though, anchors are designed to bury themselves instead of hooking a single spike into the sea-bed, but to operate properly in extreme conditions they need some help.

Anchor weight

They need to be of the correct weight for the boat. Unfortunately when new boats are sold with a basic inventory of equipment, cost-conscious builders furnish them with anchors of the minimum weight allowable for the size of boat, and anchor cables of the minimum length, usually around 15 fathoms or 30 metres. As a result there are many owners who accept these weights and lengths as a sort of standard and never question them.

The old rule-of-thumb when anchors were mainly of the old fisherman type was one pound of weight for every foot length of boat. Fisherman anchors need a lot of weight because their holding power in average to good sea-beds, which means hard sand or mud, is only about 7–10 times their weight, whereas that of a burying type anchor can be perhaps 30–80 times its weight, provided it buries properly in good holding conditions. In the smaller sizes of cruiser this pound-per-foot rule is still a good guide and, although generous, a 30-lb anchor for a 30-foot boat would enhance her chances of not dragging in a gale to an enormous extent. Usually she would be equipped with a 25-lb anchor, or even lighter than that.

The sum of it is that while a boat with a somewhat lighter anchor than desired will be adequately anchored for ninety per cent of her time, there will come occasions when she has to be anchored in poor holding ground, or in water which is deeper than would normally be chosen, or in rough water, or a bad gale. It is then that the marginally under-weight anchor will almost certainly drag, while the marginally over-weight one will probably hold. Anchoring involves a number of factors as well as weight: scope of cable, holding ground, exposure to wind, boat windage and state of sea. In an exposed anchorage there will be waves which cause the boat to roll and pitch and at times to sheer from side to side, and the snubbing of the boat at her cable can double or treble the load on the anchor.

The Romans and their contemporaries were well aware of how vital it was that the lead of the cable should not lift the anchor (a fisherman type) off the sea-bed, and many had solid lead stocks to hold them down. The same need today is satisfied by using a chain cable, or alternatively a length of chain, perhaps four fathoms, connecting a nylon rope cable to the anchor. An all-chain cable by virtue of its weight is hard to lift as the boat rises and falls to the seas and this produces a shock absorbing effect; nylon, being elastic, does the same thing, which is why other synthetics which stretch less should never be used as anchor cables.

Scope

Another false notion is that the scope of cable needed for anchoring safely is three times the depth of water at high tide. In fact, three × depth should be the *minimum* in quiet or average conditions. When rope is used a scope of five × depth is advised but again this is the minimum and it is possible that in some conditions up to 10 × depth may be needed to stop a boat from dragging. This very seldom happens because once a boat drags people tend to let out a few more fathoms and if she still drags they start their engines and go in search of a better spot.

There may not be a better spot, or the engine won't start and in any case getting under way in a crowded anchorage with a hard gale blowing can lead to more damage than dragging may cause. I like to carry 25–30 fathoms of cable and have a good long warp in reserve which can serve as a kedge warp or be tailed onto the main anchor cable in an emergency to give me a total of around 50 fathoms. Alternatively, and since my kedge is only a little smaller than the main anchor, I can moor the boat to two anchors if there isn't room astern to pay out a long main scope.

Perhaps the problem of handling a bigger anchor is unacceptable to some skippers and the twin anchor solution is more attractive, but the fact remains that the second anchor won't be used in the ordinary way and the boat will be anchored on her slightly under-weight anchor for most of the time. It means that extra vigilance is needed when the wind pipes up during the night with nobody on deck to notice her beginning to drag. Not that dragging is necessarily always serious, and a skipper should take into account what the end result might be. If a boat is surrounded by soft mud banks and shores the worst that can happen is a few hours spent with the boat lying dried out at an unsocial angle; a very different matter if there is a rocky shore or a quay wall to leeward.

The kedge

In times past small vessels were far more reliant upon their anchors because, lacking engines, anchoring was the only alternative to being carried by a foul tide or to safeguard the boat in tight corners where there was no room to sail. To these ends boats carried a number of anchors, certainly three, two main bow anchors and a substantial kedge.

The kedge, being the lightest anchor aboard, can be used for temporary anchoring in light weather, perhaps to ride out a foul tide in a calm when a boat is racing and the engine can't be used, or to stop briefly for some reason. It is also the anchor which is carried out in the dinghy and laid off when the cruiser has run aground and needs to be hauled out into deep water. It is the kedge which is dropped either at an angle from the main anchor or in line astern when there is a need to restrict the swinging circle of the yacht, perhaps when she is anchored in a narrow channel with deep water restricted to the middle.

Although it has to be light enough to be handled in and out of the dinghy it must also be capable of taking a solid hold because hauling off by kedge or mooring with one to restrict swinging room both mean that there will be a lot of load on it. Once again, scope is the key to efficiency.

Kedging off

To haul a boat off by kedge after she has run aground is the last resort when other tricks fail and if the tide is still on the flood there is no great urgency, as a rule. But if it is ebbing, especially a spring ebb, and the boat cannot be sailed off at the first attempt, the kedge will have to be laid out at lightning speed. On a 5-metre (say 16-ft spring rise) tide which is at half ebb the water may fall away at a rate of around 10 cm or, say, 4 inches in about five minutes, or if it has only just begun to ebb maybe 3–4 cm or $1\frac{1}{2}$ inches in five minutes. It may take ten minutes to launch a dinghy, bend kedge to warp and row it out.

If you run on a sandbank of unknown shape and extent, possibly in some estuary, you will usually have to try to get off in the same direction as you went on. If the bottom shelves very gradually and the ebb is running fast the case is pretty hopeless and the only thing to do with a very small craft is to turn the whole crew overboard to lighten her at once and walk her back.

Will the wind help or hinder? This is the first consideration. If you run slap up a bank with a following wind it quite obviously won't help. Get sail off her right away, push her round, and either motor off or take out the kedge in the dinghy, if you have one, and haul her into water deep enough for you to make sail again.

Most strandings occur during a beat up a channel when one tack is held for a shade too long. If the bank is fairly steep it is easy enough to push the bows through the eye of the wind and get the jib aback. This, of course, tends to drive her heel harder aground and if the crew were all forward pushing, their weight back in the cockpit may glue her so firmly to the bank that she still refuses to sail off. Let draw the jib and send them forward again.

Quite often a boat can be skimmed over the shallows after touching by heeling her so far over that her draft is lessened, but this trick doesn't work with the twin-keeler which increases the draft of her leeward keel as she heels; the opposite is true in this case, the more upright the better (Fig. 16(B)).

Larger yachts are compelled to follow a more involved drill: using kedges, rocking (sugging) to loosen the hold of the mud around the keel, and so on. For the very small cruiser in danger of sticking on a falling tide as she makes her way up some creek it is far better to have one member of the crew all ready in a life-jacket and ready to push off, than it is to follow any big-ship routine.

The kedge must be hooked over the dinghy stern and the warp is then paid down, *not* coiled or it will tangle as it runs out, on the floor of the dinghy between the rower's feet. It must not be paid out from the yacht because this would mean that the rower would be dragging the rope out, perhaps across the current, instead of paying it out behind him as he went. To pay a rope down you simply feed it in a pile just as it falls and if the pile is not disturbed the rope will run out freely without any snagging.

In perhaps eight out of ten attempts the kedge is not taken far enough out, perhaps due to haste or because it is hard work. Then there is a delay while the rower ships the oars and heaves the anchor over which means that the dinghy drifts swiftly down-wind from the chosen spot and the end result is that the kedge is laid at the wrong angle to the stranded cruiser and too close to her. Upon hauling in it takes some distance before the anchor bites hard and if the cruiser moves as the crew heave away, the scope of the kedge is shortened still more so that the anchor breaks out before the cruiser can be pulled right off.

The kedge, then, must be taken off as far as possible, which may mean joining several warps together. If it has to be taken off into deep water, such as may be the case if the cruiser is grounded on a steep-to bank or hummock, the scope taken out must be what would be given for that depth of water (3–5 times the deep water depth at minimum), even though the yacht is lying in maybe three feet depth (Fig. 17).

Perhaps the majority of us rely upon the engine to get us off in the first place, dropping all sail and motoring hard astern with all available crew weight right forward in the bows to lift her stern, but in some cases

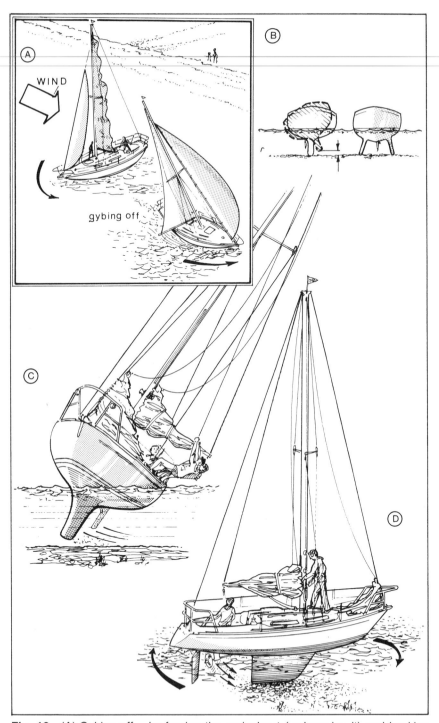

Fig. 16 (A) Gybing off – by freeing the mainsheet (or lowering it) and backing the headsail, short-keeled craft can often be turned down-wind and gybed free. (B) Heeling a boat can decrease her draught enough to get her off the mud, but in the case of a twin-keeled hull heeling her has the opposite effect of increasing her draught. (C) Sugging (rocking her) by having crew weight transferred from side to side rapidly can help free the keel from mud suction. (D) With short-keeled boats a hard burst of engine on full rudder may pivot the boat towards deeper water.

Yacht aground in 1 Metre but
kedge must be given the scope
needed for a depth of 6 Metres.

1 M

6 Metres

Fig. 17

this see-saw trick merely presses the forward end of the keel deeper and it is then better to heel the boat to reduce draught. As suggested earlier it is sometimes possible to pile all spare crew into the dinghy to get them off the cruiser, or even get them to jump overboard into the shallows – if it is really shallow. There can be a danger though when it comes time to get them back again, and non-swimmers must stay aboard.

Choosing an anchorage

Small cruisers fall betwixt and between when it comes to anchoring. Many main yacht anchorages are too deep and too exposed for really little craft. The slightest breeze starts them jumping around, and passing motor-boats can make life hell. There is also the critical business of getting ashore. The small dinghy carried by these yachts is not to be relied on for a long row in any but calm conditions. Any chance of a fouled anchor becomes more troublesome, too, if there is no anchor winch nor enough deck space for heaving and 'hanging off'.

A suitable anchorage must therefore have a maximum of three or, at the outside, four fathoms of water at high tide, reasonable shelter, a pitch well clear of power traffic, and within close reach of the shore or a landing of some sort. This all boils down to a position just outside the low-water mark in most waters, and choice of ground means care with chart and echo sounder. Big tidal ranges are a separate problem.

It is something of a guide to note the types of craft already moored there: big, deep-draught yachts along the edge of the fairway and small keel boats and cruisers edging the shallows. Echo sounders are important, because the inshore line of craft may well be on drying moorings or the soundings may rise abruptly from three or four fathoms to a drying bank. With a large-scale chart or harbour plan, a fair idea of where to lie can be planned in advance. It may not be possible to use the chosen spot when you get there, but at least there is something to aim for. The soundings (which may be shown tinted) show whether the shore is steep-to and the underlined figures give drying heights. Charts always tend to make the space seem smaller than it really is, and the creek which looks impossibly narrow is apt to grow into a wide sheet of water by the time you arrive. This is a common snare. If you arrive at dead low water on a big spring tide the scene might be very different again.

If you aim to lie afloat at low water you must first calculate the level to which the tide on the day concerned is likely to fall – chart datum figures deal with Lowest Astronomical Tide and this means that there will be times at neaps when there is more water at low tide than the chart shows, and at other times (equinoctial springs) when they relate more closely to the chart soundings shown.

If it is dead low water you obviously know whether there is enough water there for you to lie afloat – you'll go aground if there isn't. If it is dead high water, a sounding will show how much scope of cable to let go. If there is, say, four fathoms, and the tide-table shows a height for that day of only two fathoms above chart datum, then obviously there will be enough water and to spare, but since we are trying to tuck into a snug shallow-water berth we must work to rather finer limits. This means understanding how the tides work and how to establish just what depth of water there will be in any particular spot and at any particular time. This matter is dealt with under the heading 'Reductions to Soundings' later in this chapter.

Without a large-scale chart and some idea of the sea-bed contour, you may find your chosen spot fine for your ship, but only if she can stay in that precise spot, which isn't likely. Having let go the anchor and settled back on the scope, the yacht may be in very shallow water, or again the spot where the sounding was taken may be on the side of a steep underwater hillside, so that by the time the anchor is let go you may have drifted back into very deep water. The moral is always to take an approach line of soundings, three at least, and anchor where the bottom is reasonably flat and the scope of the swing embraces a circle of water deep enough to float the yacht.

If you make a mistake, and as a consequence are dried out for an hour or two, it will be no hardship in such a small boat, particularly if she is a twin-keeler, but it might delay a start or mean a muddy business getting back aboard in the dark. There are more sinister pitfalls dealt with under 'Beaching a twin keeler'.

One of the finest guarantees of a good night's rest is an anchor-weight. This is simply a weight which can be lowered down the anchor-warp or chain to a position well below the hull. It greatly increases the holding power of the anchor by directing the pull at a lower angle, and it reduces the tendency to snub and sheer a vessel in a tideway lying to her full scope. For a small cruiser of up to 30 feet length, a 14-lb weight with an outsize shackle to go over the cable can be lowered one-third to half-way down the scope (Fig. 18).

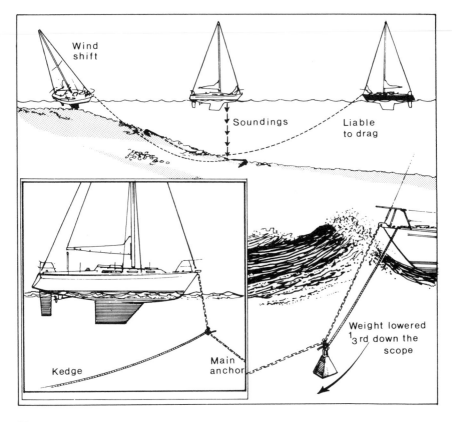

Fig. 18 Anchoring too close to a steep-to bank can mean going aground if there is an unexpected shift of wind; it is also unwise to place the anchor on the face of a sea-bed slope pulling towards deeper water, as the anchor is then more likely to drag. If the kedge is used to limit the swinging circle while at anchor, it can be bent onto the main cable and lowered to below keel depth. An anchor weight is a valuable aid to safe anchoring, increasing the holding power and softening the snubbing in a seaway.

Handling at the time of letting go naturally varies according to circumstances. You should plan your approach to a crowded anchorage before you reach it. When you have studied the chart and chosen your anchorage, rough transits will give a guide to the selected spot. They might, for instance, be: A jetty open of the next bend in the river, sail until the small creek to port opens up. This will be the spot to begin looking for a space and taking soundings (Fig. 19).

Although it seems foolish to prescribe a course of action more befiting a twenty-tonner, the broad principles hold good for any size of craft, and in practice amount only to a long, careful sizing up of the situation as you approach. For instance, sail in and have a look, then sail around and come in ready to let go. This simple habit saves a lot of

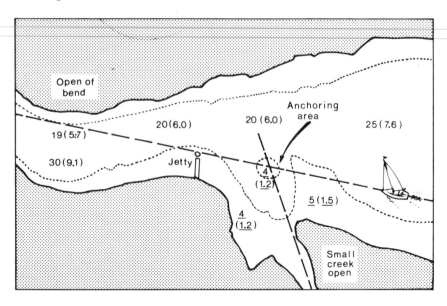

Fig. 19

trouble. It may be high water with the ebb just beginning. The moored yachts will have swung, but all their slack cable will still be ranged out along the bottom *down tide*. To anchor too close astern of one of them may mean that she'll be on top of you when the strengthening ebb causes her to lie back on her mooring. Again, at slack water there may be fine wide gaps in the ranks due to the yachts lying at different angles to each other, but as the stream begins the gaps may close. Make allowances for shallow-hulled power-boats which skate around in a wind and deep-keeled hulls liable to sheer when the wind is against the tide. Note that a yacht with a kedge out as well may mean that her swinging circle is going to be small. Suspiciously vacant areas where submerged wreckage or oyster-beds may lie should be regarded with caution.

Possible future shifts of wind should be taken into consideration, especially if the anchor lies on the side of a steep-to bed, as a strong offshore wind may drag it into deep water. In such cases it is better to let go the main anchor in the shallows and lay a kedge to keep you from swinging inshore. This is done by taking the kedge well off in the opposite direction to a scope of maybe six to one (the kedge is much lighter and needs extra scope), then making it fast to the main cable and veering a fathom or so to take it below the hull depth (see Fig. 18).

A tripping line and buoy are most essential if you are anchoring where there is a risk of fouling moorings or rocky ground. The line goes to the crown of the anchor and need be no more than five fathoms in length since it is unlikely that there will be more water than this at high water. If your anchor fouls, the buoy will be visible at slack water, even if it tows under in the current the rest of the time. By means of this line the anchor can usually be pulled free from the opposite direction. Be wary at slack water low tide, however; a tripping-line buoy can foul your rudder and later trip the anchor.

If your anchor is badly fouled you may well need help from a shipyard, or even lose both anchor and some chain. The normal method of clearing an anchor that has fouled a mooring-chain is to haul it up as far as possible at dead low water, lifting the mooring-chain off the bottom until you can reach it. A line is then passed under the mooring-chain and secured on deck. If you pay out your anchor-chain, the anchor, with luck, will fall clear, and you can then slip the mooring-chain by letting go one end of the line. It is a back-breaking job at the best of times, and may be impossible. See page 234 for note on the use of the chain collar.

Anchor noises

After a while one learns to interpret the sounds made by a small yacht at anchor, but at first every rumble is hailed as a sign of a dragging anchor. Chain will rumble loudly each time the tidal stream changes and the yacht swings and begins dragging slack lengths of chain one across the other. On stony ground the noise is even louder. The true dragging sound is very little different. Like the slack chain noise it is spasmodic, but more likely to occur as the vessel snatches at her chain or snubs to a sea. A cruiser sheering to and fro when the wind is against the tide produces a similar sound.

To check whether an anchor is holding, line up marks or lights ashore and watch them for some minutes on end. In squalls the yacht will lie back on her anchor and then move ahead under the pull of the weight of the bight of chain in the lulls, and this will tend to make marks in line shift a little. Only by watching steadily can a real drag be detected – unless, of course, the anchor is hardly holding at all. If you put your hand on the chain or rope you can feel the anchor grumbling as it jerks from hold to hold on the bottom, but do not mistake the rhythmic throbbing of the tide against the cable for a dragging hook.

If she is taking up slack cable on the turn of the tide (often the tide is flowing strongly before the yacht decides to lie back) the chain may sometimes be seen to lead taut ahead, fall slack, lead ahead again and so on. The important moment is when she finally brings up on her full scope. The chain will then lead straight out and go bar taut as it takes the load. If the anchor is going to drag then that is the moment to notice it. The chain should sink quietly back into its catenary instead of suddenly jerking and tightening again.

More and more scope will be needed in bad weather, but the chain may have to be shortened in when wind and tide are in opposition as the yacht may begin to sheer wildly around the anchorage. It is then that it is best to lie between two anchors in order to limit the range of sheering.

The above assumes the use of an all-chain cable. With a rope cable, behaviour is different since its elasticity absorbs much of the 'information', but with practice one soon learns to distinguish the clues to a dragging anchor.

Beaching a twin keeler

One of the great advantages of most twin keelers is that they can be beached. Twin keels offer a chance of sitting upright, and make it possible to have a safe berth ashore with the least amount of dinghy work. But it isn't safe to assume that any shore will be suitable for drying out, especially in strange water.

The ideal is a gently sloping shore which is level and firm, preferably the weather shore if she is to lie quietly afloat at high water. If the cruiser has made her port in the evening, her crew will want to be able to go ashore for the ritual drink and get back safely in the dark. If they put her where she'll take the ground this will either mean rowing the few yards to dry land and carrying the boat back dry-shod later on, or the other way about.

With an evening high water, it is sensible to arrange the programme ashore so that the cruiser is beached with a couple of hours still to flood. This means that she'll still be afloat roughly the same amount of time after high water, but her anchor must be taken off and dropped so that she can't wash in as the tide rises. Knowing just when you can get away from a dry berth is important for an owner cruising to a plan. It isn't much use sticking the cruiser up among the bulrushes on the top of a mid-afternoon tide if you have a passage to make next day, since she won't float until some time in the early afternoon, and the alternative is to start before dawn – not always popular with a weary crew.

Knowing height of tide and rate of rise and fall, the owner can decide how much water he'll need beneath him at high water if he is to have time enough for a later departure. Since rise and fall are slower towards the top and bottom of the tide, his boat may remain afloat in a few feet of water for perhaps three or four hours just before and just after high water. After that the level begins to fall rapidly and the boat must be moved well out if she is to remain afloat for a longer spell; merely anchoring a few yards further offshore will mean grounding again within an hour or less.

Suspiciously vacant plots along an otherwise crowded shore must be investigated. There may be an underwater groyne or row of piles, a hardway or landing, or the bottom there may be intersected with gullies into which one of the twin keels might fall with dire results. The bottom may be dotted with large chunks of masonry, or there may be a by-law forbidding anchorage there. A steep, or even moderately steep, shore has two main disadvantages. If there is a stiff onshore breeze the waves will roll straight ashore and may be eighteen inches or so in height which will mean gross discomfort afloat and some bad banging as the tide ebbs. A gently shelving shore causes the height of such waves to diminish safely before the keels begin to ground. The second snag is domestic. Most bunks are tapered to one end so that they can only be used lying with the head forward. To beach a cruiser on a steepish shore means passing the night at an odd angle if she grounds up and down. The alternative of beaching her to lie beam-on is easier for sleeping, but a constant nuisance for cooking and general moving around.

If bad weather is forecast any beach other than a flat one should be avoided, unless it is almost certain to remain a weather shore. Most blows are likely to come from south-east to sou'west, and veer around through west to north-west, which means that beaching on a shore sheltered from those quarters is usually safe. But if the bad weather is due to a depression shaping to pass to the south there's no guarantee of peace.

There is one final point to remember. A house ashore may own the foreshore rights. This means that while you may beach there below the mean low water level, you have no claim of access to the dry land. You may beach in an emergency and get ashore, of course, but be careful you don't trespass. A good many waterside house-owners spend their lives trying to defend their privacy against picnic parties which have no respect for private property. This means that you will need to use a little tact. But most of them are yachtsmen and this will open a lot of doors, for their objections are usually to noise and litter and damage to their property.

Moorings

It is a common enough practice to pick up any old mooring in a strange anchorage. This is usually quite permissible as long as one or two things are borne in mind. The mooring is private property borrowed without permission. It may have been put down to hold a light dinghy, or, if it is a yacht mooring, the owner may return in the middle of the night and even if you rouse out quickly and get off it there will be a lot of fuss all round. Ocean-racing yachts in particular are likely to return at any time of the night, and, what is more, they have to moor and get the crews back to their jobs in time. A dinghy left on a mooring 'to save his place' usually means that the owner is returning shortly. It is therefore unwise to pick up a mooring without first finding out from a neighbouring yachtsman or boatman whether it is likely to be wanted.

By law, a mooring is a permanent anchor and the owner has no right to more room than the swinging space of the boat using it. Morally, there

Plate 18 Rafted up. A variety of visitors share one common mooring buoy. Extricating a boat from the middle isn't always easy.

is little difference between putting your boat on somebody's else's mooring or putting your car into somebody else's garage, but legally the owner of a mooring is in a weaker position. However, sea-lawyering among yachtsmen is abominable. Keep it friendly if you can; and better still be independent and lie to your own anchor.

The rate of damage to boats at their moorings is ridiculously high. One rarely hears of them lifting their moorings, since most are either laid by professionals or made far heavier than necessary. The damage arises from failure due to lack of inspection (how often is a private mooring lifted?), carelessness in making it fast aboard, inadequate mooring cleats and the inevitable risk of other boats getting out of control when trying to pick up their own buoys – and not much can be done about that.

Any deep-water mooring laid in sandy waters should be inspected at least every other year as the constant scouring of sand grains between the links wears away the metal at a fantastic rate – a good reason for choosing chain a bit oversize. It should go without saying that no mixture of metals, such as copper wire to seize a shackle-pin, should be allowed, for electrolysis can ruin a mooring in a single season. Screw shackles should be avoided in any case, and the oval-pinned cable joining shackle used instead.

Permission to lay a mooring is almost always needed, and this may be the business of a local harbour board or yacht club. In deep water, where the yacht is to lie constantly afloat, a concrete 'clump' is often used. This can be a cast concrete block, flat in shape and concave on the bottom and weighing about 50 lb for each yacht ton. This would give a block of around 250 lb for an average 25–30 footer, but much depends upon locality. This should be increased in small sizes, particularly if the bottom is hard sand.

The chain is made up of a ground length (which may be heavy stuff, $\frac{7}{16}$ in or so) one-third of the depth of water, and the riding chain, which is a size larger than the normal anchor cable, and three times the depth of water. Extra length should be allowed for making fast on deck. A synthetic riding line may be substituted as long as it can be fully protected from chafe. Between the ground chain and riding chain comes a swivel, large enough to match the general breaking strains. If chain is used all the way, the buoy should be made fast to a pick-up rope one and a half times the depth of the water. This rope should be strong enough for the yacht to lie to until the yacht is properly moored. Alternatively the riding chain may be supported by a large buoy with a short length of chain left hanging to be taken aboard. In some cases the yacht may be secured direct to a strong ring on the buoy itself.

Two clump moorings may be used where space is limited – 20 lb per yacht ton. Here the weights are laid, usually up and down tide, six depths apart with the riding chain coming from a swivel in the middle of the ground chain or bridle. Old anchors may be used so long as the yacht cannot sit on them at low tide. These should be about twice the weight normally used on the yacht.

The dug mooring which dries out at low tide conforms to the same rule regarding size of chain and scope, except that the ground chain goes to a 'root' chain which in turn is secured to the sinker. The experts have a fine time stipulating the best type of sinker, but the truth is that almost anything buried to a depth of about four feet will do, whether it's an old gas cooker or half a railway sleeper. On the east coast of England, a 3-foot cross made from 4 × 4 in or 4 × 6 in timber is a favourite. These can last up to twenty years buried in the mud, witness the ancient ship finds. The chain is usually the vulnerable part of it, particularly 'black' chain (ungalvanised). Railway sleepers are especially good because, of course, the timber has been pickled to preserve it. One argument against a solid sinker such as an old flywheel deserves consideration. When beachcombers are looking for coins in the sand they look for small wet patches and beneath them, sometimes six inches down, is the coin – the moisture lies above it and the sand remains fluid. There was a case of an iron wheel which came to the surface time and time again; in the end a wooden baulk was substituted and that stayed put.

A final word about pick-up buoys. It is most important to paint on it the tonnage of the yacht for which the mooring was laid, otherwise a bigger visitor may lift it.

Going alongside

The way carried by a small cruiser when going alongside can usually be checked quite easily but there are still some basic rules to be followed.

Try for a longish approach. The straight-at-it-and-then-swing manoeuvre is for experts only. The turning circle becomes harder to judge towards the middle of the turn, and it's then that nerve fails. Lower the sails and head into the tide, even if the wind is stiff. Only if the tide is nearly slack can this law be ignored. Get a stern line ashore to stop her and watch for her stern swinging in. Fenders should be ready and in position, but keep one loose on deck in case of a last minute change of plan.

Remember the side-kick propeller effect when putting the engine astern to check headway. In theory at least, a right-handed prop will kick the stern to port when astern which makes a port-side-to berth a better bet if there is a choice. With heavier boats which cannot be checked by hand or boathook the stern line may be important, but don't rely too much on any casual bystander on the quay knowing what to do with it if you throw it to him. It is wise to tie a bowline in it so that he can drop it over a bollard rather than trust to his ability to take a proper turn.

Many wharves or quays have protruding vertical baulks of timber serving as rubbers for bigger craft. Avoid such walls if possible, since yacht-fenders are useless on them. If there is much current, use a back-spring as well as head and stern lines, otherwise the bow will hit the quay wall as she falls back.

If a boat is to be left alone, springs are essential or she will never stay on her fenders. The action of a spring is to prevent the yacht from ranging fore and aft on the swell or as the wind catches her rig. Head and stern lines moor her to the quay and breast-ropes (if used) hold her close against it, but the springs are the ropes which protect the topsides; they need only be of very light line but they cannot be dispensed with.

If a fin-keel is to take the bottom at low water you must take steps to hold her upright. If she lies outwards from the foot of the quay she may be hard to get up on the next flood, and if she leans too sharply towards the wall, her spars may be damaged (Fig. 20).

There are two methods. One is to hold her at a list by means of a line from the mast to the shore (preferably no higher than the cross-trees), and the second is to give her a natural list by shifting ballast or chain, or just loose gear, onto the side-deck. If the tide has far to fall the second method is the only practical one, although, in such small craft, anyone moving around down below may cause her to fall the wrong way if there is no masthead line to the shore as an extra safeguard.

The shape of the fin-keel is important. Drying out alongside is quite impractical with some craft because of the angle of the bottom of the fin which makes them go down bow-heavy. It is also vital to know what the bottom of the wall is like, whether it is littered with rubble, smooth mud, or sand.

With a fair list inwards (five degrees or so) the hull must be kept in constant contact with the wall, otherwise if she dries out at some distance from it she will lean her mast against it. The first time she goes down the crew must obviously be in attendance, but if a proper list can be maintained and the hull kept close to the wall, there is no reason why she shouldn't be left to get on with it alone in future. To be certain of this it is far better to get her in trim and watch from the quay the first time, giving her no further help unless needed.

A simple dodge for holding the hull against the wall is to hang two good heavy weights to the middle of the bights of the head and stern lines. This keeps tension on them all the time. Another tip to remember, this time if the crew are living aboard and need to wake up just before she begins to touch down, is the bell and leadline trick. The lead should be a heavy one, which means that a rock from ashore will do the job better. Suspend it overboard on codline a little below keel level. Make a bowline on the inboard end, tuck the bight through a ventilator or crack in the door and peg the frying-pan (bell) handle into the bowline. When the rock takes the bottom the line goes slack and down falls the pan with a crash to wake the dead.

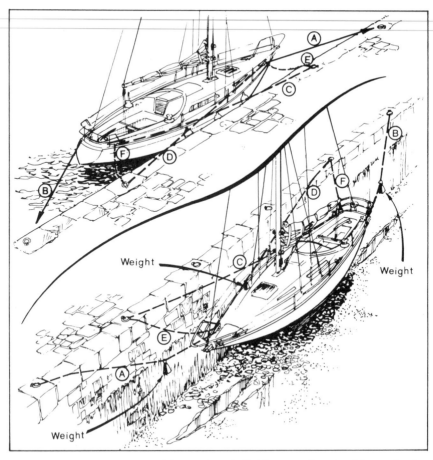

Fig. 20 The use of springs (shown dotted, C–D) prevents a boat from slewing her bow and stern against the wall. E–F are bow and stern breast ropes, A–B are head and stern ropes. When drying out against a wall the boat must be held firmly but not tightly against the wall, well fendered, and in some cases a line from the masthead can be used to incline her so that she dries out leaning against the wall. If a strong wind is blowing off the wall, masthead windage may cause the boat to list outwards at the critical moment of grounding on the ebb. Conversely a strong on-wall wind can heel her too steeply against the wall and the mast may be damaged. In windy weather stand by the boat while drying out.

The visitors' berth

Arrival at a popular marina or yacht haven during the height of the cruising season usually means that the visitors' berth will be fairly crowded with yachts berthed alongside one another. This also applies to trot moorings where boats lie between large posts. There is always a great sense of community. Everybody would prefer to be the only yacht there but since this cannot be, people make the best of it and the essential aim is not to inconvenience others more than is necessary. Boats are arriving and departing all the time or in bunches according to tide but there is a usual exodus in the morning and a trickle of arrivals from late afternoon. This of course means that crews of yachts already there are constantly having to juggle with warps and shift berths. If the marina is reached via a lock gate the upheaval can occur whenever the lock is scheduled to open.

Arrival at a visitors' berth which is already well occupied should be slow, head to current if there is any and with fenders already in position. Great care must be taken to look aloft in case the spreaders of boats should tangle, an event which doesn't normally occur when boats are upright, but with crew lining the contact sides of both boats, heeling them together, it is likely to happen and expensive damage can be done. If your crew has been ashore while boats have been leaving or arriving, look aloft very carefully for signs of damage because not everybody is honest and a damaged spreader could mean a lost mast later. If there is a choice in the matter when you arrive, try to berth bow to stern so that the two masts don't come opposite each other.

Berthing in a fresh breeze is not always easy and crews of boats already berthed will be as anxious as you are to see the job done safely. A certain amount of gratuitous advice may be flying around; accept it in good part even if you don't act on it and if the manoeuvre begins to go wrong, forget pride and accept any help that is appropriate.

Rafting up

Sometimes boats will 'raft up'; this means that four, five or maybe more boats lie alongside each other with only the inside boat actually alongside the jetty, and there may be several of these rafts. If there is wind, current or movement of the water caused by passing shipping it can be imagined that not only the inside boats but those in the middle take a lot of bumping, grinding and pressure. If the wind or current is affecting the trot laterally there is also a tendency for the whole raft to be slewed sideways.

For these reasons the general aim is for the biggest boats to lie nearest the jetty, smallest on the outside, but of course it isn't always practicable to juggle around so drastically, although as it is for the general good of all it is wise not to argue. What is to be avoided is arriving, mooring up to the outside boat and enjoying the benefit of his shore warps. The unwritten but holy rule is that every boat must have bow and stern lines taken ashore. Half the time they may not be taking any strain, but in fresh conditions the raft will need every line ashore that can be provided to stop it from sagging away. The other berthing lines needed are bow and stern lines to the neighbouring inside yacht and one if not

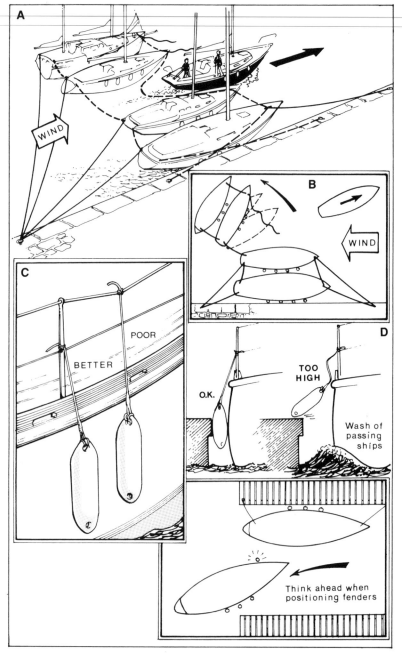

Fig. 21 Rafting up. Inset (B) shows what can happen if a departing yacht leaves the middle of the raft on its windward side. It is better if possible to leave to leeward (A), closing the gap as she does so.

Fenders should not be hitched to the guardrail wires but to stanchions (C), and if possible to their bases. The height at which a fender is suspended is also important especially if the yacht is rolling a little (D).

two springs according to conditions and as springs are intended to stop any fore and aft movement of adjoining boats they are the only means of keeping the raft as a whole in a tidy bunch.

It is when a yacht leaves from the middle of the raft that the greatest care is needed. A raft of boats, each moored firmly to its neighbour and with a series of long bow and stern lines fanning out shorewards to hold the whole raft, is secure enough, but when one boat leaves from the middle (Fig. 21) the wind can open up the whole thing like a book if the opening left is on the *windward* side of the raft. There isn't always the choice of leaving down wind and it is the moral responsibility of the departing crew to make sure that the gap is closed before it can widen out of control. If the crews of neighbouring boats are about they will take care of things, but if they are not it is best to leave one crew member behind to do so, picking him up again by circling and going alongside the outside yacht.

The procedure for leaving is first to take in the long bow and stern shore lines, let go your other lines and take those from one of the neighbour boats round your stern and secure them loosely. If there is a fresh head wind or current all this latter part will have to be done quickly, easing your own boat slow ahead and tightening in the linking ropes to close the gap the instant you are clear, not forgetting the all-important springs.

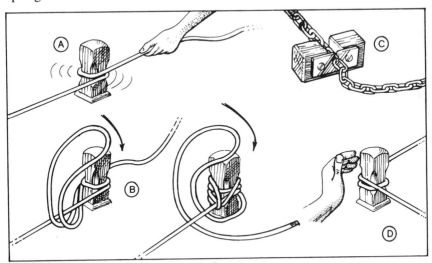

Fig. 22 Handling ropes under strain, 'Surging' (A) must be done with care, keeping the hands well clear and the rope low so that it won't jump off the post. The tug-boat hitch (B) is a reliable way of securing a towrope or anchor cable, it will never jam. Never use a clove hitch. C: a chain stopper, in this case a slotted steel plate, is a great boon in rough weather when trying to control an anchor chain. D: checking a surged rope with the base of the hand – this is the only safe way.

Life in a raft is not very peaceful, especially for the inside boats, because there is a constant traffic of other crews, bound shorewards or the other way, across their decks. Another unwritten law is that you should always try to cross other boats via the foredeck to preserve the cockpit privacy of other crews, but this is a matter of judgement and an open forehatch can be embarrassing for all. Don't jump onto side decks, shake rigging violently or pull yourself up by other people's guardrails, and when returning aboard late at night tread softly and keep your voices low.

Reduction to soundings

Sounding with the echo sounder is, or should be, one of the mainstays of piloting a small cruiser. It is the means of correlating the tide-table with the soundings shown on the chart.

First you must understand how the tides behave. It would be easy to assume wrongly that the height of tide in the tide-table simply shows how high the level of the water will rise from the figures shown on the chart, that it will rise a long way at springs and not so far at neaps, sinking to chart datum at each low water. The truth is a bit different.

The level of the tide oscillates equally above and below a *Mean Tide Level*, rather like the lift in a tall building. If the half-way floor of the building is called Mean Tide Level, the tide-lift goes up and down one floor above and below (at neaps) and spring tides rise and fall two floors above and below it. These are average tides, they can range further or not so far on other occasions and on some occasions come the really big spring tides which sink even lower and rise even higher but always equally either side of that mean level.

This is a very simplistic explanation of the *movement* of tides and they are all measured from a chart datum, which in fact the level very rarely reaches. It is based on the Lowest Astronomical Tide (LAT). The *range* of tide is the total distance between low and high water levels, the *height* of tide refers to the height measured up from chart datum and the *rise* of tide means the distance of sea level from datum on a flooding tide. Nautical almanacs contain much more detailed explanations of tidal movement and it is important to have a thorough grasp of the tidal mechanics.

To get back to actualities, the yacht which is anchored at high water neaps on a 5-metre tide is not going to fall 5 metres on the ebb, she is going to fall the distance which the tide happens to be *ranging* on that particular day, perhaps only 4 metres. Knowing the range is the key to the whole thing. First you need to know Mean Tide Level or MTL for the locality (this can usually be found in the nautical almanac); double it and subtract the height at HW for that day. For example, MTL 3 metres,

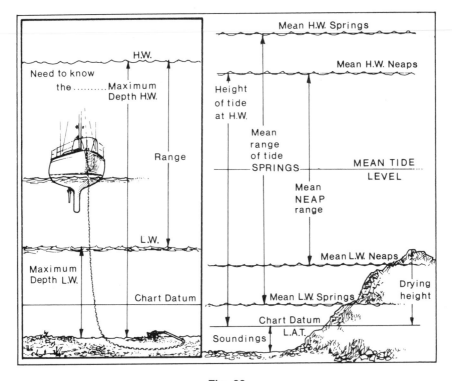

Fig. 23

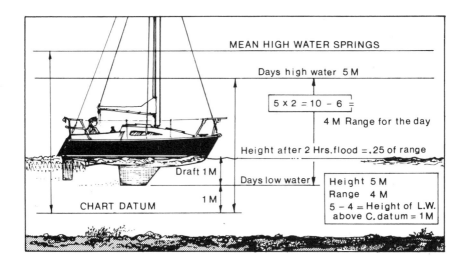

Fig. 24

height 5 metres: $3 \times 2 = 6 - 5 = 1$ metre, which means that there will be 1 metre of water above chart datum (from which height of tide is measured). This leaves a range of 4 metres for the day. Another rough method of finding range is to double the height for the day and subtract from it Mean High Water Springs thus: Day's height 4 metres $\times 2 = 8$ metres. MHWS 5 metres or $8 - 5 = 3$ metres range that day.

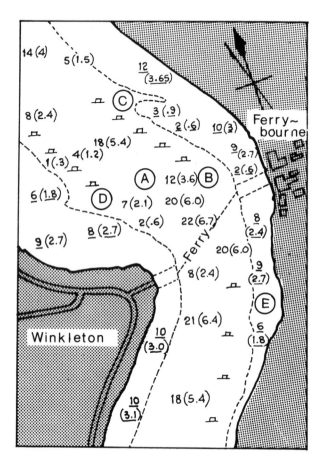

Fig. 25 Choice of anchorage. (A) is right in the fairway where tidal rates are higher and where it will be choppy when wind and current are in opposition. (B) is also liable to be choppy where the stream follows the steep-to curve of the river. (C) is a long way from the landing if the foreshore is soft mud, also it is more exposed to strong sou'westerly winds. (D) is better, although the steep-to drying bank would be a problem in a sudden wind shift; there might also be a tidal back eddy. (E) is on a drying bank, suitable perhaps for a twin keeler although in a strong sou'westerly the boat might pound badly as the tide floated or beached her. In all, not an ideal anchorage. Better to move further up or down the river when a comfortable overnight stop is needed.

Almanacs contain accurate graphs and tables for working out exactly what the range will be, but it should never be forgotten that all figures are based upon tide-tables which are *predictions*, and barometric pressure, wind-driven tidal surge or regression, flood water from estuaries and the effects upon range of being, perhaps, up at the head of some long and winding creek where the range may be much less than may be experienced on the coast, all mean that the figures shown in the tables may sometimes be inaccurate. The yachtsman approaching an anchorage may not have time to work things out to fine limits and he simply needs to know whether there will be enough depth at low tide in the spot he has chosen.

The chart will show him soundings, which are the depth of water *below* chart datum and the drying heights (figures have a small line under them) which represent the height of dry sea-bed left at any low water which reaches chart datum. Since chart datum is the Lowest Astronomical Tide it means that very rarely will the sea level sink so low and many of the drying heights given in fact seldom show, or remain just awash at low tide at springs and be well covered (although not well covered enough to anchor over) at low water neaps.

If he arrives at the chosen anchorage at dead low water there is no problem, he finds a suitable spot and anchors, merely veering enough scope of cable to allow for the depth at the next high tide. If he arrives at dead high water he takes a sounding, mentally subtracts the range for the day and if this leaves him enough depth he is satisfied. Should he arrive at exactly half tide, be it ebb or flood, he knows that he must subtract half the range from the depth his echo sounder shows. When the state of tide is just after HW or perhaps just before MTL he can fudge a bit, always keeping plenty of depth in hand so that guesswork is acceptable.

Because the tide level rises and falls faster around the middle of the rise or fall – either side of MTL in fact – the rough rule is that in the first two hours (of rise or ebb) the level alters one-quarter of the range, in the third hour one-half and by the fourth hour three-quarters. This is based upon a 6-hour interval between high and low water whereas the interval is more in the order of 6 hours 20 minutes and varying, but for rough calculations that can be ignored. The sum can be done as a percentage. The level rises (or falls) hourly by 10%, 15%, 25%, 25%, 15%, 10%. In practice this means that a boat may arrive at, say, the fourth hour of the flood, when 10 + 15 + 25 + 25 = 75% of the range has risen and if a sounding is taken and the figure subtracted from it the crew will know how much depth to expect at low tide.

CHAPTER EIGHT
Sailing by Eye

Allowing for tide

There is nothing frighteningly technical about navigating coastwise and making short sea crossings, and the term 'pilotage' fits the case better. The simpler it can be the better because the constrictions of a small chart table and the jerky motion of a small yacht at sea are not conducive to complex mental exercises. Accuracy should be strived for as a matter of habit no matter how basic the navigation because it is when the weather is rough and chartwork becomes increasingly difficult that the habit of accuracy keeps you from getting careless.

Ancient Norse pilots sailed by eye, studying the headlands and committing them to memory, reading the look of the land. In today's small cruisers and despite the advantages of charts, tide-tables and compasses plus the electronics, being able to visualise the chart as the land and studying the land with the chart in mind is still at the core of the art. The one big difference is that we read the chart from a bird's eye angle and read the land in a horizontal plane. To interpret the land we see as the chart is rather like looking at the front of a building and then studying a plan of it to relate one to the other.

Most navigational troubles arise from losing sense of orientation. It is possible to get lost in full view of a recognisable stretch of coastline simply through having failed to look at it properly in the bustle of laying courses, plotting tides and doing sums. It only needs a fix to go wrong and we suddenly become aware that the land doesn't look at all as we had expected it to look. The art of conning a boat along the coast is a relaxed one in which one leans comfortably over the hatch coaming staring quietly at the passing coastline and taking an occasional glance at the chart.

Plotting is often a labour in a bit of a sea. Watching the coast calls for no instruments, and fixes upon buoys and shore-marks are only for confirmation. The compass course may be used when there is risk of suddenly losing visibility or it may be a simple matter of convenience for steering straight. At other times it is really only important if there are offlying dangers athwart the course, which have to be given a known safe berth, or in verifying a transit when there is doubt about the identification of one of the objects.

It is possible to navigate clear along a coastline without looking at the instruments, simply by noting the natural transits provided by headlands, piers, rocks and so on. By laying a ruler on the chart, for instance, the yachtsman may notice a headland which, at a certain point, becomes obscured behind a bulge in the coast. By watching for it he gets a position line which is indisputable and if, at the same time, a glance ashore shows a small bay or group of rocks coming abeam he has his second line – rough, of course, but a succession of such transit fixes takes him safely down the coast without him once becoming involved in the complexity of chart work which seems to be considered so vital.

I mention this habit of studying the coast first for an important reason. There are times when a man has his hands far too full sailing the boat to indulge in lengthy sessions on the chart. If he can 'see' his way along it will stand him in good stead. But first he must learn to see the coast as a chart and the chart as a coast. This chapter deals with pilotage by eye and the look of the land from seaward. Later on the use of compass, calculation of tidal effect, laying a course offshore and so on will be dealt with stage by stage.

The look of the land

Each coastal region has its own typical features. The East Coast man is often terrified of West Coast rockiness and the deep-water man, accustomed to rock-fringed coasts, is nervous of navigating among the shallows of the Thames Estuary.

The low-lying coastline is particularly difficult to identify. The shape of the sea-bed usually continues the run of the flat shore, and it is therefore shallow for a long way out to sea. This means that the cruiser is forced to stay well out, and details on shore become harder to identify. The absence of pronounced headlands, cliffs, distinctive bays and rocky outcrops complicates things further. Headlands run out to sea so gradually that the exact point where the land finishes and sea begins is hard to decide. On this kind of coast the navigator becomes a buoy-hopper. He concentrates entirely on buoys and ignores the land, and he can easily lose his sense of position if he makes a mistake in a compass course between buoys.

The low coastline rises and falls in hazy undulations and it's difficult to decide whether a gradual fading away into the sea is due to the height of the land diminishing or the coastline receding. The only clues are such objects as houses, trees and people ashore. Compare them constantly through the binoculars and note their relative sizes at different spots along the coastline.

The direction of natural light must be reckoned with. If the sun is low and behind the land there will be a featureless monotony of bluish shadow in which a block of flats may look no different from a church tower, or a clump of trees may masquerade as a prominent spur of ground shown on the chart. On the other hand the sunlight shining full onshore can pick out a strip of wet road and make it appear to be a white tower, while the actual tower is muted by the shadow of a cloud. You must therefore never accept the obvious without due thought.

A hilly coast is far easier to correlate to the chart. The yacht is usually closer inshore and bays and headlands are more distinct, also villages and small towns do not straggle, each is contained more compactly in its valley. There is only the risk of one headland looking much like another, especially with the effect of sunshine and cloud shadow to alter the apparent contours.

Seen from well offshore coastal contours can be deceptive if there are ranges of hills inland. The switchback effect of the more distant hills may be quite different from the outline of those along the actual coast and although this coastal profile may be lower than the distant inland hills it is this that the navigator sees, hiding the inland hills, as he draws closer in. From sea level also bays and headlands are seen in foreshortened form and often it is only low-slanting sunlight, casting shadow, which reveals the shallower bays and headlands at all (by shallow I mean in the horizontal view, and not depth of water). Consequently he may sail straight past a minor headland only to find it, as he thinks, some miles further on when he reaches a second headland made more conspicuous by its angle and the shadow it casts, or the effect of sunlight on a cliff face (Fig. 26).

It is quite simple to con a cruiser along the coast by identifying features as they come into line, once you have mastered the chart symbols and learned to match land to paper. In tricky waters infested with rocks and sandbanks it is no substitute for careful plotting of compass bearings, but it dispenses with much of it in straightforward waters, while the safe transit method of keeping an offing from inshore dangers is better than any mechanical plot.

Many transits (objects in line) are marked on the chart for the guidance of the navigator approaching a river or passage between dangers, and most of these are man-made beacons, towers and so forth. The coastline furnishes many, many more which are there for the finding.

In Fig. 27 the cruiser is coasting offshore along the unbroken arrowed line. At A, headlands are in transit, and at B a headland hides the bulge in the coastline astern. Yet another transit of sorts comes up as the bay opens up from C, and at D the navigator finds a safe transit to see him past the shoal. By glancing at the church tower he knows that he will not be in the danger area until it is lost to view behind the land, while by keeping the Mew Stone astern *inside* Pol Point he can stay outside the danger area.

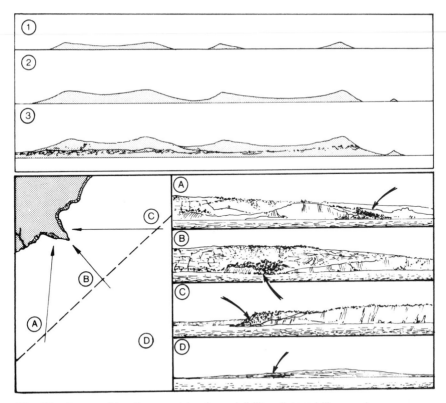

Fig. 26 Approaching the coast in clear visibility, distant hills may be seen as a row of islands (1). Nearer inshore (2) the foreground is still overshadowed by the inland contour, but close inshore the inland hills are hidden and the skyline shape of the coast is quite changed (3).

The small headland seen from positions (A), (B) and (C) may be hard to distinguish against the rest of the coastline although from the chart it would promise to be easily identified. At position D, well offshore, only a slight sharpening of detail indicates its position.

There will be buoys to aid him, naturally, but it isn't always so easy for the inexperienced navigator to be certain of the identity of a buoy until he is close. The buoy which appears where he would *like* to see it may not be the one he is hoping to find, and, of course, there is no excuse for not checking the compass bearings between buoys as they are passed. Many of them form useful transits in their own right, but it must be borne in mind that at close hand the swinging room of a moored buoy upsets the angles a lot, especially if it should be a little out of position. Buoys and lightships rarely get out of position, but occasionally they do so and they ought not to be relied upon implicitly.

The chart usually gives a picture of compactness with the buoys in cosy proximity to each other. In reality the details are unexpectedly distant, and the whole picture greatly extended. An observer takes in the

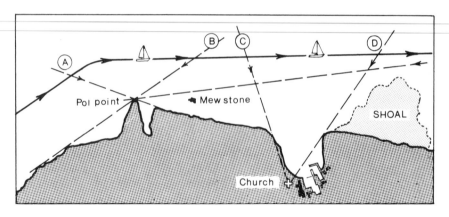

Fig. 27

whole chart-coast at a glance, but the land is seen as a mass which tapers in perspective on either hand. The buoys marked on the chart would need to be engraved as pin-pricks to approximate to their correct scale, and it is important to think of them as pin-pricks. At a distance of three miles a really large buoy can just about be seen, though probably not identified, and the smaller buoys without topmarks are not visible until within one and a half miles. The navigator studying his chart may expect to see half a dozen buoys all within a small area and he may get worried because they don't show up. In coasting, it is a common mistake to look too close inshore for an expected buoy probably marking an offlying spit. In fact, it may be visible as a tiny black peppercorn apparently far out to sea. But once you reach it, the coastline behind it appears close again due to the effect of foreshortening. Practice with the ordinary Ordnance Survey map ashore helps a lot by giving you a feeling of distance away from land. Coasting and keeping a safe distance offshore are largely a matter of judgement. The navigator may cover his chart with fixes, but when the shore is featureless and barren of seamarks it is judgement which counts.

Distance by eye

It is deceptive to attempt to judge distance through binoculars. Distance blurs detail even though the object may be visible for a long way. A large tree at between one and a half and two miles can be seen in crisp detail in a good light, but if a pencil is held at arm's length, the tree will be no taller than the lead. At four miles the tree is seen with rounded outlines, and shadows are blue, with the foliage masses appearing to have been dabbed on roughly, though the shapes of trees are still quite individual. At eight miles trees are simply blue humps and can easily be confused with, say, a water tower or a row of houses.

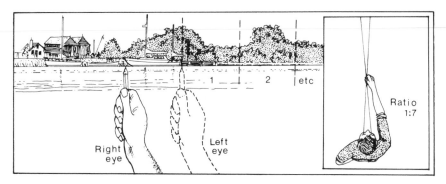

Fig. 28 Judging distance roughly. Hold a pencil at arm's length and gaze beyond it with the left eye closed. Line it up with some object as a reference point and then open the left eye and close the right one – the pencil will appear to jump to the right (dotted line). If the amount of the jump is multiplied by seven, visually, the total distance will be roughly equal to the distance off. The ratio of distance between eyes is roughly one-seventh of the length of the average arm. As a further check, at 60 yards a person's features are visible and at 120 yards the eyes, nose and mouth are seen as dots.

A small building with a white or pale facing wall becomes blurred and loses sharp edges at a mile and a half although darker windows and doors are still recognisable. At four miles these details have gone and the shape is almost lost. At six miles it has become a dab of colour without shape. Caravan parks at five miles are scattered chips of white, cars can be seen if they are moving and hedgerows are about the size of a pencil line.

The effect of lighting is again very important. A coastline under the full blaze of early morning sunshine is crisp in detail and appears closer than it does with the detail lost in shadow. At dusk, with the light behind the land making it a flat silhouette and the reflection of high ground extending across the water, it is often hard to form any true estimate. This is especially true at night and many a cruiser has navigated inshore to find an anchorage, and finally anchored at what seems to be a perilously close distance from the shore; but daylight finds her stuck out in the open a mile from land. The black land mass and its reflection seem to loom far higher than they really are.

Weather also affects one's judgement of distance. The vivid clarity which often comes in advance of rain and wind can mess up the estimates; the pearly haze of a hot day, which so often accompanies easterly weather, or the refraction which seems to jack up the whole coastline, must all be reckoned with. Refraction, extending the height of shore buildings to a grotesque proportion, can fool the navigator into thinking that a row of particularly nasty bungalows are actually oil storage tanks. The beach also becomes a prominent feature, to be searched for anxiously on the chart, though it is really just a narrow strip of shingle.

The effect of the earth's curvature when one is looking for shore-marks also comes into the picture when visibility is very clear. A harbour wall, sole clue to a small port perhaps, may be 'dipped' just below the horizon when the town behind it is vividly seen in detail, and at night whole rows of shore lights can be seen jauntily nipping up and down with a disturbing ripple effect.

The look of the water

Without a certain knowledge of position, a passage down the coast becomes rather frightening. Every wind ripple or tidal swirl becomes, in the imagination, an 'uncharted' rock. The look of the water is a necessary study.

In rocky coastal districts the colour of the water is significant. Blue-black for the deeps, paler blue and then green for shoal patches, with black shadows marking underwater rocks covered with weed – and in sunshine the pilot can get plenty of warning of shoaling water. On the east coast of England, however, it is rare to find clear water and a one-metre patch or a ten-metre channel may look the same. In fact the swirl and underwater currents and eddies of a fast tide may bring sand to the surface and imitate a shoal where none exists. The movement of the water is another matter altogether.

Plate 19 Tidal overfalls. It is easy to think that these smooth slicks or 'kelds' are an indication of shallow water.

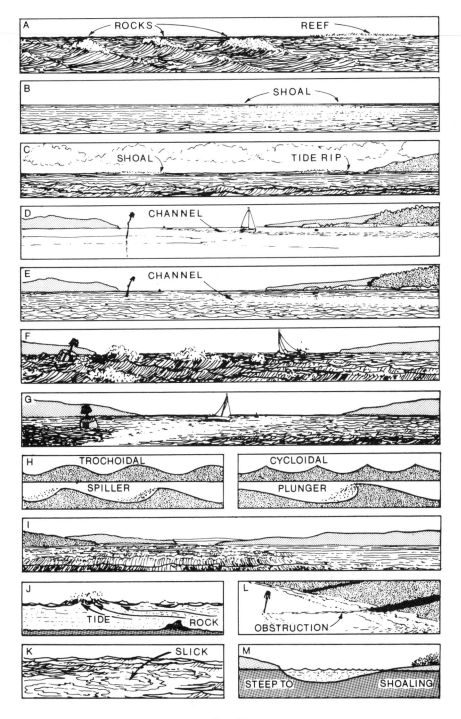

Fig. 29

In Fig. 29 some of the many faces of the sea are shown. At A unbalanced breaking crests give warning of rocks beneath. This is familiar deep-water rocky coast stuff and there may be ample water above the rocks, but they must still be avoided. The sheen on the water above a sandbank, B, is often imitated by a 'hole' in the wind on a quiet day, but with the least breeze there will be a subtle change in the surface of the water which is unmistakable. C shows how a tidal overfall may look very similar to a shoal or reef. At D a calm sea allows the tidal stream running through the deeper water of the channel to reveal its whereabouts by a rippling of the surface. Note how the awash shoal by the beacon is barely distinguishable from the water around it. The same channel in a light breeze E may be marked by a slick of smooth water if the stream is flowing, with the wind, fast enough to prevent the formation of wavelets. At F, however, wind against tide has raised a steep sea in the deep water, while the regular wave-formation indicates shallower water where the fast tide is not felt. G shows the same channel when the stream is running with the wind and the higher waves are seen over the shallower water. Open-sea waves of a trochoidal type of swell (H) may be left-overs from a distant storm, they may be high but they are usually harmless. In shoaling water the crests may spill forward, and again not necessarily be troublesome. The cycloidal wind-driven wave, which increases in size according to 'fetch' or distance unimpeded by land, frequently becomes a plunger in shoal water and must be avoided. The shallow bar I seen from seaward is deceptive because only the backs of the breaking waves are seen. Overfalls are often caused by an abrupt rise in the sea-bed, J, which forces the tidal current on the surface, but an isolated rocky outcrop may also be the cause. It is dangerous to venture close to any overfall unless the exact depth of water is known. To skirt it in order to stay on a making tack, for instance, is risky since the actual water disturbance takes place at various distances from the rock itself. A fast tide in deep water creates 'smooths' or slicks which may be frightening, suggesting as they do some unseen rock, K. The yacht may be spun completely around in a slick, but the real danger comes if there is a sea running, when a 'race' may develop which can overpower a small boat. The ripple above an underwater obstruction, L, is a good guide close inshore when the outer mark may have passed unnoticed further out to seaward. At M is a section of shore showing the difference between shoal and steep-to coasts. Note how the diminishing size of wave in shallow water, due to the slacker tidal stream, is a guide to the nature of the bottom.

Working the tidal currents offshore

Although the modern cruiser with her diesel engine can motor or motor-sail against most of the normal tidal currents met with, and unlike the old

Plate 20 Water breaking over a recently covered shoal patch. (*Photo: courtesy Yachting Monthly*)

engineless sailing barges, which had to work the tides and anchor when they were foul, the cruiser must still work her tides with care if her passages are going to be fast and enjoyable. You might for instance flog a foul tide in the river under engine in order to reach the fair run of tide along the coast, whereas an engineless vessel would have had to be under way perhaps at an ungodly hour in order to take the last of the ebb downriver. Despite her engine, at sea with wind and current both contrary, progress is miserably slow.

This means that catching a fair tide *may* involve getting under way at strange hours of the day or night although there is always a choice of two starting times per twenty-four hours, and a tide which begins to run fair at, say, 3 am, will also be starting fair again at between 3 and 4 pm following. The skipper must decide whether it is better to get going at 3 am (which may mean setting the alarm clock at 2 am) and thereafter have a whole long summer's day for making the passage, or whether to start after midday, motor against a steadily weakening foul tide and complete the passage with a fair tide. It may depend upon the length of the passage and its expected duration and whether it is necessary to complete it during daylight. It is usually better to start a passage against a foul tide if you have to rather than finish it punching a foul tide, when everybody is tired and impatient to get in and moor up.

On a coastal passage long enough to mean that it can't be completed on one fair tide and which is also a beat to windward it is usually better to arrange the tacks so that the boat is making a long offshore tack shortly before the current goes foul, tacking inshore again to reach the coast ready for the fair stream. This is because tidal rates are usually stronger inshore, weaker some ten miles offshore, and also there is the possibility of getting a slight wind shift offshore since the wind tends to follow the coast and when you are tacking dead to windward any shift means that one tack will be more favourable than the other.

In tacking terms there are about eight hours of usable fair current to count on per tide. Of this about six hours are actually fair, although very weak at the beginning and end, and an hour at each end of the period when there is a period of slack and turning. This varies according to locality of course and only a study of the tidal atlas or tidal information on the chart can show what actually happens. If the tide is seen in the atlas to be turning fair at, say, 10 am offshore it will probably mean getting under way by 8 am in order to be offshore and punching the last trickle of foul tide prior to it turning fair. All too often people lose precious hours by miscalculating how long it may take to get from berth to passage start.

A long beat is tiring, perhaps wet and a cause of seasickness aboard, and a fair tide, running contrary to the wind direction, kicks up a worse sea than a foul tide when both are together. With a weak crew, short one-tide passages coastwise are preferred provided there is convenient shelter at the end of them, but this often means deviating many miles in order to reach a river or port and losing much time when coming out again in time for the next fair stream. Consequently crews prefer to keep plugging away until the main coastal passage is completed. It is a skipper's job to assess his party and decide whether people are up to this grim pressing on; it is better to go in somewhere and start fresh the next day than have a boat-load of grim, unhappy people who are really supposed to be enjoying themselves.

Sometimes there is the alternative of motor-sailing the foul tide for the peak rate hours, or anchoring for maybe four hours in some sheltered cove, or in calm weather, if there isn't a swell, of lying to a kedge anchor for a while. With light head winds and a decision to keep going it is better to take the headsail off, sheet the mainsail flat and motor quietly dead to windward. With an autopilot this is a time when one member of crew as lookout can allow the rest of the party to relax in their bunks.

On a tide-hopping passage when it is planned to reach a haven soon after the fair stream has ended, the presence of a headland mid-way can make hard work of it. With a fair stream the accelerated tidal rates off the headland, albeit favourable in direction, can turn a beat into a very wet ride indeed and the aim should be to make an offshore tack before reaching it, then tack back as soon as the headland is roughly abeam, thereby missing the rough overfalls off the headland. On occasion a boat

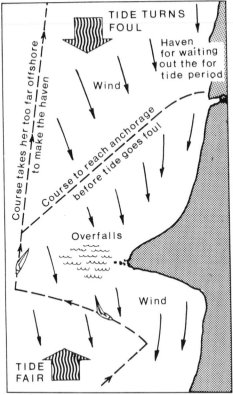

Fig. 30

may be reaching the headland on the last of a fair stream and again she should tack offshore in search of a slacker foul tide to follow. Then (Fig. 30) the wind direction offshore may shift, making the port tack favourable. The navigator must judge whether to bear off to reach the haven before the stream goes foul, or to stand on up the coast while it remains fair. In the first instance he may start off haven-wards on a fast broad reach only to find the wind heading him when closer in, just about the time when the foul current is beginning. In the second instance, standing on a bit parallel to the coast and still closehauled, he may misjudge it and, upon tacking to head inshore for the haven, find that he now has to crab in across a strengthening foul tide.

There is often a safe alternative, although not one that sailing purists would contemplate. With a short passage to the next destination against a head wind and around a headland it is often possible to find an inshore passage between headland and overfalls. It is only safe if it is easy to navigate and without hidden rocks. The navigator skipper may sail so far as possible then stow the sails and motor close inshore, getting well beyond the point before sailing again. One hazard must be watched for though, and that is the buoyed marker lines of the crab fisherman which are often barely visible – although these days, when electronic position-finders are to be found in small fishing craft, it is becoming just as likely to encounter crab pot markers far out at sea.

Plotting a compass course

The steering compass may have been part of the inventory when the boat was bought, particularly if second-hand, and therefore the choice will have been made for you and the tendency is to accept it without questioning whether or not it is the sort you need. Sooner or later, maybe in rain or thick fog, you will have to trust it – even though it is telling you to head in one direction while your instincts are telling you something quite different. No matter how accurately our ancient ancestors may have been able to judge direction, modern man can become disorientated among the aisles of a supermarket.

Most of the requirements of a good steering compass, such as clarity, the damping of the movement so that it doesn't spin and whirl when the boat is bouncing around, and its frictional freedom, can be practically guaranteed by buying from a top class manufacturer – although this doesn't mean that because a second-hand compass was made by a good company it is necessarily in its original condition and not in need of overhaul. Pivot wear, for instance, can make a compass card sluggish.

Pivot wear is a common problem and it can occur very quickly with cheap compasses. When a boat is afloat she is moving a little the whole time for months on end, and the needle point of the pivot is subject to constant wear. The only way to stop this is to stow the compass on its side when not in use. A check on pivot freedom can be made by using a small magnet to deflect the compass 45 degrees to either side, then whipping the magnet out of range and watching the card settle. It should settle within 20–25 seconds to within one degree of the true (correct) reading and on its first return swing it should not go more than about 12 degrees past its correct position before swinging back. It is not always obvious that a pivot is worn, particularly if you do a lot of motoring, because engine vibration keeps the card 'afloat' on its needle.

Dome-type compasses have the advantage that what is known as 'swirl', the drag effect of the fluid in the bowl, is less pronounced and the design also makes the card easier to read from various angles. Any steering compass must be large enough to be read easily from the helmsman's position, which with tiller steering means well off-centre to port or starboard. There is a pronounced parallax effect from these angles and the compass design should allow for this by means of vertical lines complementary to the central lubber line. Night illumination is important. Luminous markings are not enough because while the luminosity may be adequate in near-total darkness, it is useless in semi-darkness or in

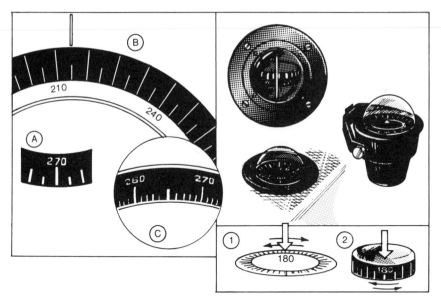

Fig. 31 (A) a side-reading card may show only a fraction of the whole compass and it is read from the front, while the top-reading card (B) is lined up with the lubber line on the far side from the viewer. Many are divided into 5-degree increments for easier reading, others show each degree (C). The bulkhead compass (right) is front-reading and can be mounted in a position where it is least likely to be damaged; a similar but top-reading version can be recessed into the cockpit bridge deck. The dome pattern (right lower), and also top-reading, has the advantage of minimising the swirl of the liquid. The big difference in use between top and side-reading, though (bottom, 1 and 2), lies in the fact that the apparent swing of the card when the helm is used is opposite.

moonlight. Some form of rheostat on low power electric lighting is far better. A brightly lit compass on a dark night ruins night vision and exerts a sort of hypnotic effect on helmsmen which is sleep-inducing unless the power of the light can be turned down a bit.

Most compasses nowadays are marked off in 5-degree divisions of a 360-degree card, with bolder lines for tens and the main cardinals. This is for easier visibility and it acknowledges the fact that steering a small boat to one or two degrees is not possible anyway, which may seem a bit odd considering the effort which a navigator is supposed to go to in order to lay a course to the final degree of accuracy. In practical terms the navigator orders a course to the nearest five degrees, or tells the helmsman to steer 'up' a bit or 'just below' a particular course given.

A card diameter of about four inches minimum is necessary for a helmsman to be able to steer with any real accuracy. It is a mistake to choose a small compass because an accurate course is as essential to a small vessel as to a large one; also, individual eyesight varies.

Steering compasses vary between the horizontally mounted types, maybe on a pedestal base, in larger craft perhaps on the top of the steering wheel pedestal, and the vertically mounted ones, perhaps recessed into the cockpit bulkhead. They can be flat or spherical, the former being read on the top and the latter on the side – as it might be if it were the rim of an upturned dish. There is an odd difference between these two types. The flat card can be seen in its entirety, like the compass rose on the chart, and quite a lot of use can be made of this feature by sighting across the whole card for rough bearings or by studying it in relation to surroundings as an aid to orientation. The side-reading card on the other hand really only allows the ship's heading to be read clearly, although many do have a small flat card on top. The real oddity is the relationship of card movement to tiller movement. On a flat card the course is lined up with the lubber line on the opposite side to the viewer and the tiller movement appears to push or pull the card to and fro, whereas with a front-reading or edge-reading card the viewer is looking at and lining up the side of the card nearest to him – it being calibrated to permit this. Accordingly the tiller movements have an opposite seeming effect on the card movement. With a wheel which is turned in the direction it is intended that the bows should turn, the whole bag of tricks is opposite. The card of course doesn't move, the card remains aligned with magnetic north and the boat turns around it. The wheel versus tiller, side-reading versus top, can cause problems when sailing in a strange boat, although any combination of the above is easy to get used to after half an hour or so at the helm.

The bulkhead compass has other advantages, though. It can pierce the bulkhead and allow it to be read from either side, which can be useful for the navigator below. It is also almost flush fitting, which means that it is not vulnerable to snarling by the mainsheet and it is also usually easier to find a position on the bulkhead where the compass is least affected by deviational influences such as the engine, the contents of cockpit lockers, and so on.

The compass deviation is a subject about which books are written, or whole chapters of books at least. For our purposes we'll have to accept that any magnetic compass in a small cruiser is going to be affected by boat metalwork, ferrous metals on the inside of the bulkhead such as the cooker perhaps, or a fire extinguisher and various moveable items – in some cases even the sheath knife worn by somebody sitting nearby. The engine and its electrical currents can cause most of the trouble and even this is not a constant because the heeling of the boat causes the metal mass to move from side to side under the compass. Neither is deviation constant; the compass may be deviated by 4 degrees on, say, a westerly heading, but as the compass north remains aligned to magnetic north while the boat turns, the metal masses are also turned relative to the north-seeking card. Typically a deviation of perhaps 4 degrees plus on west might show little error on north and south and 4 degrees minus on east – but that is an over-simplification. Compass deviation must be studied a little. A compass can and perhaps should be professionally adjusted in a new boat and a deviation card issued; thereafter a skipper must check his compass at least once a season.

Perhaps the vital thing is not so much adjusting a compass to give the minimum deviation, as knowing the *amount* of deviation so that it can be allowed for. Having a reliable and accurate hand-bearing compass for taking bearings in plotting positions is part of the navigator's first needs. Once its accuracy is proved (plotting an exact position from bearings taken from the rubber dinghy is as simple a way as any), a hand-bearing compass can be used for making regular checks of the steering compass. A fore-and-aft bearing taken from a position on the boat's centreline well clear of any metal, including standing rigging, and noted against a simultaneous compass reading, only takes a minute.

The True north bogey

From the very beginning professional navigators (and their pupils) use True north as a basis for all calculation on the chart, converting to magnetic by applying local variation and any deviation there may be to arrive at a course to steer, and converting back to True when a compass bearing has been taken and it is to be plotted on the chart. They *think* True, but it is only the shifting influences of the earth's magnetic field and the imperfect siting of a compass in a boat that produce variation and deviation and make conversion necessary. The professional converts back and forth instinctively without having to think whether to add or subtract. The trouble is that the number of degrees involved can sometimes be considerable and to add, say, 7 degrees instead of subtracting it would mean a disastrous 14-degree error.

To a newcomer to small boat navigation this can be a serious risk, especially to a tired navigator. I think that either a beginner should learn to work in True north from the very beginning and learn to *think* in True north, or it is safer to cheat. The only thing that matters is that a navigator should be able to order safe compass headings and plot accurate bearings on the chart. This is a heresy which will annoy many people, but I am unrepentant.

Given a chart which is of reasonably recent issue, the printed magnetic rose will be accurate to within maybe 1 or at most 2 degrees, this being the amount by which magnetic variation has altered since the particular chart was originally printed. This means that a navigator can work directly off the magnetic part of the compass rose, applying the tiny discrepancy perhaps, but in no great trouble if not. Ship's deviation must be applied and the problem of whether to add or subtract remains, but if the compass is reasonably accurate any unhappy error made by getting things back-to-front will still be small compared to the huge one resulting from a misapplication of variation.

Earlier I insisted that although navigation in small boat coasting, or on short sea passages, was quite simple, accuracy should still be strived for, and so it should because a string of minor inaccuracies can accumulate into a single large one. The choice as to whether to work correctly in True or fudge the issue is an individual one. Some people have tidy, mathematical minds and others haven't. Perhaps it is safer for the latter to cut out the possibility of major errors at the expense of a little accuracy. An understanding of True is still necessary now and again. Bearings in almanacs and pilot books are given in True, for example bearings for the entry of a river. There is still no need to wrestle with mental arithmetic; just lay the rules across the chart rose on the True bearing and read its magnetic equivalent – give or take a degree.

Plotting tidal set

A stream which is either dead against her or dead astern obviously only affects the yacht's time of arrival, but if it sets *across* the course the navigator will have to make due allowance for it. The simple instance of a boat sailing across a river to reach a point on the far bank will show that the helmsman gauges the extent to which he must head into the current entirely by eye, and he may have to head up 45 degrees off course to get there. When he reaches the slacker stream near the bank he adjusts his angle again, and so on. The navigator who cannot see his destination must calculate the angle by means of tide-table and tidal atlas. Hour by hour the tidal stream alters in strength and direction, and hour by hour the sailing boat may alter her speed and direction according to the dictates of the wind.

The navigator notes his time of departure. He turns to his Nautical Almanac and looks up the tidal atlas appropriate to his part of the coast. These atlases consist of a series of chartlets showing, by means of arrows, the direction of the stream hour by hour, and, by means of figures, the rate of the stream for both neap tides and spring tides.

Perhaps he is crossing the mouth of the Thames Estuary and it is ten o'clock in the morning. The atlas is based on the Dover tide times (in this case also upon Sheerness) so that a check shows it to be, let's say, two hours after high water at Dover. Turning to the appropriate chartlet he sees that a weak stream is setting across his course from west to east – maybe half a knot. In the next three hours, however, the stream will increase to $1-1\frac{1}{2}$ knots (first figure neaps, second figure spring tides). At the speed he is sailing (three knots perhaps) it may take him four hours to reach his destination and saying, just for the hell of it, that the tides are at springs, it means he will be set to the east about five miles during that time. Later, the stream will slacken and then begin running from the opposite direction, and if, during his passage, his speed falls so low that the whole thing takes him twice as long, he might expect to get pushed back again that five miles. Meanwhile (see Fig. 32) he lays off a course to steer which will keep him on the straight and narrow. Setting off the five miles down tide (Point 'A') from his starting-point and then setting the dividers at the distance he expects to sail during the four-hour span – twelve miles in this case – he places one point at the five-mile down-tide position (Point 'A') and swings the other point to cut the course line (Point 'B'). He rules in the line between the two points of the dividers, and this gives the direction in which he must steer to keep his ship proceeding in the direction in which he wants to go. The point where the dividers (Point 'B') have cut the course line will be his position in four hours' time.

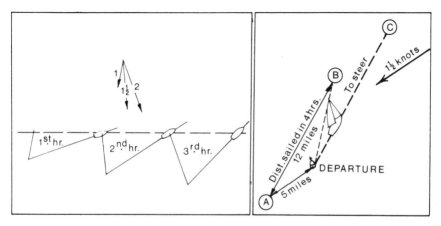

Fig. 32

Four hours is a long time ahead to forecast the sailing speed of a small boat. A motor boat, counting on keeping up an exact speed the whole time, can be navigated the whole way in one go. We know how long she'll take to cover the distance and can set off the tidal effect in one step. Under sail it is often safer to take it hour by hour, adjusting the course steered according to the increase or decrease in speed of boat and rate of tide.

It may so happen that the route across the estuary is a buoy-hopping one, zigzagging, sometimes up-tide, sometimes down. In thick weather the compass courses will have to be worked out for every change. In normal weather, when each buoy can be seen from the preceding one, it is the best practice possible to plot every fresh change just as if the visibility were poor; the disparity, if any, between course steered by eye and course plotted will reveal any inaccuracies in your allowances for tide.

Since tidal streams rarely set exactly up and down but tend to deviate towards the beginning and end of each run, you must allow for this if plotting is to be accurate. If you make a plot hourly or half-hourly – and in a thickly buoyed area this isn't too frequent – some account of this deviation from the straight stream will be taken, but on a long hop across open water, with a steady breeze and some hope of a steady speed, a four-hour plot may be ample. In this case the whole tide effect, both rate by the hour and direction, can be plotted in advance and the resultant course steered. But it is important to remember that the yacht is not going to travel along a straight line. As the tide effect strengthens and slackens she will go forward along her sailed course but will be carried down and then back in a long curve. As destination may be the first concern of the navigator, where the yacht goes in the process may not seem so important. However, should there be a shoal or a danger of some sort along this curve, the vessel may be in trouble, despite the fact that the straight line ruled on the chart skirts it safely (Fig. 33).

A sailing cruiser meandering quietly to her destination across a relatively large expanse of open water and taking long enough about it to allow several tides to elapse is a rather different case. She may plot and

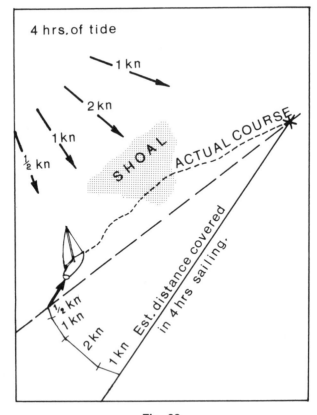

Fig. 33

allow for tide at regular periods in the manner described or, since her time of arrival under sail alone cannot be estimated with certainty, she can sail the direct course from A to B and simply plot her tidal wanderings either side of the course line. Ultimately she will be near enough to her goal for a prediction to be made and a tidal stream allowance worked out. For a crew of two or three men, of whom only one is navigating, this is the easier method. It wouldn't do for an offshore racer, but it is safe, it is easier in a small cruiser, and it places no strain upon the watchkeeping.

A study of the tidal atlases shows that the streams sweep along the coasts, filling the rivers and setting up eddies in bays, building up to very high levels in some places (study the various tide height tables) and only reaching modest heights at others. The French Channel coasts and the Bristol Channel have tides which range to the thirty-foot mark and over, while the English south coast may have its highest levels of only half that figure. The rate of the tidal streams varies just as much. The fastest stream in some areas may not exceed three knots while speeds of seven and eight knots are not rare around the Brittany headlands. At times, the course to steer, plotted in advance, may seem quite mad. The coast may be distant and the sea calm, yet the tide has the cruiser in an iron grip, and only by carefully planning beforehand can one get her to port in reasonable time. So many carelessly navigated yachts can be seen shooting up and down the French coasts, aiming uncertainly at some harbour and never quite hitting it, that the lesson for the man in the very small cruiser, making a cross-Channel passage, is to study the tides with painstaking thoroughness. Half a mile down-tide on arrival can mean either frantic motoring to make up or six hours or so spent waiting for the turn of the tide and the risk of missing one's harbour if the wind goes light.

The atlases are as accurate as plain mathematics can make them, but the streams vary quite a lot depending upon prevailing wind and atmospheric pressure. Prolonged north to north-west winds in the North Sea can jam the tide up in the narrows and cause devastating flooding (the 1953 disaster is a case in point). At other times, tides may become erratic, with fierce ebbs, perhaps. Thus, a tongue in the cheek is not out of place. The tidal atlases published by the Admiralty have a graph which enables one to interpolate between Spring and Neap.

The making tack

So far, the yacht has been considered as luckily blessed with a free wind and able to sail any course which is plotted. We can allow ourselves a bitter laugh at this presumption. Facts show that about half our time seems to be spent hard on the wind. Once the system of plotting and allowing for tidal set is understood, the added disadvantage of having to lay a course which can be sailed becomes just a matter of compromise. The yacht beating along a track which cuts athwart the run of the tide must seek to lee-bow when she can. The wind rarely stays constant for long, and sooner or later the yacht will find one tack more advantageous than the other. Her final track may show an apparently haphazard stagger across the channel. The extent to which it diverges from the most direct line will depend entirely upon the navigator's skill at marrying the course sailed with the allowance for tide.

The simple example would be a yacht on a cross-Channel passage facing a head wind. If she tacks down-tide it will carry her many miles to leeward of her destination, but if she makes her tack a lee-bowed one, the end of the tide run will see her somewhere not so far from her planned course. In a river she may even sheer straight across on one tack.

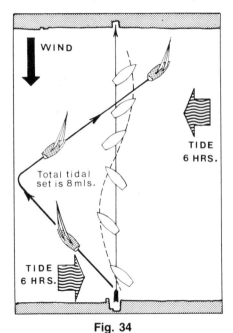

WIND

TIDE
6 HRS.

Total tidal
set is 8 mls.

TIDE
6 HRS.

Fig. 34

A long passage in which several tides may ebb and flow and which the yacht lee-bows, should see her far ahead of another which simply drifts up and down the Channel (Fig. 34). Lee-bowing has the effect of reducing the loss of ground from leeway and it enables the yacht to stay somewhere near her desired track even if the wind shifts its direction. Even if the direction of the wind allows her to lie almost directly on the bearing of her destination, a strong cross-tide may make the losing tack more profitable, although, of course, this would only apply to a short passage involving one tide. If the tide could be counted upon to turn and shove the yacht back on her track later, the making tack would certainly pay better.

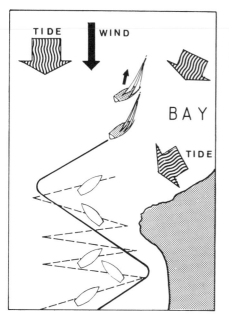

Fig. 35 The hard struggle to beat against a foul current while passing a headland may, if there is a significantly deep bay beyond it, provide an opportunity to lee-bow a current coming out of the bay.

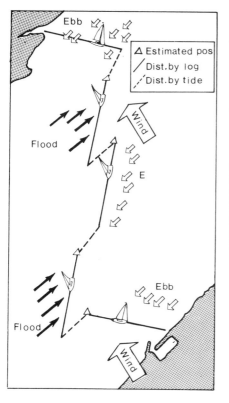

Fig. 36 Three ebbs and two flood streams are to elapse during the passage, the yacht has a head wind and her speed cannot be predicted ahead. She lee-bows the tide for much of the time, tacking when it suits. Dotted lines indicate the amount of tidal set to be plotted each time her DR position is worked up (for simplicity, leeway etc. have been omitted). She has reached a point where she can stem the coastal current with the option of freeing sheets if needed. A powerboat passage with its duration known in advance might have assumed that tides would cancel and a simple lay-off for the extra ebb might have been made. This would assume that tidal rates were fairly equal.

129

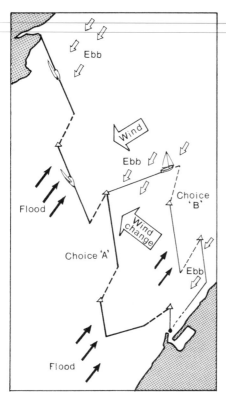

Fig. 37 A changing wind affects strategy in this case. She has dropped down channel with the ebb and held the same reaching course when the flood began to lee-bow her. The wind comes ahead and she is faced with a choice of tack. Choice A carries her well down the coast so that she can take the next flood up to her port. Choice B, a lee-bowing course, takes her longer in the end since she spends less time on the more direct making tack.

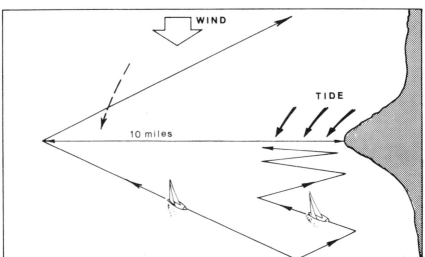

Fig. 38 With the current about to turn foul off a headland it is usually better to pass the headland in two long offshore tacks rather than attempting to beat inshore where rates are stronger.

Other deflections from course

The helmsman can make a farce of the finest course ever plotted. One cannot expect ocean racing accuracy from the helmsman of a small cruiser. He will make the best course he can consistent with the distractions of sunbathing, yarning, eating and drinking canned ale. This doesn't matter as long as all are enjoying themselves, but it is still important to have a shrewd idea of on which side of the course line to expect the greatest errors. On the wind people may tend to eat up to windward a shade, sailing in a series of long luffs. If they are pinching, a good deal of leeway may also be expected. On a run, fear of a gybe shows in an error upwind or at least towards the direction opposite the boom. Without getting acid about it, the navigator must induce his companions to try noting their average course steered – the fact that their errors are so plain will in any case improve their steering. Leeway can be checked by taking a bearing of the wake while the ship is being sailed as straight as possible; the result, checked against the compass course, is a rough guide, but it cannot be applied to all on-the-wind courses for leeway will vary with the conditions.

Distance and speed

The modern yacht log may be anything from the towing rotator variety to the latest in electronics with through-hull impellers or inside-hull doppler type. It is as accurate an instrument as one might hope to find dealing with such erratic things as wind, water and sailing craft. It is a costly device for the small-boat man to buy if he is only likely to use it once or twice in the course of a season, but it is vital that he should have some idea of his speed through the water and hence distance travelled through the water if his navigation is to be anything but a series of guesses. A log gives speed through the water; speed and direction over the ground is a combination of current and boat speed.

One soon develops a sense of tide. On a hazy day out of sight of land or moored buoys the cruiser may drift along apparently making no more than a knot, but in real terms of speed over the ground she may be sliding down the invisible coastline at four knots, three of them being tidal current. Just as a beetle scuttling over the carpet can be given a lot of extra exercise if the carpet is pulled, or deflected from its target if pulled sideways, so also is a boat deflected, aided or opposed on a chosen course by the moving carpet of the tidal sea.

Accumulated errors

Pilotage is full of possibilities for errors, mostly small, but capable of accumulating. A one-degree error in the course steered results in an error of one mile at the end of a 60-mile passage. It is rare to hold one heading for such a distance in the confined waters of the British Isles. Neither can we steer to one degree, and a couple of degrees steered off course by luffing up more than one should on a windward course is easily done; to be a mile out at the end of a thirty-mile passage when hoping to find a buoy in hazy conditions is likely enough.

Take the case of a boat on passage between two buoys which are ten miles apart. The navigator has made a careful departure from his first buoy, noted the log reading (or zeroed it), estimated tidal set, possible leeway perhaps, and arrived at a course to steer. There may be a tidal set against the starboard side and the boat, closehauled, will be making some leeway. There may be a little deviation on that heading and there could be some helm error if the helmsman was consistently steering upwind of the course in the gusts. The navigator, feeling queasy perhaps, may have allowed his parallel rules to slip the odd degree when reading off his plotted course and perhaps if he is working from the magnetic rose of the chart, it might mean another half degree of error. If the navigator allows too little or too much for tidal set and leeway, if the helmsman's errors are not owned up to or noticed, and the deviation is considered too little to bother about (or not even known about), the total error could be sizeable. If the navigator was working to True north bearings and made a mistake, it could be catastrophic. And yet despite all these errors they might bring the expected buoy bang on the nose or near enough and never realise that it was pure luck. The errors had cancelled each other out.

Fortunately it is rare to find that all these small errors combine into one huge one; most of the time some of them at least cancel each other out, thus the helmsman's two-degree upwind error might be cancelled out by a stronger current on the bow than the navigator allowed for, leeway may offset any deviation and so on, and the end result is acceptable. Just occasionally, though, they join forces and the navigator is well and truly lost – a phenomenon put down to abnormal tidal surge perhaps.

Not all errors are foreseeable. Tidal set can certainly be greater on occasion than as shown in the atlas, affected by barometric and local conditions, or there can be an unexpected surface drift of perhaps nearly one knot if the wind has been blowing steadily from one quarter for some days. Leeway also varies according to speed, angle of sailing, heeling and sea conditions and it takes some while before a navigator can assess it correctly. Then we must also remember the bitter fact that while a navigator can perform miracles in calm, gentle weather and on a steady chart table, his accuracy is liable to plummet in a rough seaway, when in rain and murk accuracy is most important.

At the end of the distance run with no mark in sight, which way should the navigator head in search of it? If the logbook entries have been made in detail throughout the passage he can first check back through all his workings, perhaps belatedly with a little more care, check too on the succession of helmsmen and what they think they averaged port or starboard of the course. At the end of it all he may have a hunch that the buoy might be, say, somewhere to port, but if turning to port means running downwind in search of the buoy, nobody will be very happy.

It largely depends upon how urgent it is to find that buoy; whether to search at all, whether to simply press on – this is a decision for the skipper. The press-on-and-hope philosophy is human enough, but on occasion it can be dangerous and it might just be that the only *safe* decision is to turn the boat and go back. Even this option is far from safe because it means virtually starting a new passage without a known starting position and the boat, although being steered on a reciprocal heading, may in fact be covering quite a different stretch of water, subject to tidal set, different leeway, deviation and course steered.

Today's position-finding electronics (provided an owner can understand the instruction manual) can obviate the problem completely, but more modest navigating equipment might include a radio direction finder and VHF radio. In an emergency the VHF radio might yield a fix by courtesy of the coastguard, but this facility must not be regarded as part of a small boat navigator's regular armoury. RDF on the other hand certainly *is* part of it, but it takes a lot of practice to become proficient in its use. Taking a compass fix in bad weather is difficult in any case, even when it is a visual one at a shore object a couple of miles or so away. Taking a bearing on the null of a radio signal from a station perhaps twenty or more miles away is more so, and big errors can occur. There are many reasons for this apart from the actual distance of the radio beacon and the motion of the boat. There is the angle of the bearing in terms of crossing a fix, whether the signal is passing over land, signal distortion due to interference from the yacht's rigging and the accuracy and deviation of the RDF compass.

Much depends upon what you hope to achieve with an RDF, how simple it is to use and how competent you are. Some navigators live with the RDF in hand at sea continually updating their fixes, checking them against their DR and so familiar with the art that they have memorised most of the morse identification signals. On the other hand there are very simple, basic RDF instruments which are at their best being used to pinpoint a beacon which is perhaps only just over the horizon, or not visible due to haze. Used in this way with strong or nearby beacons providing a single position line these basic instruments can often confirm a DR position, but inaccurate fine tuning may make them inadequate for proper fixing.

Much also depends on how a boat is crewed. In cases where the skipper is navigator and master of destiny aboard there will be times when half an hour spent down below waiting for the various beacons to come up on schedule, then plotting them, will be out of the question because there is too much happening on deck.

Coping with all the various possible errors begins right at the commencement of the passage by being ready with a course to steer as soon as the chosen departure point is abeam and the log is zeroed. In normal visibility the departure point may remain visible astern for half an hour or more and if careful back bearings are taken and plotted it will be seen whether the boat is making good her ordered course and it can be modified if necessary. Thereafter the navigator can sit quietly below for a while monitoring the course being steered by holding a hand-bearing compass steady against the chart table. What the hand bearing is actually reading down below isn't important, it is the average of the swings and curves off course that matters.

CHAPTER NINE
The Chart, Fixes and Drift

Never economise on charts. The belief that a single small-scale chart showing all the ports and rivers you plan to visit on a cruise is the most sensible buy soon leads to grey hairs. The small-scale passage charts covering large areas of coast are intended to be used by vessels following the sea-lanes around the coasts. They show all the principal lights and give all the relevant details of headlands, soundings, nature of bottom and so forth, but once the vessel, no matter how small, makes for a river or begins to coast close to the land she begins to need more detailed information. The small-scale chart may show an offlying shoal, but not all the small unlit buoys around it, and the cruiser, seeing a beacon pole far to seaward, may search his passage chart in vain.

The chart folder might include one general passage chart showing the whole cruising areas, and as many large-scale charts and river plans as are likely to be needed, also one or two which you may be forced to need. For instance on a long passage along an exposed coastline, it's wise to have a chart of available shelter. To back up this information, a yachtsman's pilot book is needed. There is a wide choice available, but it is important to bear in mind that no pilot book can stay up-to-date indefinitely, particularly those dealing with shallow and changing coastlines, new harbours and changes of buoyage. A nautical almanac is also indispensible, as are tidal atlases.

To outline all the information to be found on any chart would take far more room than I have to spare here, but the details in regular use by yachtsmen can be noted.

Buoyage, soundings, coastal features, compass rose and scale of sea-miles claim first attention, but the wealth of additional detail given in symbol form must be learned by close study – the whorl which indicates a tidal eddy, the different types of pecked line denoting three-, five-, ten-metre lines, and so on. The various ways of indicating whether a wreck is dangerous to surface navigation or quite harmless (save to anchors), the nature of the sea-bed and types of rock and reef are all listed in almanacs so that you can recognise them on the charts.

The system of buoyage used on charts is international in principle although the general design of the buoys may differ. Other systems, the

French quadrantal system for instance, are easy to pick up. On the chart, buoys are shown in symbol and underlined with a centre dot to show actual position; bearings plotted upon buoys should be taken from this point. Lit buoys have a tinted halo to distinguish them, and the light characteristic in abbreviation beside it (see Night Sailing, Chapter 11). Colour tinting makes the modern chart easier to read at a glance, with drying banks and shoreline distinct from shoal water which doesn't quite dry out and deep soundings, while dry land remains a uniform tone. Chart scale is all-important and before working on a new chart its scale should be noted. The changeover to metric depths can also catch the careless and the unwary.

Drying heights are underlined and the figures then refer to the drying heights of the seabed exposed by a tide which reaches or comes somewhere near chart datum. A drying height of, for example, $\underline{3}$ metres might rarely dry below 2 or 2.5 metres and at neaps it may not dry at all, or remain just awash.

The chart compass rose can either be a circle marked in 360 degrees with zero on the True north line and the principal points of N, NNE, NE, ENE and so on indicated, or it will be the more commonly found True rose with the magnetic rose inside it and offset to the extent of magnetic variation in that particular area.

Compass 'points' bear no relationship to degrees and they are seldom used nowadays, a point being equal to $11\frac{1}{4}$ degrees. In the past all courses and bearings were given in points, but this is no longer so.

The charts mark coastal features according to their value as means of identification. Thus, if a church is marked it will be a prominent one. Cliffs are shown as a bird's-eye view, principal coastal roads are given and some charts give contours to indicate land heights. High hills have their height in feet above Mean High Water Springs. Gasometers, windmills, quarries, high chimneys, and so on, are all indicated by appropriate symbols. Most chart symbols are self-explanatory, but as there is no room to reproduce the whole lot in these pages, your only alternative is to settle down with chart and almanac and study them.

Unlike those on a land map, which gives a separate scale of miles, the distances measured on a chart must be taken from the side-margins (latitude). A sea-mile is equal to 1 minute of latitude and 60 minutes make 1 degree of latitude. (A knot is purely a measurement of speed – sea-miles per hour. One cannot speak of being six knots away from land, nor is it correct to speak of six knots per hour, knots are just knots.) It must be emphasised that all references to 'miles' in this book are to sea- and not to land-miles.

Charts are always drawn on Mercator's Projection, which gives a true picture of angles and bearings, but only by distorting the scale, which becomes larger as it nears the poles. On small-scale charts this change in scale is quite noticeable. It is therefore usual to measure distance by using that part of the side margin which is on more or less the same line of latitude. The usual procedure is to set the dividers at the distance to be measured and then place one point on a convenient figure of the scale and read off above it. Alternatively, setting the dividers to a five- or ten-mile span, they can then be 'walked' across the chart.

Large-scale charts or plans do sometimes give a separate scale of sea-miles in the title, divided into smaller distances of one cable for the purpose of estimating safe navigable distances from rocks, wharves and so on. A cable is one-tenth of a sea-mile, and near enough to 200 yards for purposes of distance judging. It is worth remembering this as pilot books refer to safe offings from river-banks, cliffs and so on in terms of cable-lengths, which appear in a separate scale on the chart.

Bearings and fixes

There are few things so reassuring to the man in some doubt as to which side of safety his ship is lying as a set of bearings taken with an accurate hand-bearing compass on identified lights or landmarks. The procedure is simple. The bearing read on the compass-card is plotted on the chart from the identified mark. Several such bearings taken within an approximate right angle will intersect: the intersection is the ship's position – or should be.

Two bearings only, taken inaccurately (Fig. 39), can yield a nice variety of possible positions, particularly if the marks are spaced at a narrow angle as shown at A. The addition of a third bearing clinches the matter in the form of a 'cocked hat'. The relative size of this headgear largely determines the accuracy of the fix. It is, however, possible to produce a tidy little hat when the bearings are well adrift, but it is more likely to be wide and obvious to see. The important thing is that inaccuracy should be limited to small errors, and be consistent.

The bearing compass must be pretty dead-beat, that is to say it must return smartly to its true orientation after a wild swing caused by the cavorting cruiser. It will often be impossible to get the card to centre exactly on a bearing and the average of the swing must be taken. Thus, the navigator looking at the object over his compass sees it swooping around in the sights and the card swooping to and fro in the prism. Steady helmsmanship and patience are required. Never take a hasty bearing if it is an important one, and never tell an inexperienced crew to do it unless it is a routine check and not vital. When using a hand-bearing compass make sure you are holding it clear of iron stanchions, steel rigging or neighbouring iron.

Since accuracy is important it may be necessary to correct the chart bearing for change in Variation before plotting it. In general, a chart which is one or two years older than the date shown on the compass rose

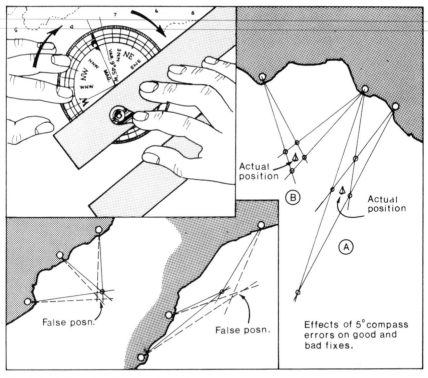

Fig. 39 A fix using the hand-bearing compass can produce convincing looking positions, but these can be well adrift if the bearings are narrow (A) or there is a compass error or if the bearings are carelessly taken; wide angles (B) are also unreliable.

will be so little adrift that one can get away with plotting straight from it. For instance, the chart shows that Magnetic Variation at that position was 9 degrees and 45 minutes west of True north in 1986 and that it is decreasing by 8 minutes annually. In two years Magnetic north has crept nearer to True north by 16 minutes. There are 60 minutes to 1 degree so the error is just over a quarter of a degree or the thickness of a very fine pencil line. Had the chart been ten years out of date (although corrected for other little anachronisms, we hope) the error would have been $10 \times 8 = 1$ degree 20 minutes. When one remembers that the bearing may be taken in rough weather giving another 2 degrees error and that the compass may have been nestling against the backstay at the time and been deviated by another couple of degrees, the possible total error of 5 degrees 20 minutes is going to matter. All efforts towards accuracy should be made provided the results are plottable.

To correct the chart for, say, a 1½-degree decrease of *easterly* error, one must visualise holding the parallel rules (or whatever gadget is in use) steady on the bearing just taken with the compass and turning the chart

1½ degrees clockwise or to the east (Fig. 39). If the bearing taken was 70 degrees, the swing to the east will decrease it to 68½ degrees.

If a bearing is to be read from the chart and then sought with the hand-bearing compass, the same rule must naturally be followed. The case of a yachtsman faced with lights in line or a line of safe bearing is one in point here. From the chart he notes that the bearing must be 120 degrees magnetic for a safe course. The chart is 2 degrees out of date, so he would look for a bearing of 118 degrees with his compass. In point of fact, any really serious situation involving a yes or no of safety which rested on a matter of 2 degrees would be rather nasty.

Generally speaking, practically all the bearings taken in small yachts are confirmatory ones. Position is known within reasonable limits from dead-reckoning; the bearings confirm and implement. Among the most important are sets of bearings taken to give a fix at the end of a long passage offshore when DR is possibly a bit adrift. On this score, the temptation to trust in a fuzzy bearing taken on the distant 'loom' of a light, before the light itself has cleared the horizon, must be resisted mightily. Such bearings, taken at right angles to the course as a check on distance to the land ahead, can be wildly adrift. Take them by all means but don't rely on them simply because they 'confirm' DR position, for both can be out. Beware, too, the bearings taken on buoys. These can be, and quite often are, a little out of position after very hard weather. Moreover, if they are close at hand, the range of the buoy on its mooring can account for inaccuracy. Whenever buoys are the sole means of fixing, take a set of shots on every buoy which is in a position to give a cross. Four or five bearings in fact – that is, if the result is of serious importance.

On a coastal run, and with a fast tide under the cruiser, you must take bearings in quick succession. To take one, plot it, and then take two more is bound to give a poor result as the yacht will have travelled a long way between the first and last bearings.

Our old die-hards, those monsters of possible inaccuracy, the running fix and the double-the-angle-on-the-bow, must come into the picture here. Perhaps I am hard on them, but these fixes, being subject to failure because of the unknown speed of the cruiser over the ground, do produce an 'answer' which fairly screams reliability while remaining forever suspect. The great advantage of a running fix is that you only need one shore object; two bearings are taken of it separated by a log run distance, then the first bearing is transferred to give a cross with the second (Fig. 40). The whole thing then depends on the accuracy not of the log, but of the distance sailed over the ground. At slack water the fix can be very accurate, but in a fast and only estimated run of tide it can be well out.

Doubling the angle, while being another one-object trick, also relies upon one's knowing the tide effect. In this case, though, a tidal stream

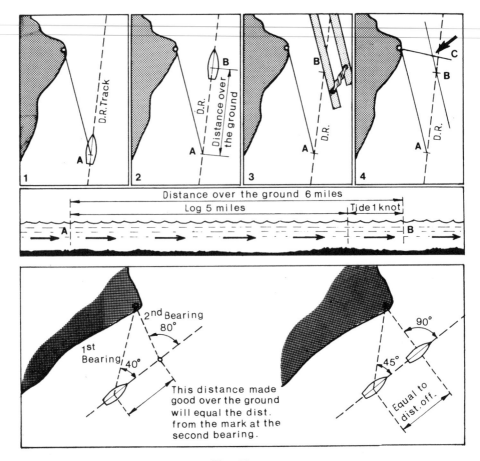

Fig. 40

which is either dead fair or dead foul does not matter so long as it can be calculated, but any cross-current or the effect of excessive leeway will ruin the fix. With the cruiser sailing a straight course past the object a bearing is taken – we will say that it is plotted and makes an angle of 40 degrees to the course-line (Fig. 40). If the yacht sails on until a bearing can be taken which will give an angle of 80 degrees to her course, the distance measured along the course-line between bearings will then be the same as her distance from the object at the time of the second bearing. What must be remembered is that it is the *angle to the course-line* which must be doubled and not the actual magnetic bearing. This means that when you have plotted the first bearing and used a protractor to measure the angle, you must use the protractor again to strike off a doubled angle which can then be read off against the compass-rose to determine its actual magnetic bearing. Armed with this knowledge the navigator waits, compass in hand, until the bearing comes 'on'.

Distance off by the four-point method is a good mental check for the man who is only able to leave the helm for short and hectic rushes to the chart. The object must be well ahead. He waits until it bears four points (45 degrees anyway) on his bow, then he reads the log and notes the time. He sails on, waiting again until the object bears full on his beam or eight points (90 degrees). By reading his log again and mentally adjusting the result for tide effect he now has his distance from the object (Fig. 40). Again it can be seen that a difference of a knot of tide can mean a big error in a thirty-minute interval between bearings, but since, in darkness, the yachtsman may not know his distance off within two miles or more, the method is still of some comfort to him.

Plotting drift

Most people start the engine once speed falls to near-calm, and calculating position in light variable weather and in tidal waters after a few hours of fitful going is an uncertain art. Wind shifts mean repeated alterations of course, and flat calms punctuate the whole performance. Sooner or later, though, the breeze will harden and the cruiser will begin to move. It is then, from that moment, that the certainty of a good landfall rests upon the amount of care which has gone into plotting the drift. One tends to relax, potter with the gear, or swim over the side if the sun is hot, but the plotting is not to be neglected.

As soon as the speed drops and all signs of calm are manifest – possibly the fog as well – the navigator must check log, time and tide and put his latest calculated position on the chart. As the speed falls still further he can amend the position hourly until the log-readings are no longer to be trusted, and from then on he calculates drift (Fig. 41A).

We'll suppose that the period of calm and light airs has lasted all day from 8 am until 6 pm when the cruiser is sailing properly again. The navigator may not have put a position on the chart since early morning but he has filled the logbook with careful entries of every alteration of course made in the fluky airs and the estimated distance sailed on each course. Distrusting the almost vertical log-line (or maybe not having one at all), he will have done the best he can by calculating speed through water either with some sort of chip-log or drag-log or basing his calculations on the fact that one knot is equivalent to (nearly) 100 feet per minute.

He begins, however, by plotting the tidal drift from the time of his last good DR position. It is to be noted here that the effect is not 'so much east' and 'so much west' (or north and south) but a gradual circling effect as the tidal stream has flowed, slackened, turned and ebbed again. With an Admiralty chart, he will have been able to plot his tide by finding the nearest code letter to his position on the chart and referring to the

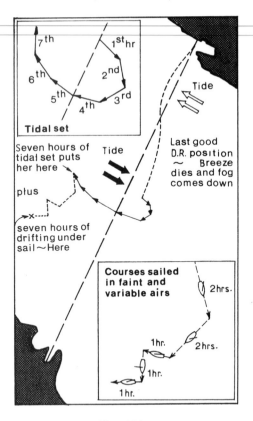

Fig. 41A

tidal stream table found elsewhere on the sheet. Thus in the last eight hours he may have been set south-east a mile, south half a mile, south-west half a mile, and then west for five, west-north-west a mile, and so on. This is all plotted, and when the final position is reached he begins to plot the actual sailing courses for the period. The ultimate result is (if he has taken due care and the tides have run according to the plan) his departure point from thenceforward. While all this was being worked out he would, of course, have given the helmsman a snap course to steer, having noted time and log-reading at the onset.

CHAPTER TEN

Planning a Port-to-Port Passage

The great virtue in detailed passage planning is not so much that the passage plan can be followed step by step in detail, thereby cutting out the amount of chartwork and navigation needed during the passage, as that having once thought the passage through and identified the problems, listed any lights to be seen, tidal changes, RDF beacons which can be used and so on, we are familiar with the picture as a whole. Later, relevant passages in the pilot book, digested earlier, are familiar and tidal information and the whole tidal pattern needs only a bit of revision. The hard truth of the matter is that once at sea and making the passage under sail the carefully worked out series of courses, distances and times may go straight up the spout. A change in the anticipated wind direction, or a flat calm, or any of a number of things can render the original passage plan obsolete. It is seldom that a passage plan does work out exactly, but the problems are all on now familiar territory.

The imaginary passage plan which follows concerns a short hop between two rivers. All that it really involves is the tidal pattern and the decision on starting time in order to cross a bar at the river entrance on arrival. A power boat would have no problem at all other than calculating distance and speed. The local high water time of midday and midnight in Ex river is of course a simplification and merely indicates at what hours the current will be ebbing or flowing in the river (Fig. 41B).

A sailing purist or an owner without an engine (rare these days) might decide to drop down the river Ex on the last of the river ebb at around 5 am and since the wind is offshore and the land will provide shelter he might anchor outside the river, waiting until the foul tide slackens prior to turning fair at 0700. Alternatively, since the foul tide would be weakening and he has a broad reaching wind off the land he might be able to dispense with anchoring and make ground against the tide. There are maybe seven hours in which to cover the twenty miles of coasting, with a fair tide most of the way. Thereafter he would have to beat into the entrance of the river Wye with the last of the flood. Catching this bit of flood into the river is his target because, engineless, he won't be able to do it once the ebb begins to run out over the bar. So he beats his way inside and when the ebb starts after 1250 he anchors and waits for the whole ebb to run its course; probably resuming the beat up-river about 1900 that evening.

A second owner has no inhibitions about use of engine, nor does he bother much about working the tides, his only target is to reach the river Wye in time to be able to cross the bar – latest time an hour after local HW (1350). So the crew breakfast in leisurely fashion at 0800, get under way at 0900 punching the by then strong flood in the river Ex and clearing the river mouth by 1000. He does have a fair wind in the river, though, and under sail plus engine he might do a bit better than that. He can now enjoy over three hours of sailing with a fair tide under him, making perhaps 5 knots over the ground, but by 1300 and with the tide slackening and due to turn foul soon, he has a last five miles to cover before he can reach the bar – and 1350 is supposed to be the latest time he should cross (one hour after local HW). With full sail and engine screaming flat out the yacht races for the bar, crosses it a bit naughtily well after the proper

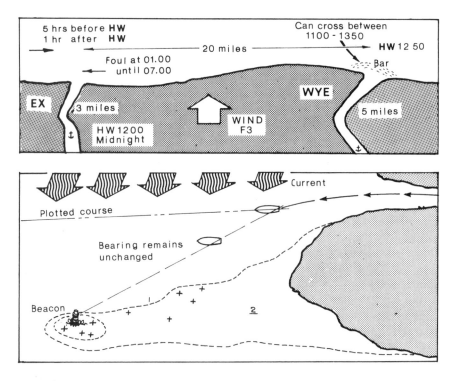

Fig. 41 (B) A common hazard when leaving a river with a strong cross-tidal current along the coast outside the mouth is that there is a temptation to head straight out to sea, perhaps keeping some beacon to buoy 'safely' on the bow. Unless regular bearings are taken the beacon may remain on a *constant* bearing due to the set of the current and the yacht is in fact being set towards it or the shoal it guards.

time, but with a flat sea she scrapes over, and then follow two hours of hard motoring against the whole of the river ebb. He anchors at about 1630 after a seven-hour passage, mainly under engine.

A third owner doesn't mind motoring either, but he does study the tides and he strikes a compromise, setting as his target the earliest time he can cross the bar, which is about 1100. There will be twenty miles of coasting prior to that and since the tide will be fair after 0700 he has four hours of it in which to reach his goal. He should be able to average five knots over the ground all right. In short, he must get going early enough to be outside at 0700. They probably get under way at 0600, eating breakfast as they drop down the river under a touch of engine. Having arrived at the river Wye there is enough flood left to have that delight of delights, a crisp beat up a new river on a fair tide.

Planning a cruise

The tendency in planning a cruise is to be over-ambitious. To have a general objective is good, but one should be prepared to enjoy cruising for its own sake rather than as a form of transport to a particular place.

New owners who are short of experience are better advised to choose an area which has plenty of scope for day-sailing and short hops between fresh anchorages. The Solent is a classic example of a place where it is possible to sail every day for a fortnight and never anchor twice in the same place at night. Falmouth, the East Coast rivers and creeks, the Clyde and many more areas are to be found which are ideal training grounds. The man who takes his family to sea for the first time is well advised to choose short-hop cruising if he is not to risk putting them off for ever after.

Sailing to a schedule can ruin a cruise, the eternal urge to press on is tiring and the feeling of being a water gypsy is lost. Plans should be elastic to allow for a little dallying and it is better to spend an extra day in a place that everybody enjoys, and then miss out on one of the scheduled stops to make up lost time later.

The answer to the eternal question 'How far can we get?' is like the length of the proverbial piece of string, but with settled weather, good sailing breezes, some fair and some foul, a small family cruiser might cover getting on for a couple of hundred miles in ten days, sailing during daylight and having the occasional day in. The same boat with a tougher crew who want to push harder, sail at night, and use every fair breeze, could double this distance. We are presupposing of course, that the winds, if not always fair, are never so foul that the cruiser is weather-bound in port for days on end. Some cruisers never get further than a few miles down the coast, and there they stay until the weather lets up a bit. The Solent type of cruise which offers more sheltered sailing has a big advantage here.

With wind and weather permitting and an energetic crew, it is possible to make a twenty-four hour passage which covers between eighty and one hundred miles. Two days at sea for a crew of three experienced hands is no hardship in good weather and such a passage would take them most of the way down-Channel. For the small cruiser it would be rare to have it easy for much longer than that, and the long passage cannot be reckoned on – one can only take the chance if it arises.

In a fortnight an experienced crew might cruise from, say, the Solent to Cherbourg, down to St Malo, back to Weymouth, and thence to the Solent again. A total distance of about 250 miles but including two Channel crossings and perhaps three or four nights at sea in light weather; a total sailing time of between a possible 70, or in light weather a probable 115, sailing hours which, divided up, means something like an average of 8–9 hours a day for a fortnight. The essential thing about this type of cruise is to have time in hand in case you are delayed by the weather.

Plans must be made on the chart if estimates are to be realistic. It is safer to call fourteen days nine actual sailing days to allow for delay, poor weather, and so on, and of the nine, perhaps only four will be real distance-coverers.

Prevailing wind is important. A one-way cruise from Falmouth to the Solent would be far more likely to come off than the same distance from east to west. For the same reason, a cross-Channel passage to, say, Le Havre from the Solent is more likely to go according to plan than one from Chichester to Alderney – the first is a reach and the second a close fetch in prevailing westerlies. The return passage must be remembered, of course, and time kept in hand once more.

It is unwise to arrange a cruise to coincide with top spring tides, especially in such areas as the Brittany coast or Bristol Channel where heights rise to 30 or 40 feet (Bay of Mont St Michel). Seas are rougher, many shallow-water anchorages dry out, anchor scope is much greater and it will often be impossible to make headway against foul tidal streams. Important also to note times of ebbs to avoid when entering rivers.

The matter of the weather is anybody's gamble, but it is possible to gamble a little upon the likelihood of certain months of the summer being better than others. According to records taken over the years May is likely to start with a cold spell and end with hot sun and thundery tendencies. June is famed for cold nights, sunny days and frequent rain. Thunderstorms in July, hot and dull days alternating, ending up with a questionable few weeks when gales so often cause havoc among yachts. The first weeks of August tend to be stormy too. Mid-July and mid-August would seem to be hot spell periods frequently.

Late August and early September are likely to give troubled weather – hot days sandwiched between rough patches. A settled spell often arrives after the first few days of September and may last until the middle or last week of the month. This is the time for small craft to be content to stay around home waters as the equinox arrives with a tendency to bad gales. If a late autumn cruise is planned, early October is often safer if the bad weather has passed by.

Trailer cruising is becoming ever more popular. Using the boat as a caravan, there are big advantages in trailing to some ideal cruising area, or for that matter trailing on the Continent. The AA and RAC can give advice upon cost of shipment and so forth.

Going foreign

In a book such as this there is a very real danger attached to giving detailed information about government regulations because books (one likes to think) have a shelf life of some years and consequently a buyer may fall between revised editions. Although the movement of thousands of small yachts between countries of different nationalities means that bureaucracy is kept to the minimum (usually, at any rate), there are still a few very important requirements which are ignored at one's peril. The reader is urged to contact the office of HM Customs and Excise for current information and to write to the Royal Yachting Association, Victoria Way, Woking, Surrey, for booklet information on entry procedures affecting other countries. The following is a very much abbreviated outline of general requirements, affecting the Atlantic-facing European countries.

Ownership: Most countries insist on proof of ownership of the boat. The Small Ships Registration procedure conducted by the Royal Yachting Association, unlike earlier forms of registration in the UK, is simple and cheap.

Skipper's qualification: Although not currently required by the UK authorities, some documentary evidence of competence may be needed in other countries, particularly if the yacht enters inland waterways. There are various certificates available to owners who have the necessary skills, but of course they have to be awarded. In any case studying for a certificate of competence (they are on different levels) is very much to an owner's advantage. The RYA conducts them through recognised sailing schools.

Passports: All members of crew must have valid passports and a crew list should be made available for port officials, which also states that the vessel is being used for pleasure only. The skipper is responsible for making sure that all aboard carry passports.

Customs: It is necessary to clear outwards from the UK, to notify HM Customs if the departure is cancelled or delayed, and to clear inwards on return within two hours of arrival, by phone if this is the only way. The Q flag must be shown aloft on re-entry, or at night the flag (yellow) must be illuminated in some way. Fuller details of forms required are usually in nautical almanacs.

Animals: It is strictly forbidden to bring animals back to the UK and very heavy fines are involved for disregarding this rule.

The Q flag: The safe rule is to fly it when entering any foreign waters and to seek clearance at a port where customs and immigration offices are to be found. Usually one has to seek out the customs office in France.

Dutiable goods: Again, seek out the latest regulations before sailing out of home waters and make sure that you understand foreign laws. Duty free stores are widely available abroad, but remember that the 'ration' allowed upon re-entering the UK is not recognised in other countries. Once you might take aboard sufficient tobacco, spirits, etc., for use while cruising and leave the right amount for re-entering the UK, but nowadays the whole amount may be sealed into a locker by French (and other) customs and it has to be declared at any other French ports visited thereafter. The Q flag has to be displayed each time and the stores may only be broached when leaving French waters. It is better to leave shopping for your full permitted allocation until the final port.

Again, ask HM Customs and Excise for the correct forms and read up well on immigration, quarantine, VAT and duty.

CHAPTER ELEVEN
Night Sailing

There is nothing particularly alarming about sailing at night. Whether by accident or design every cruising yachtsman finds himself at sea in the dark sooner or later. As long as he is prepared for it, a night passage lengthens cruising scope and broadens his experience.

The main differences between day and night sailing boil down to a few important details. The danger from big ships increases but landfalls are usually easier by reason of coastal lights. Judgement of speed, wind strength and sea conditions is harder, the man overboard risk becomes more serious, chart-reading and coastal comparison, although easier on the score of identifying buoys, become harder in reckoning distances. And the weather can change without anyone noticing. To all this must be added the sense of emergency which most first-timers are apt to feel; and the important point that man is not a nocturnal animal and has to readjust his habits and instincts.

It is very unwise to attempt a night passage until basic chart-reading is not only mastered, but has become a habit. The need to have a 'feeling of position' on the chart is more necessary than ever, since there is no recognisable feature of land to cling to, and all the navigator has by way of substitute is a panorama of lights, some moving, some flashing and others fixed. By day, one can look at the coastline some eight miles away and be in no doubts of a safe offing. By night, a powerful lighthouse to the inexperienced eye looms uncomfortably close, and in no time at all one hears breakers where none exist – which is the first step to hollow-eyed despair and fun all round.

The first night passage

If possible the first night sail should begin in daylight, allowing the darkness to come upon the yacht when she is already nicely under way, her course tracked on the chart, the buoys of any channels already noted, and so on. This also offers a chance to watch the lights of large shipping and get some idea of distance by relative height and width between lights. The crew will have settled down and the ship will be in good order with everything in readiness for darkness.

Leaving the moorings in darkness means wholesale confusion and much coming and going with torches, looking for gear, groping about in lockers for almanacs and so on. The outcome of it all is that by the time the yacht is well under way and there is time to think about the little matter of navigation, she will be in the thick of that panorama of lights and the navigator will be hard pushed to sort himself out.

If for no better reason than that man is not a nocturnal animal, night sailing demands an even greater degree of care; but just at the time when this care is really needed, yachtsmen are most likely to be sunk in cold and sleepy apathy, caring little how they steer and less how they navigate. More offshore races are lost by night than by day. The crew which may be on the ball all day may subside into lethargy soon after dark so that by dawn better crewed yachts are lost in the distance ahead.

Brilliant moonlit nights are a joy at any time, but unfortunately they are the exception rather than the rule. Dark nights play havoc with sense of proportion and the yacht seems to be tearing along in a rising wind and sea when she is probably sailing well in moderate conditions. It is easy to doubt one's common sense. Lights will be seen where none could be and even the compass may be suspected. There is only one answer to this state of affairs: heave-to and think it out.

Most nights at sea can be divided into three phases: the early part of the night when tiredness is yet to come and when people are alert and warm and sailing the yacht, next to the state of intolerable sleepiness when it is almost impossible to keep the eyes open, and thirdly the early hours before dawn when apathy sets in. One becomes cold and a prey to sea-sickness, and the reluctance to move an inch from the cockpit results in many a yacht drifting under double-reefed main in a falling breeze or conversely being dangerously over-driven. It is only by understanding the likelihood of these conditions that a skipper can stay in proper control.

Watch-keeping

Sleep on a night passage is only vital if there is any likelihood of having to remain at sea for an indefinite time. This is mild heresy, of course, for the reason that one never can tell how long a passage may last, but there are plenty of times when with settled weather and shelter in easy reach along the line a fair guess can be made. The point of the argument is that it is a silly habit to let sleep for sleep's sake rule the ship. The man who lies in his bunk gloomily ticking off the hours of sleep which *he* has missed (the others have always had more) becomes so obsessed with the thought that nothing else can possibly matter. One night at sea without more than a nap or two is no hardship. As long as a man can lie down and rest for his spell below there is no need for panic. The fact that he can't get to sleep simply means that he's in no desperate need of it. By the next day he will be able to sleep, and if a second night should follow, he will have only to close his eyes and that will be that. On a single night-passage it is far more important to change watches often, every hour even, and keep the ship sailing than it is for the two- or three-man crew to be determined to get their sleep during their watch below, and to hell with what's happening up top.

Watches are essential, of course. A man must *know* that he is free to have a rest. The all-night marathons with everyone hanging around in the cockpit feeling that it is in some way 'not quite cricket' to go below are bad seamanship and lead to ill-feeling. Systems vary, a three-man crew of experienced people may choose a two-hour trick each, which means a clear four hours of rest for each. No beginner should be left entirely alone on watch, though.

A typical watch system for a three-person crew which includes an experienced skipper and two less experienced crew and which might be suitable for a 2-night passage, might be designed to give the skipper the 'graveyard' watch when people are most vulnerable to sleepiness. He would be on instant call during the other's watch.

2-person crew	skipper	crew	skipper	all hands
2000–0000	0000–0400	0400–1000	1000–1600	1600–2000

This system gives the skipper a good, solid morning sleep and the all-hands spell in the early evening allows the main meal to be cooked and a social drink, perhaps, before preparing for the next night. In all probability the skipper will get far less sleep than the other two, but this is the price of being boss.

The essential about this second arrangement is that 'instant call'. It must be absolutely understood that the skipper is to be called for anything which is in the least sense unusual, change of wind force or direction, appearance of lights or any steamer seen close enough to distinguish her side-lights. In thickish weather of course the skipper will have an all-night session. No skipper has the right to resent being awakened on a false alarm, because it is only the knowledge that he can be sure of being given a shake which allows the system to work. For a three-man crew a stand-by system works well if all the crew are of fairly equal experience. One man stays on watch for three (or four) hours, according to the expected duration of the passage. He then comes off watch, or off the tiller at least, and stands by while the next man does his trick. He then goes off and goes below for three or four hours while the third man comes on watch and the second man does stand-by duty. The system means that each man is on watch for a spell, available for a spell, and definitely off for a spell. During his stand-by, he can doze, cook or relieve the helmsman so that he can feed. The plan also ensures that nobody comes on watch half-asleep to take charge of the ship unprepared.

An autopilot comes into its own on night passages, allowing crew to move around the cockpit, to brew up, enter the log and do all the little jobs that help stave off sleepiness. A single person on watch must always remain harnessed and never wander forward on deck without alerting his stand-by.

Preparation for a night passage

It is bad policy for a skipper to decide on a night run purely on the spur of the moment. Ordinary people who spend a third of their lives in bed lack the adaptability of the professional seagoer. After a day of energetic swimming or dashing about ashore, it is poor preparation to spring a night passage on them just as they are getting ready to turn in. This sort of thing may, or may not, be tolerable for the larger crew of an offshore racer but certainly is not good policy for a three-man boat. Since the decision to go or stay usually rests upon the BBC weather forecast at ten minutes to six, there is plenty of time to warn the rest of the crew in the afternoon, giving them a chance to rest up in advance. Once the decision is made, either way, there should be no vacillation. The 'shall we, shan't we' skipper is a pest.

A really good, though not outsize, supper is important. A celebratory rich meal with drinks is a bad foundation for night passage; such a meal will only cause sleepiness and probably seasickness. Take the opportunity to fill thermos flasks or to mix the ingredients for cocoa so that successive brew-ups only need hot water adding. Sort out oilskins and spare warm clothing and stow them where they can be found without disturbing the resting watch. Sort out the charts in the order they may be needed and mark in courses and distances for easy reference, page-mark the pilot book after carefully reading any appropriate bits. You will need to read it all again, but later, when the mind is fogged by sleepiness, it will help to be reading what is already familiar. Note any prominent light buoy characteristics on a separate scrap of paper or pad and keep it in a pocket. Knowing which light sequences to look for without repeated scrambles to and from the chart makes it easier to watch for them as they come up.

The tidal stream situation will be checked in the ordinary way, but notes on when it changes etc. save wearisome checking by artificial light. See that torches, flares, spare bulbs and batteries can all be found easily. Check over the gear on deck and see that reefing pennants are rove off. Not having to search for a single thing is the mark of a well-run ship, no matter how small.

Night sailing is often cold and wet. Even if there is no rain, it is surprising how wet one can get from dew-fall. The only true protection from cold is plenty of proper feeding beforehand. Multiple layers of clothing on the upper part of the body are not really satisfactory. Clothing should keep the wind out and the body-heat in, therefore loose wool under oilskins is warmer than tight clothing. Looseness is the real secret. Plenty to do and plenty to chew is a sound rule for a night watch. Regular log entries and shortish watches, plenty of nuts, raisins, boiled sweets, glucose and so on. Incidentally, glucose is no more energy-giving than sugar but it is less thirst-promoting and is digested more quickly. Let the change of watch brew-up be a routine as long as weather permits. In quiet weather the ritual of putting on the kettle helps to make the last of the watch go quickly and a hot drink for both oncomers and offgoers is good sense.

Steering

Steering by night is the true test of sailing instinct. The man who is a slave to the burgee is at an immediate disadvantage. The sails are only a pale blur, there is very little help to be had from the eyes, and one sails by the feel of wind on cheek or neck and by the sensed speed, tiller pressure and angle of heel. The rattle of a luff or leech brings hearing into a new importance, perhaps, but keeping a good windward course is much more a matter of feeling.

Most compasses rely on luminous marks for their lighting. The snag about this is that the brightness wears off in time, and whereas the card may be easy to read on a very dark night, it will be too faint to see in semi-darkness or bright moonlight. This is not quite the serious drawback that it may seem. Compass staring is a habit to shun. All that is really necessary is to glance at the card occasionally – it should be easy to read naturally, but with practice one can manage fairly well by having a small torch with a red bulb (so as not to spoil night vision) and keep it in one hand the whole time.

'A star to steer her by' is very practical poetry. It is rare that the sky is completely overcast at night and any star which is at a convenient height to line up with some part of the rigging will serve as a steering-mark. The procedure is to glance at the compass to check course and then look for a star, say between cap shrouds and mast. The movement of the yacht will cause it to arc wildly back and forth, but the mean of the swing can be judged and the course steered by it.

One must remember that most stars are moving across the sky, and it is bad to steer for too long without checking the course. From time to time it may be necessary to pick out another star. If the course is a windward one, and making ground is therefore the only important thing, it is far better to forget the compass completely save for noting the average course made for the navigator's benefit. This will mean that every little lift of wind will be used instead of ploughing along like a shopper with a basket on wheels, indifferent to anything but direction.

Night vision

Night vision must be protected at all costs, and if by any remote chance the compass has an electrically-illuminated binnacle, it should be fitted with a rheostat to control the degree of light. A glaringly bright compass ruins night vision and also hypnotises the helmsman. In fact it can put a tired man to sleep.

It may take five to ten minutes to accustom the eyes to darkness after scrambling into oilskins by the light of a torch on the cabin sole. The old watch should never hand over and bolt below to the blankets without hanging on for a while until his relief has got used to the darkness. It should also be the practice to point out the sights and advise him of any peculiarities of the wind. The sort of thing might go as follows: 'I half-imagined a loom from Berry Head over there and that's Torquay reflecting from that cloud (the town lights). There's a steamer crossing safe ahead but I've been watching one astern for some time'. The briefing can be more detailed but some sort of 'picture' is essential to the man who has just come blinking sleepily into the cockpit.

One sometimes marvels at the difference between the night vision of an old hand and an inexperienced yachtsman. The difference is not in better eyesight but in knowing what to *expect* to see. If a particular light is expected and overdue one can begin to see lights everywhere. Looking for lights should never be a matter of straining to see. The best way is to let the eyes wander almost lazily backwards and forwards across the horizon. The light is more likely to be spotted through the corner of the eye than by direct sight. This is because the most sensitive part of the retina of the eye is not exactly the centre.

Without appearing to be personal a skipper should try to find out how well his crew can see in the dark. Some people have a distinct defect in their night vision, typically taking a very long time to readjust from lighted cabin to darkness, or they may have some degree of colour-blindness, finding it hard to distinguish red from green or yellow from blue. This could be a bit tricky if trying to judge whether the navigation light of an approaching ship was port or starboard, or whether a buoy light was red or green.

On a small yacht cruising at sea – and let's stress the word *cruising* – the helmsman is the best look-out. His gaze is ceaselessly roving from ship to horizon, back and forth. He is alert and in control, he has the best opportunity to gauge his speed against that of other shipping and he has sense of direction to help in spotting lights. Incidentally, if a landfall light is expected, it is wise to look now and then in the 'impossible' direction – odd things happen.

Coastal lights

Many years ago I received two sharp and never-forgotten lessons about coastal lights. The first taught me to discriminate and the second taught me scrupulous care. On that first occasion I had the watch while sailing along the West Brittany coast. Suddenly it seemed that the coast became alive with lights – flashing, occulting, fixed and moving. I panicked. Inside five minutes I had taken ten different bearings and couldn't plot one of them. I called the skipper. He looked, grinned, identified three lights, took their bearings, plotted them and then went back to bed. The lesson learned was that faced with a mass of lights one need only pick out those which assist. The rest, unless they lie athwart the course, can be left alone.

The second lesson I gave myself. We expected to pick up a distant lighthouse at a certain time. Dead on time the helmsman called out that he could see it. I asked for a bearing, plotted it, altered course and patted myself on the back. Within half an hour we were squared away and sailing hard with the engine running flat out trying to get clear of a sluicing tide and a reef – my distant lighthouse had turned out to be an unexpected buoy near at hand. We had been off course on landfall, and I had neglected to check and time the light. Moral, never 'guess' the identity of a light without checking it.

Lights of buoys, lightships and lighthouses, shore beacons and harbour lights are all identifiable by their colour, character, timing and range. The chart informs and the almanac lists them. On the face of it there should be no difficulty. The loom (glow from below the horizon) of a distant lighthouse or lightship gives long warning of its identity. Next comes the river mouth or harbour entrance with a sequence of lit buoys or beacons. Then there are leading lights which may need to be kept in line (transit) during the approach, or perhaps taking the form of a sector light which shows a safe white, with red and sometimes green sectors on either side. There are quick flashing, group flashing, fixed or occulting lights. Individually they are simple to understand, collectively they are liable to be as perplexing as twenty masters to one dog.

Another source of confusion when looking for lights, either navigational marks or the lights of shipping, is that while a white light represents a power of 100%, a red one is visible at only 30% and a green light as low as 20%. In short, in a group of distant buoys the white flashes may be easily visible and an essential red flashing one may not, which could lead a navigator to believe that they were somewhere else, with predictable anguish and perhaps an unwise change of course.

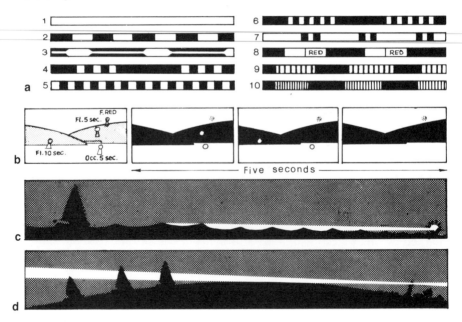

Fig. 42 (a) Reading top to bottom. (White indicates period of light, black period of eclipse.) (1) Fixed. (2) Flashing. (3) Fixed and flashing. (4) Group flashing. (5) Quick flashing. (6) Group interrupted quick flash. (7) Occulting. (8) Alternating. (9) Interrupted very quick flash. (10) Interrupted ultra quick flash. (b) Although four lights are visible ashore, each has a different characteristic and it is extremely unlikely to see all 'on' at the same moment. In five seconds the pattern might alter as shown and the eye must try to retain a picture of how they lie in position to each other so that comparison with the chart is possible. (c) Wave crests can cause a distant light to appear to be flashing in a different sequence to that which is expected. Thus intervening crests could cause a group five light to appear as a group four. (d) A distant light as it appears above the horizon can provide a rough but useful means of judging distance off: the two sums, height of light to horizon and height of eye to horizon, can be taken separately and looked up in the sea horizon tables of the almanac.

Viewing the coast by night and looking at the chart of that area brings out one major difference. The lights marked on the chart can all be seen at once, but in actual fact they can only be seen in irregular groups just as they happen to flash at that particular moment, and second by second the picture alters (Fig. 42). Add to this the altering angles caused by the moving ship, the loss from view of some lights as they are obscured by an island or headland and the emergence of new lights as the coast opens up, and the confusion becomes easy to appreciate.

The surest proof of the good navigator, compared to the beginner, is his chart after a completed passage. The one will show only a track-line ticked here and there by a neat three-point fix, the other will be smothered in little wigwams – indication of a constant taking and plotting of bearings which continues from dusk till dawn. By knowing where you are at the start and 'feeling' your position relative to the chart, it is usually possible to con the ship by eye alone, working from a previously noted list of buoy timings and watching them as they appear and disappear along the coast.

A stop-watch is not essential to night sailing but, as I have mentioned before, for the beginner it is a great help. Looking at the sweep hand of a watch means taking one's eyes off the buoy and it is easier if there are two on deck, so that the mate can keep his eye on the flash and call out 'now'. Lights are timed from the first flash of one group to the first flash of the next, whether occulting (light on steadily, and going out at fixed intervals, flashes of darkness in fact) or group flashing. With practice the timing can be done by judgement alone. Some people count seconds by saying 'One thousand two thousand three thousand' and so on (note the absence of punctuation). Others favour 'I-reckon-that's-one-I-reckon-that's-two', etc. Try out both methods against a stop-watch. The tendency is to count too fast.

One of the disadvantages of navigating a very small yacht is the low eye-level. Buoy lights which are seen steadily flashing from a higher platform are often seen intermittently as yacht and buoy rise and fall among the seas (Fig. 42). This doesn't stop you from seeing the light, but it does play hell with the light sequence. For instance a buoy may be expected to flash four times every fifteen seconds. One count may show two flashes, another gives four and a third three. Sooner or later the whole sequence is seen, but the temptation is to guess. Sometimes ships' lights (such as fishing vessels off the French coast) can be confused with navigational lights, when they dip regularly in the swell or the troughs of seas.

The height of the eye above sea level is a good thing to know since the 'Table of Lights Seen and Just Dipping' can be used to estimate distance away. A shortened table is given at the end of the book and the use is self-explanatory. Knowing height of eye and height of light from the chart or almanac Lights' List, the appropriate cross-reference provides distance away. This naturally means the actual light and not the loom, which varies in range according to the weather. Sometimes it is possible to see both St Catherine's Lighthouse on the Isle of Wight and the Barfleur light on the French coast when in mid-Channel, although naturally this can't be relied upon.

The 'Lights Seen Dipping' table comes into its own on a cross-Channel passage. Once the loom of the light is seen it is only a matter of standing and waiting for the first blink of the light at sea-level as it climbs the curvature of the horizon. While on the subject of dipping lights, a warning. Fixed shore lights, nothing to do with navigation, sometimes give a convincing impersonation of flashing lights when seen from low down. Car headlights on a busy road, sweeping around a bend, do much the same thing, and to the beginner it all adds to the confusion.

A navigator must not forget to take the power of lights into account. He expects to find the buoy which appears in a prominent position on the chart more easily than the rest. It may be of minor importance or there may be others nearer to his position at the time. What he sees is a line of lights, some faint and others bright; the one he wants may be insignificant. After looking the chart over the temptation is to pick out the buoys as you expect to come to them and ignore anything five miles beyond. This doesn't always work out. As long as you can identify enough lights to fix your position and keep an eye on your track, nothing else matters much. Tick off the lights as you pass them, and pass them on the proper side unless they are merely marking a big-ship channel.

The visible range of main navigation buoys, if known, can be used to give approximations of distance away although the 'Lights Seen Dipping' tables don't include heights above sea level as low as those of buoys. A class 1 cardinal buoy as laid by Trinity House has a light height of 6 metres, a class 2 buoy 3 metres, and a LANBY (a high intensity light and fog signal float) 13 metres. By use of the Horizon Distance table in the almanac and taking the height of light and height of observer's eye as two separate distances from the horizon, then adding them, we can get some rough idea of distance. For example: observer's eye level above the sea 2 metres and height of light 3 metres, total distance from light 6.5 miles. This assumes a white light.

Approaches

Landfall and arrival in darkness are usually easier than in daylight – for identification of the coast at least. In practice, many people feel far happier to be bowling inshore in daylight, searching for their marks along a hazy and anonymous coastline, than they do at night when the way in may be unmistakable. By daylight they can see how far away they are, but night gives a feeling of sailing straight ashore, when, as like as not, the yacht is still five miles off. Dawn is the best time for an approach because you will have come inshore on the shore lights and there will be strengthening daylight to assist in piloting the river or harbour entrance.

Coming to an anchor in the dark is tricky. Shore lights can dazzle you and the reflections across intervening water confuse sense of distance – usually we over-estimate and end up anchored far from the shore.

When anchored among local yachts on their moorings and clear of the main channel it is rarely necessary to rig a riding-light although it is wise to remember that legally you should do so and should some other arrival in the dark hit you this might win or lose a claims case. Whether used or not, no cruising yacht can afford to be without one aboard. The chances are that the time will come when the only vacant berth for

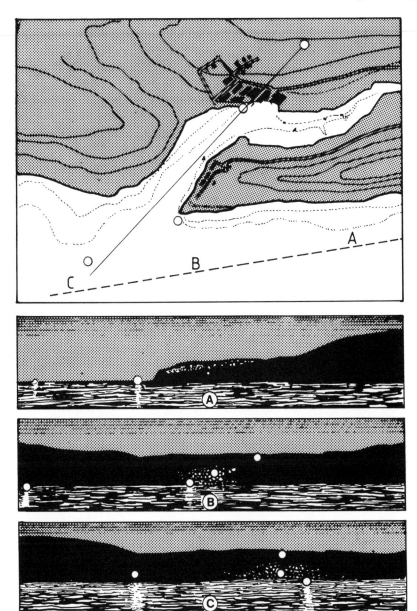

Fig. 43 As the coast slips by the shore lights alter second by second according to their characteristics, and they also change bearing. The chart here shows four lights at the small port; two (solid line) are leading lights, one on the shore and the other on the hillside; the pecked line is the yacht's course. At (A) the loom of the town lights just shows over the shoulder of land, and two buoy lights, one more distant and fainter, can be seen. At (B) the leading lights have appeared, but they are still wide apart. At (C) the leading lights are in line and the yacht can come on course for entry.

anchoring is on the fringe of the yacht anchorage and bordering the navigable channel. A riding-light may make the difference between safe sleep and a bad crack from a returning fishing-boat. Oil-lamps are messy but quite reliable. The hurricane lamp from the local ironmonger is definitely not proof against a fresh breeze, let alone a hurricane, and a proper yacht riding-light is the only safe type. An electric light run off a 6-volt bell battery is effective, but the fittings must be watertight, and a stock of spare batteries carried, as they soon run down. A simple make-shift is to lead the wire flex from the battery below deck up to the bulb and holder which are contained in a pill bottle with the neck corked. Better is proper engine-charged lighting and a wandering lead to the light.

Safety at night

Although the alarms of navigation and weather are more pressing on the imagination, by far the greatest dangers at sea are from being run down by a big ship or the risk of going overboard. There is only one safe rule for navigating steamer lanes by night or in thick weather in a small boat and that is to *assume your own yacht to be invisible*. The value of the radar reflector is discussed in another part of this book, but suffice to say now that no yacht should go to sea without one. Having said that, the rule of invisibility should still be acted upon since the radar reflector is *not* a guarantee of safety.

The rule that 'power gives way to sail' was made in the days of the big commercial sailing ships which handled slowly and couldn't hope to manoeuvre clear of a power ship. Today, there are such matters as Traffic Separation Zones and local dock and harbour board regulations to consider, which frequently give full rights of way to large commercial ships.

Most yachts' sidelights may not be visible for more than a mile. (One cheap plastic combination light powered by torch battery was visible at fifty yards on a rainy night.) The big ship steaming at twelve or fifteen knots or possibly much more has only a matter of a couple of minutes or less in which to do something after a light is sighted. Suppose then that the look-out sees 'something' ahead. He phones the bridge and the officer of the watch takes his night glasses and walks to the wing of the bridge. He has to decide what it is and *which way* it is travelling, then he has to give an order to the quartermaster on the wheel. A very young officer may hesitate for a minute – big ships are not to be swung off course at a whim, especially if there are other big ships ahead. The small yacht may have been holding course and speed in accordance with the rules, relying on the Law instead of interpreting it with common sense. Alternatively, to play safe the skipper of the yacht may begin flashing a torch and this, from a steamer's bridge, may completely destroy all idea of which way the yacht is moving or indeed that it is a sailing craft in the first place.

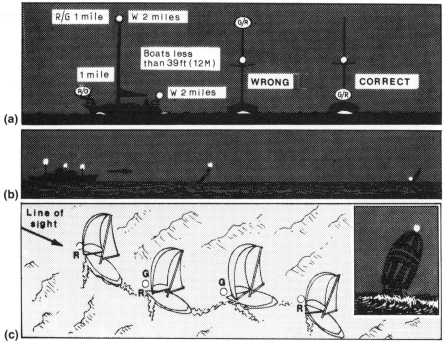

Fig. 44 (a) A combination masthead light must not be above the white steaming light, and if fitted there should be a port/starboard combined navigation light on the pulpit to replace the masthead one when under power. (b) Although combination masthead lights are more easily visible it must be remembered that it is possible for the lookout on a ship to misjudge the distance of the yacht, being unsure whether the light seen is on the bow or at masthead. (c) If the yacht is sheering around in a seaway, particularly if on a run, a watcher on a ship ahead may see alternating red, green, both, red, etc., and be uncertain about the yacht's real course.

Small sidelights on a heeling yacht are pointing at sea and sky respectively. They are also gyrating wildly and half the time invisible by reason of lost direction. Pulpit lights of combination pattern rarely have a satisfactory dividing screen with the result that, seen from nearly ahead, they show alternating red, green, red, green. This confusion completely destroys any notion of direction. Tri-colour masthead lights, now accepted under International ruling, are the best answer.

However bright your lights you must still leave a reserve for error. Some yachts have pulpit lights and others masthead navigation lights and an observer on a ship's bridge may not realise which you have. If he assumes it is a pulpit light he may think you further away than you are – if in fact it is a masthead light. Couple to this the possibility that he is viewing from an angle at which your lights are changing from red to green and back again as the yacht rolls and screws around in a seaway, and the situation could become nasty (Fig. 44).

The safe rule is to decide very early whether the two vessels are on a collision course and, very early, shape to pass astern. This need only mean altering course until the bow is aimed at the big ship's stern and following her round.

The rule for recognising a collision course is quite simple. A bearing taken on the other ship will read the same when taken some minutes later if they are converging. If the bearing has increased or decreased you will be passing clear ahead or astern. A simple rule-of-thumb method which will be used to save rooting out the bearing compass (the steering compass isn't always suitable) is to settle the yacht on as straight a course as possible and sit quite rigid. Let any part of the yacht's deck or rigging fall in line with the distant ship and then, remaining motionless, watch carefully to see if the lights of the big ship draw ahead or fall astern (Fig. 45). Naturally if there is much sea movement this 'bearing' will be no more than an average line-up, but the odds are that any doubts will be resolved one way or the other.

It is misleading to waver and haver at such time. Assuming that you have been seen (for once) you should think carefully, alter course if necessary and then sail straight. The sight of pin-point lights changing colour and angle back and forth is dangerous. As mentioned earlier, flashing of torches is harmful too. Shine a torch steadily at the ship and when she is closer, pan it slowly on to the sails and then slowly back to the ship. Even this hallowed routine is of questionable value. The only sure and safe course when in actual danger of being run down is to light a white flare. These flares can be bought from any good yacht chandler for a small sum and a stock of half a dozen (you may need several in a real emergency) is as fine an insurance as all the navigation lights on sale. Big ships recognise the meaning of a white flare as a warning of presence and they won't attempt a forceable rescue.

Fig. 45 A first check on what may be a converging situation. The person at the helm, steering as straight as possible, sits absolutely still and sights the other vessel against some part of the yacht. If the relative angle of the other vessel remains unaltered a collision must be avoided by altering course to pass astern.

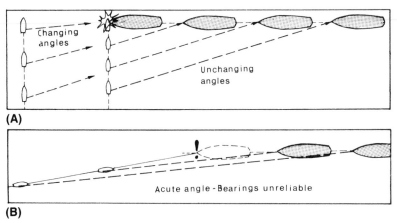

(A)

(B)

Fig. 46 The changing angles at (A) indicate that the vessels should pass clear, whereas at (B) a collision state exists. These angles, however, are very narrow ones and such bearings are not only unreliable but standing on could confuse the other vessel and therefore a bold course alteration is needed.

Becalmed and helpless, a sailing vessel has to do *something* and the white flare is the answer. Do remember, though, that it must be shown in good time, giving the big ship a chance to alter course. Once the flare is finished, keep a torch alight and have a second flare ready in case she doesn't seem to be altering.

Judging the distance of a big ship at night is very difficult for the inexperienced man. At a distance of about $2\frac{1}{4}$ sea-miles, an ordinary large freighter crossing ahead looks very large, but also remote. With the little finger at arm's length both her masthead lights can be covered. It is this appearance of remoteness which is most misleading. Take the case of an express train seen approaching from the distance and head-on. For a long while it is visible as a black vertical rectangle which simply grows gradually larger. It is only in the last quarter of a mile that it suddenly seems to accelerate, and then it does so breathtakingly.

The big ship at sea is much the same to watch. First the remote pin-points of light at the mastheads, next the red and green sidelights and then a long spell during which they steadily grow wider apart and higher. Quite suddenly the lights develop haloes, light spills from portholes, deck lights are seen, and the black bulk of the superstructure. In an instant it has become a vast, reeling, shimmering mass of movement, her engines are heard and the intervening water is lit by her reflection. If she is head-on it will be too late to bother about flares, only your cool action at the helm can avert the danger. On a rainy night the blurred lights are even harder to judge.

Ships at sea by night show direction firstly by the position of the two masthead lights, the lower of the two being forward and thus giving the clue to her direction of travel, and secondly by the sidelights. It takes quite some while before a beginner can glance at a cluster of lights and say at once, 'Passing safe astern port-side-to'. Distance away is less easy, since one has no idea of the size of a ship beyond the number of lighted ports and her speed relative to her apparent size.

Whatever you decide to do about avoiding her or revealing your own presence, do be sure to glance in the opposite direction as well. The whereabouts of any other big ships, though of no concern to you, may dictate how the steamer is to be turned. Other more distant ships may not know why your steamer is suddenly bearing to port, but they will probably have to alter course as well, and you are in the middle.

For much the same reason never be too sure that a big ship has seen you just because she may have 'seemed' to alter course. She may be altering to clear another big ship miles away and there is no guarantee that she won't suddenly swing back if the distant ship has behaved unexpectedly. Having seen yourself clear, keep an eye on the ship until you are quite safe.

Not all lights are easy to identify. Fishing-boats are one of the inshore hazards for the coasting yacht and here there is no question of forcing a right of way, sail versus power. You are expected to know (or at least do some lightning thumb-work in a book a find out) the significance of any unusual arrangement of lights, and the trawler with her gear down or the drifter lying to her nets must be given a wide berth. Not only are they not under proper command since they can't manoeuvre, but their gear extends beyond them and often at surface level. The arrangement of their lights makes this quite plain. The cluster lights which illuminate the decks for working are the first clue to the fisherman, unless on passage, of course. Even under way and not fishing the lights may be in use for clearing the catch and they may be so bright that the navigation lights are quite hard to distinguish. The biggest illusion is in thinking a small fishing-boat to be a big ship far away and then suddenly see her roll and pitch dead ahead and close to. The inshore fishermen are wonderful friends to yachtsmen, but woe betide the man who transgresses the fisherman's rights at sea.

Tugs towing at sea, naval craft on manoeuvres, behaving in a very odd manner and, of course, fellow yachtsmen, all add their quota to the endless puzzles of lights in combination. Yachts meeting yachts can be the biggest headache of all sometimes. Many people sail without any lights at all, reasoning that as they can't be seen by steamers, what the hell? Others have a nasty habit of switching on a masthead or spreader light for identification. Both are risky habits, and the latter is illegal. Sailing yachts are required to carry only sidelights and a sternlight. In yachts under 12 metres they may be combined in a single lantern at the masthead. The sidelights must be visible from 1 mile and the sternlight 2 miles. Sailing vessels over 12 metres must carry the same sidelights and sternlight as a power-driven vessel of their size.

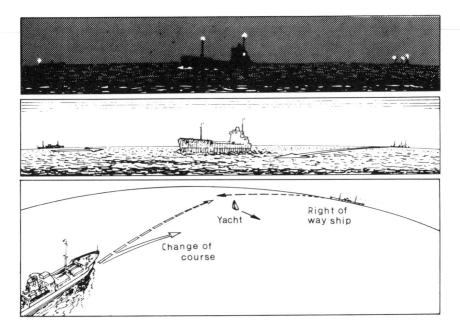

Fig. 47 Lights in a busy channel such as a separation lane must be watched constantly. Although all vessels in the lane will be proceeding in the same direction they will be doing so at different speeds and perhaps at different angles. To cross the traffic in a low speed yacht means having to judge whether it is possible to pass close astern of one vessel without falling foul of others astern and beyond. In busy lanes it is safer to motor so that speed can be regulated, rather than making abrupt and probably illegal course alterations.
Be wary when big ships change course for no apparent reason: a potential collision situation may be developing at long range and perhaps on radar, when the yachtsman passing between is quite unaware of this.

A yacht under power becomes a power-driven vessel. If she is also carrying sail and *behaving* as a sailing vessel under the Rules and an accident occurs, she may be liable; if she behaves as a powered vessel she must make the fact plain, if necessary lowering sails. At night she must show a white light on the mast with a forward arc of 225 degrees and at least 3 foot above her sidelights.

Crossing a busy estuary channel at night is about the nastiest part of navigating in the dark. Big ships are, by reason of narrow fairways, restricted to straight courses and in certain port areas, such as Southampton Water, they have absolute right of way. The small yacht must wait her chance to cross much as a pedestrian waits at a busy crossing. A good plan is to make for one of the channel buoys and stay close to it (don't sail round and round it) until there is a chance to cross the deep-water channel. Once in the middle it may even be necessary to alter course up or down stream so that a big ship can go by. Whatever happens don't begin zigzagging around. Try not to tack across a channel at such a time, take it full-and-by and get across fast and then work up the opposite shore in shallow water and safety. (See Additional Notes on page 229.)

CHAPTER TWELVE
Fog

Although anyone with a choice in the matter and some previous experience of being at sea in a small boat in fog would settle for staying at anchor when the visibility begins to drop, fog is such a stealthy danger that one is often at sea when it begins to roll. The typical sea fog accompanied by faint airs and perhaps the swell which is the aftermath of an earlier blow is the most damnable of all conditions. Avoid it at all costs, but if it can't be avoided, concentrate if possible on piloting the boat out of the way of the big ships and let passage-making take second place.

If the approach of fog is stealthy at least the conditions giving rise to fog can often be noted, and an eye kept lifted for the disappearance of the horizon or the long flat-topped bank until the true extent of it is realised.

A fog bank is really a cloud. Warm air holds moisture but as it cools, perhaps by coming into contact with the cooler air rising from the sea, the moisture has to be deposited and the cloud rains. If the cloud is already at sea level the droplets have insufficient distance to fall to gain size and become raindrops and so they remain as drifting vapour. A fine 'mizzle' often accompanies fog.

Warm wind blowing over cool water, sea haze, the sun a yellow ball or a warm, soggy-feeling wind, all are fog signs – signs that the warm air has almost reached 'dew point' when the moisture will begin to be squeezed out. The night-time cooling of the earth can give rise to fog conditions. A slowly moving cold front coupled with night cooling is also a cause, although the arrival of a warm front is more usual. It is possible, especially along the western Brittany coasts, to come up with thick fog driving in on a gale-force wind, quite terrible conditions.

There is often a fog tendency during settled weather, and if weather forecasts repeatedly give fog warnings in certain areas they can be anticipated in other areas if the conditions seem to be spreading. The warm steady wind, warmer than the water, and the sudden muzzy appearance of lights at night, are signs that the navigator should take a set of bearings while there is still time.

The constant checking of position is the wise navigator's only armament against the fog. He knows that he can be lost in a bank while the rest of the coast is still clear, or the reverse can be true. It is the true test of accurate dead reckoning, since the only visual assistance is the compass, the chart, the water, log and echo sounder.

Hearing in fog becomes the most important of the senses while being the one most subject to trickery. The yachtsman must be able to hear. If he is unlucky enough to be out among big ships he must hear and hope to be heard.

The decision which so often has to be made is whether to drift under sail at a couple of knots or less, straining to hear every siren, thump of engines, ringing of bells, and so on, thus having some idea of the nearness of other ships (if not their direction), or whether to use power and motor as fast as possible out of the danger area while being deafened to all save the clatter of the engine. There can be no single answer. The owner should bear in mind two things. Whether it be sail or power he *must* have smart steerageway on his craft at all times if he is caught in dense shipping, for it will be *his* action which will avert trouble in an emergency. The second point to remember is that hearing a very distant siren is no assurance that the ship can be dismissed as unimportant. Many big passenger ships today actually minimise the use of siren. Relying on radar, they move through the fog quickly and silently. The yachtsman has only his ears and his eyes.

Radar

The old radar bogey is slowly but surely taking a proper significance in the minds of seagoing yachtsmen. For some years we thought we were safely visible on the radar screen of every ship in the locality. We were visible in just the same way that a particular pebble is visible in a photograph of a section of beach – it can be seen if you look for it.

Wave crests give a yacht-like echo – a confused and indistinct signal which takes second place in importance to the big echo of another vessel of similar size. The advice of one Trinity House pilot was that, in fog, the radar screen should take a secondary place and more reliance should be put upon seamanship and sound signals. In fact, there are cases of ships moving through thick fog at 18 knots. Collisions between the giants are becoming more and more frequent and the reason is usually one of speed and the difficulty of deciding whether the signal on the screen is moving to port or to starboard. The clever development of 'True Motion' radar shows the picture as though the observer were at the base instead of in the centre of the screen and gives each echo a little tail which suggests direction of travel. It has provided new standards of safety among the big ships, but for the small ship the situation remains a matter of luck.

Wood is a bad reflector, even waves are probably better. Beams are absorbed instead of being thrown back and even when a yacht is visible to the naked eye, and in quiet conditions at that, the radar picture may be too indistinct for positive action to be taken by a steamer's bridge. Metallic paint is no good as a reflector since the overlapping flakes of alloy which comprise the paint simply absorb instead of reflecting. An aluminium mast, caught when it is vertical, provides a good reflector, but as soon as it heels, the reflective properties become poor.

If the radar is (let's say) tuned to picking up targets at close range such as channel buoys or fishing vessels then the small yacht can expect to be seen, but a big ship at sea is like a car on a motorway – the drivers are looking far ahead. Again, clutter control can be used to isolate important signals from the mess of wave signals and the weak reflection of canvas and wood is lost along with the wave clutter. As wind and sea increase, radar range decreases. From being able (when desired) to pick out a rowing boat three miles away, the radar loses the echo of a 30-foot yacht completely in as little as a force 4 breeze – or in the sea which goes with it at least. In a gale, quite large coasters can be missed.

Nevertheless, the radar reflector offers such amazing improvement in the chance of being picked up by a big ship scanner that there cannot be any choice in the matter of whether it is worthwhile carrying one. Any yacht even remotely liable to fall foul of the steamer lines in fog or thick weather should have one. The eighteen-inch corner reflector set in the rigging can give a reflection equivalent to a two-hundred-ton ship even in a force 4 or 5 wind and sea.

One might argue that at that rate why not be content to look like a fifty-ton ship with a four-and-a-half inch reflector? It just doesn't work that way. The smallest size practicable might be one foot in breadth but, when one considers that the echo is then similar to that of a sixty-foot hull while a *two*-foot reflector gives an echo similar to that of a one-thousand-ton ship, the disparity in size becomes trifling and a thing to be gladly borne.

The principle of the reflector is that of a prism. It offers a series of right-angle corners wherein the radar signal is caught and bounced back, and it follows that the angles must be exact right angles if it is to work. For this reason home-made reflectors (and they are simple to make) must be accurately cut and put together and protected from damage when aloft.

The biggest problem on the small yacht is where to hang the reflector. If it is hoisted on a signal halyard the motion of the yacht causes it to snatch and jerk so badly that it is destined to come crashing down within the hour and it may easily damage somebody below. Perhaps lashing to the standing backstays (if fitted) is a safer alternative. It is of great importance to hoist the octahedral corner reflector in the right aspect. If such a reflector is simply placed down on deck or table, it automatically assumes its correct aspect. Hoisting 'point-up' is absolutely wrong and reduces efficiency – so also does inaccuracy of the angles and 3

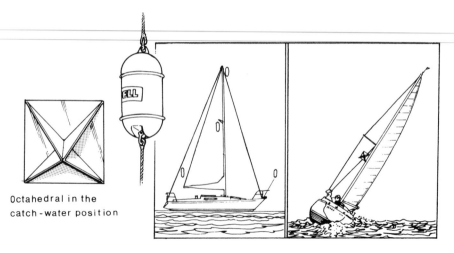

Octahedral in the
catch-water position

Fig. 48 A radar reflector in today's conditions is at times the most vital piece of equipment aboard a yacht. The common octahedral type (left) must be at least 18 inches corner-to-corner diagonally and displayed in the 'catch-water' position, the aspect it adopts when placed on a flat surface. If displayed point upwards as much as 40–50% of its efficiency can be lost. The more sophisticated versions enclosed in a casing, such as the Firdell shown, overcome aspect problems and the critical angles of the plates are protected from damage. Displaying a reflector is often a problem. Backstay position lacks height and therefore limits effective range. Crosstree position is better although vulnerable to sail contact, but the masthead mounting is ideal and the staff mounted bow position is also good. Find out the best angle of acceptance for your reflector; (right) a heeling yacht can reduce the efficiency sharply by as much as 30%.

degrees out of true in any corner reduces effectiveness by up to 50 per cent. Height above sea-level should be at least 15 feet and the higher the better.

The octahedral corner reflector is not the only type available to yachtsmen by any means. There are other designs, all based upon the multi-reflecting angles principle but enclosed in a protective outer casing. Most are more efficient than the simple corner reflector because they have wider angles of acceptance, in short a boat can heel over further before the reflective efficiency curve falls away. For a sailing yacht this is very important and a reflector that might suit a powerboat would not do for a well pressed sailing craft. Nonetheless it is wise to take note of what pilot boats, police boats, customs launches and other official craft carry because the choice would have been made after extensive testing.

Sound and sight

You will often hear mention of the strange tricks which fog can play upon sound, both volume and direction – the 'lanes of silence'. The strange truth of it seems to be that while fog itself and high humidity have only a small effect upon sound, changes of temperature and wind have a much greater one.

The effect of wind is well known. In a fresh breeze a whistle buoy, audible six miles downwind, may be barely heard only half a mile upwind – and wind with fog is not unknown. Temperature layers of warm and cold air lie over the earth's surface at varying altitudes and if air temperature increases with altitude, sound waves follow it and may pass over your head at fairly close range, while if temperature *decreases* above, the sound may travel in the warmer air at sea level.

Lanes of silence, then, are what are known as skip zones, areas over which sound may travel in a high curve, carried by temperature, or wind belts which rise and then fall to sea level, sometimes many miles away. Not only is the range of sound affected but also direction because wind currents snake and twist in the atmosphere.

Hence the sudden and clearly audible foghorn or lighthouse fog signal heard briefly and then after a short distance of sailing not heard again until it blasts out close at hand. Hence also the doubtful benefit of trying to take bearings of such sounds. Listening in fog is second nature; having been deprived of the full use of one sense the other senses are asked to compensate. This is the dilemma of motoring in a fog calm: with the engine running, only a watch kept in the bows can hear, although the boat is under control for sudden emergencies, whereas lying becalmed means being able to hear, but being a sitting duck too!

Sound is often heard more clearly from above the deck or up the mast – a little impractical on the small cruiser. It is also possible to hear bell-buoys or submarine fog signals by pressing an ear to the hull below water level, but only the very roughest idea of direction is possible.

A small boat is a surprisingly noisy place when serious listening is needed. The movement of sails and water, rattle of gear, clunk of rudder, and so on, make it very hard to concentrate. The momentary lulls in the noise make it even worse. Listen in each direction, cupping the ears and shutting the eyes – not a pretty sight perhaps, but a great aid to concentration. It is better to have two people listening, both to say aloud 'there' if the sought-for siren is heard. The 'snap' effect then disallows prompted imagination.

Look aloft often in fog. If the blue sky can be seen the bank is obviously a shallow one – it may be very little higher than your mast, which means that big ships can possibly see each other if not you. Seek constantly to judge the range of visibility. With nothing but fog and water around this is very hard to do. An empty box fifty yards away looks for an awful moment like some huge, square tanker looming up. Drop overboard a rolled up paper ball or a bean tin and watch it to see how soon it vanishes. If the visibility is, say, two hundred yards you can reckon that sighting another vessel is going to leave no time for second thoughts, ten or fifteen seconds at best.

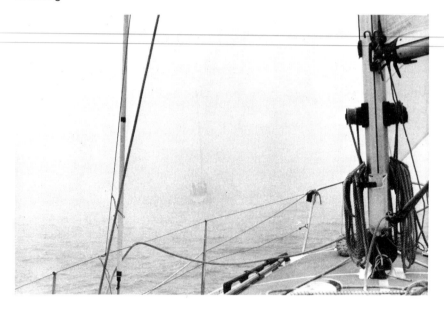

Plate 21 Visibility 100 yards. Note how dark features of the boat ahead show up more clearly than light ones.

The first glimpse of a large vessel in fog is like a sudden densening of the fog. In a flash there are gleams of white from paint and bow-wave. In that moment you will have to form an impression of her heading and decide what to do. The position of the bow-wave may be the real clue: central below the denser mass of fog if the ship is head on, to one side or the other (Fig. 49) if she is shaping to pass ahead or astern or to port or starboard of you.

Careful adherence to the Separation Zones is mandatory but it is also plain good sense and all yachtsmen should know where these rules apply.

Land seen through fog can develop just as rapidly. A first glimpse might be a row of semi-detached villas apparently built among the clouds and a depressing foretaste of the Life to Come. I have sailed slap into a tiny bay when attempting to round a headland, and seen sheep high overhead and seagulls standing on rocks just yards away.

Fog can also affect the true contour of the land by enveloping the background cliffs and leaving the low sand-hills standing importantly and deceptively high.

Disorientation

It is easy to become completely disorientated in fog, especially at night and under power. Ordinarily we take our sense of direction from some reference point, the land if visible, the wind direction if we're sailing, or

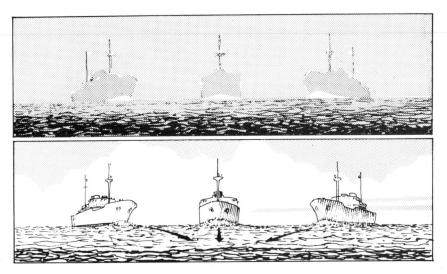

Fig. 49 In a fogbank the first glimpse had of a dangerously close large vessel may be a sudden densening of the murk followed a second later by gleams of pale upperworks and the white bow-wave. For the yachtsman there may only be a second in which to decide which way to put the helm.

the compass, and as the boat swings along we refer to it, often unconsciously. The moon if visible is another reference, or a buoy being passed at a distance. In fog there is nothing to see but the water a few yards around the boat, beyond that there is a featureless nothing.

Orientation in fog centres on the compass course, yet it is all too easy to get a feeling that the course is inexplicably wrong, that the boat should be heading more to port perhaps, because we know that somewhere out there to starboard there is land. The sound of a ship's siren can also cause this uneasiness and a desire to steer away from it. This is when a nervous helmsman can go off course and suddenly another listener on board, who heard the siren on the port bow perhaps, hears one broad on the port beam – the same one, but the helmsman has wandered off. The engine is cut and everybody listens, it comes again from the port bow and all are now certain that there are two ships out there.

A worse cause of total disorientation is a sudden emergency calling for a change of course (an echo sounder reading perhaps) or a gybe while sailing. With the compass card spinning the helmsman may panic. Around him the featureless grey murk whirls and eddies. The wind direction shifts, increases, then decreases again. Only the compass can settle the matter. Imagine, though, what might happen if somebody fell overboard during fog.

Whatever happens the helmsman must follow the course; even if the boat is slowed down for listening, he must maintain the heading or if he cannot do so, tell the skipper that the boat is pointing 'twenty degrees off to starboard'. The rest of the crew can then reorientate themselves to sounds from new angles.

In the main, then, the first concern is to get clear of steamship routes. Far offshore this means having some notion of where they lie, but with the slow-moving cruiser it may take many hours to sail into one of the few relatively quiet areas and a pretty accurate DR plot to ensure that you are in one. For the coasting cruiser the aim is to get into shallow water and stay there, to avoid headlands where shipping tends to converge, and to be on the look-out for inshore fishing craft and coasters.

It is obviously not always practicable to steam straight inshore and into a mass of rocks and reefs, especially where strong tides are running, but it is also unlikely that any big ship will venture even remotely near such a coastline. If it is possible to lie to a kedge on a long (very long) light nylon line, so much the better. In conditions of calm this sort of kedging is common ocean-racing practice and, at all events, it is safe, if not particularly comfortable in a swell. There is the added advantage that once the anchor has taken hold, the rate and direction of tidal stream become known, which is very important to navigation in fog.

One drawback should be mentioned, though. To other inshore vessels which are under way, other yachts, fishing boats or even small coasters, the last thing expected will be an anchored yacht. In the first instance they will assume that she is under way also and with perhaps only seconds of warning the helmsman may apply helm the wrong way. It is very important therefore to choose your kedging spot with care, and to maintain a listening watch on deck the whole time.

Be sure too that the tidal stream is not excessive because a thin line cannot be hauled in easily due to the force of water, even when the motor is helping the boat ahead. The line will seem to curve straight down below the bows and it will throb and vibrate so much that everybody will be certain that the anchor is dragging – which of course it may be; dragging, though, is usually accompanied by momentary sagging off of the bows and the sight of the line straightening out briefly as it bites again.

Echo sounders in fog

Contour navigation is particularly valuable in thick weather. Basically it consists of a steady series of soundings taken while studying the chart depths in the area where the yacht is considered to be. She may be approaching the coast along a course which should take her into a bay, but due to the usual regrettable little inaccuracies in the pilot's ancient art her approach may be along one of several possible lines. She may be heading for the point or she may be missing the bay altogether. A study of the chart shows how the sea-bed rises towards the land in each area.

Along the DR plot it may rise from twenty fathoms to five fathoms in the space of five miles, but to east and west it may rise abruptly within the distance of a mile and a half. By sounding until bottom at the twenty-fathom line is found, noting the log-reading and time, and then continuing to take soundings at, say, quarter-mile intervals, a picture of the sea-bed is built up. This can be plotted with an even greater degree of accuracy along an uneven sea-bed which, plotted down on tracing paper to chart scale, can be juggled around on the chart until trace fits chart. The soundings must be reduced to datum figures by adjusting them for height of tide in each case, of course.

Inevitably there are large areas of sea-bed with no distinguishing features at all and only a very gradual slope. A very careful study of the chart soundings is needed to see whether the slope is consistent for a few miles and if it is, it may be possible to zigzag off and on, zigging shorewards perhaps until the echo sounder reads five metres, then zagging offshore at right angles to the first heading until it reads perhaps ten metres, etc. This off-and-on technique is useful when following a river bank.

Echo sounders can also be used to even greater effect if the cruiser is faced with having to cross the mouth of an estuary in thick fog. It should be pointed out yet again, though, that if this involves crossing a busy steamer route it is best left untried. If the channel buoys are fitted with radar reflectors then it is a fair bet that some small coaster at least will be buoy-hopping to catch his tide to the docks.

If the crossing is to be attempted, a careful study of the course in advance will show what is to be expected if the yacht can be kept to her course. She may cross shallows for two miles, hit a deep patch for half a mile, cross a bank and another deep, then the main channel and so on. Making due allowance for cross-currents to stay on this track, the possibilities of *not* staying on it must also be allowed for, and the course laid down-tide of any dangers such as wrecks or drying banks. It will be very hard to have faith in the tidal allowance which may appear necessary since nothing will be seen but the seemingly motionless water around the cruiser. If it is possible to lay the course to include channel buoys so much the better, but faith in a carefully plotted course is preferable to time wasted searching for buoys which may be only a hundred yards away yet invisible.

Creek crawling

Quite often fog will form in valleys and rivers while it is clear a few miles out to sea. Such *convection* fog usually clears altogether by noon, but if one is anchored well up some river this is scant comfort. If the river is a quiet one free from commercial shipping, it does no harm at all to

navigate it seawards, either to anchor at the mouth or to go on your way
to sea if it appears to be clearer or clearing.

With visibility down to perhaps fifty yards, buoy-to-buoy courses,
with due allowance for tidal stream, can be not only quite accurate but
also very enjoyable as a little and harmless adventure. The vital factor is
being able to rely upon the accuracy of compass and log/speed
instrument. On short courses of maybe a couple of hundred yards
between buoys or charted marks such as withies or beacons, exact
compass accuracy is less important, although it is worth remembering the
one-in-sixty rule that to be one degree off-course means a mile off in
sixty, because in fog it is easy to miss a mark. More critical is to measure
the chart distance in cable lengths (ten to the nautical mile) and watch the
log. Current can only be with or against you which means sighting it
earlier or not getting too worried if it doesn't show up on the dot. The
echo sounder can be read at the same time.

The tidal rate can be estimated roughly before leaving the anchor or
mooring. Take a plastic deck bucket and a long length of small line, stout
fishing line perhaps, bend on the line and drop the bucket overboard so
that the current carries the bucket away. If the operation is timed by stop-
watch, on the basis that 100 feet per minute equals one knot, even a fifty-
foot run will be productive. The following short table may be used.

$\frac{1}{2}$ knot = 100 ft in 2 min
1 knot = 100 ft in 1 min
2 knots = 100 ft in $\frac{1}{2}$ min
3 knots = 100 ft in 20 sec
4 knots = 100 ft in 15 sec

In fact, of course, it would be sheer idiocy to get under way down a
river in thick fog with a tidal stream of much more than a couple of knots,
particularly if it was under you.

It is worth mentioning in passing that this table can be used in a
different way if, for instance, the yacht is offshore in fairly shallow water,
totally becalmed in fog and the navigator wishes to know how the tide is
setting and at what rate. This time instead of a bucket which drifts away
from a moored yacht we use a weight heavy enough to lie on the sea-bed
while the yacht drifts away from it and a run of 100 feet is paid out
against the stop-watch.

Back to the creek crawl. Another simple table is needed, this time
relating to speed in knots and distances in cables. Thus if the distance
from buoy to buoy is 2 cables and the boat is making 3 knots it will take 4
minutes; to this must be applied the tidal rate, adding to or subtracting
from the speed of the boat to reach a speed over the ground figure. The
table only reads up to 4 knots and 5 cables. Some interpolation may be
needed but this isn't difficult. A wise plan is to have a dummy run during
clear weather and just for the fun of it.

Cables	Speed in knots			
	1	2	3	4
1	6	3	2	$1\frac{1}{2}$
2	12	6	4	3
3	18	9	6	$4\frac{1}{2}$
4	24	12	8	6
5	30	15	10	$7\frac{1}{2}$
		minutes		

It may well be that having run the calculated distance and not found the buoy a search may have to be made. With a fifty-yard visibility there would be a 100-yard lane of visibility with the boat at its centre. If the tide is foul the distance has probably been underestimated and if fair the buoy may have been passed. If the former it is better to begin a search while the tide is carrying the yacht downstream. Turn 90 degrees either way and hold course for maybe 15 seconds, then turn 180 degrees and hold for 30 seconds, then back for 15 seconds. This in theory brings the boat back to her original starting point when the downstream course can be resumed for a short distance and the search repeated. According to boat speed, width of channel and strength of current, this search can be modified.

There are times when a particular buoy or mark must be left on a particular hand, perhaps upon penalty of running aground. This is perhaps a case for nudging along the safe side of the river on the echo sounder – less simple if there are moored yachts lining the river, in which case be sure to pass down-tide of each, tight around the sterns perhaps. The important thing is to *pilot* the boat rather than just blunder through the fog guessing and hoping.

Sound signals

Vessels of under 12 metres in length are not obliged to carry the foghorns, bells and gongs used by larger craft, but they must have an efficient sound signal of some sort. Having said that, it is easy enough to equip a small yacht with a horn of some sort, and a frying pan struck with a spanner substitutes for a bell if needed.

A sailing vessel under way in fog must sound off one long and two short blasts at intervals of not more than two minutes, and by long and short blasts we mean 4–5 seconds and 1 second. Not only sailing craft use this signal but other 'hampered' vessels such as trawlers, vessels constrained by the draught, vessels out of control, and so forth.

If the sailing yacht is *motoring*, however, whether she has sails hoisted or not, she must behave as a powered vessel and sound one prolonged blast at not more than two-minute intervals, and if stopped but technically under way, two such blasts with a two-second interval between them.

There are a variety of different horn sounds made by various types of vessel, or performing different functions, and it is as well to have a page marker in the almanac at the appropriate place when proceeding through fog. At anchor it is different again. At intervals of not more than one minute a bell is rung (or frying pan hit) for a five-second period; large vessels also use gongs to distinguish bow from stern.

The essential thing about all this is that it is not simply a question of complying with the rules – that doesn't matter a damn; what matters is *being heard*. On another vessel, most probably with engines running, squeaks and distant tinkles from yachts are lost in the sounds of ship and parting water. For this reason it is worth experimenting a little. A frying pan suspended can make a loud clang when struck but the kedge hung from the boom may be better. Likewise the horn; the popular aerosol-type sold in yacht chandlers are very piercing, but there is the absurd problem that in very dense, wet fog the reed 'freezes' as the gas is emitted, reducing them to a feeble sound. Mouth-blown horns, or even a bugle, are often better, and more certainly more reliable. Remember that two small vessels navigating in silence are well able to sink each other.

Big ships are no longer dependent upon sounds made or heard, but for small craft listening is still the main defence in fog. While more and more sophisticated radar, radio fixing, and Decca, Sat-nav and the rest guide big ships through the murk, we are still mainly reliant on our senses. Yacht radar is becoming more commonplace along with position-fixing electronics but in the context of this book cruising is still fairly unsophisticated. What has to be borne in mind is that the big ship people are very much occupied with avoiding each other, and the presence of yachts among them cannot be given as much attention as the possibility of a full-scale collision.

CHAPTER THIRTEEN
Choosing Your Weather

If there is any one subject which merits extra study by the small-boat man it is meteorology. Unfortunately single-observer met. study can present only a very limited view of the whole weather jigsaw. Nevertheless, what is happening there and then in one small part of a large-scale weather pattern and what is likely to happen within the next hour or so are important for the lone observant yachtsman to know.

The broader picture of the weather situation is provided by the shipping forecasts, but important though these may be, they are several hours old by the time they are broadcast, and in rapidly developing weather systems several hours can mean the difference between deciding to make a passage and staying in shelter.

For the very small boat, bad weather is not restricted to gales. A force 5 breeze, under certain conditions of sea, is gale enough for a family cruiser. It is the ability to glance at the sky and the barometer and make a shrewd guess at what is likely to happen within the next few hours that really matters.

No small boat should be put to sea in the face of a truly bad forecast. The trough mentioned on the shipping forecast may mean no more than cloud and a shift of wind. On the other hand it can develop quickly, the bottom can drop out of it, and it may give rise to six hours or so of truly nasty weather. The observer at sea notes what the professionals tell him and takes over from there to draw his own conclusions in his own particular bit of ocean.

To watch the weather one must watch it all the time. To perk up and become a weekend weather-prophet while ignoring the shift and change of weather during the rest of the week is only playing with it. The man who owns three barometers, one on board his boat, one at home and one in the office, may seem to be making rather a meal of things, but his weather-picture is a non-stop one. He notes the weather map in his daily paper, glances at the sky whenever he happens to think of it and maybe hears the shipping forecast before he sets out for his office. By the weekend he can go aboard his boat aware of the present trends. The fine Friday, curse of the weekender, is a fair example of this. With a chain of small lows chasing in all the week, a sudden calm and sunny day on

Friday is often an ominous sign – a ridge perhaps, heaped up before yet another depression. The observer who has been watching cynically all the week may choose to ring up his local Met. office if the official forecast sounds cagey. At all events he is on his toes.

It is always depressing to embark upon a study of met., learning the typical formations of 'fronts' and trying to identify ideal cloud shapes from the pictures. Our weather is such a mess that such identification is usually about as difficult as trying to distinguish a Dutchman from a Frenchman by racial characteristics. Now and then comes the perfect example, but most of the time it is the general character of the sky which is our guide. Anyone can forecast a thunderstorm. Sky, atmosphere and general feeling cannot be mistaken. To the old-time fisherman almost any weather change was as obvious. Now and then he was absolutely wrong – wrong to the extent of heavy loss of life, but then he had no shipping forecast to fill in the background story. We have that one great advantage, but we cannot afford to stop thinking for ourselves as well.

The sky

As a sure indication of weather-to-come the sky is very unreliable, more often than not a collection of odds and ends of cloud, left-overs from weather patterns which have passed by. Each alteration of temperature and humidity brings forth a fresh crop of clouds of one sort or another. Some, but only some of them, are significant to the layman. On the whole, it is held that soft and cushiony-looking clouds are associated with or precede fine weather and moderate winds, while those which have hard, jagged edges, or appear to be greasy, are forerunners of wind and rain. Clouds taken as confirmation therefore have value. A forecast of coming bad weather, due to arrive maybe some time the following day, might be viewed with more urgency for the present if the sky took on that distinctive lowering of the cloud base. On the other hand, of course, it might just be a trough running in advance of the true bad weather and due to be followed by a narrow belt of finer weather before the real low comes in. From this it can be seen that to assume the bad stuff to have come and gone might lead to a risky decision to go to sea and hence the importance of close link between forecast and observation.

The ragged clouds which look like torn paper and which the East Coast fishermen used to call 'bawlies' are a good indication of wind to come, not necessarily gale force but the stiff breeze of high summer. Flying across an otherwise still sky first thing in the morning, bawlies are rarely wrong. They are in fact just what they look to be – tattered scraps of cloud blown off the top of some slow-moving bank and forerunners of a general fill-in of the wind in that area within a few hours.

The much quoted rhyme about 'mackerel skies and mares' tales making great ships carry low sails' is a true enough warning of an approaching depression. The ice cirrus cloud of a high altitude wind is the jet stream whipping off the top of an advancing storm front, but it isn't always so easy to be sure of defining the signs correctly. Some people prefer to describe this type of sky as being 'scratched by a hen'. It is a piece of the jigsaw which may fit the general picture.

Sky colour is perhaps of more use than cloud type. The 'red at night' which is held to be the sailor's delight must not be truly red, though, and, in fact, livid sky colours at any time are something to be wary of. A pink or rosy sunset may be good, a bold yellow one bad. Pale yellow tinged with green is a sign of rain. In the latitudes of the British Isles a deep, hard blue sky is a sign of wind too. Pale blue on the other hand is a fine weather sky. Grey early morning skies are usually a sign of a settled day to come, but the low bank on the horizon, held to be sure sign of fine weather, is a bit uncertain; at best it is a negative sign. If the morning cloud-bank is high, though, high wind may well follow.

The thundercloud bears careful watching. If it is high and the top is rounded it is a potential squall-maker. The warm lower air rises, becomes unstable at high altitudes and plunges down to spread out across the water in all directions. A black cloud isn't necessarily a sign of a squall, although one must keep an eye on the water beneath it for signs of wind. The familiar anvil-shaped thundercloud is usually a safer proposition than the high one, since it is a thundercloud which has started to disintegrate.

The all-too-familiar solid mass of low cloud associated with nothing in particular and thoroughly gloomy in appearance, which covers the skies for so many days in one of our average summers, is usually a sign of stable air if nothing else. Stratified cloud is usually a sign of stable air conditions – not that there is much to be said for the alto-stratus which flies in advance of bad weather. The big, beautifully sculptured cumuloform clouds often mean unstable air liable to result in squalls as warm lower air rises and then returns in a down-blast. If the upper cloud is moving in a contrary direction to the lower cloud these squalls may give rise to sudden wind shifts, but when both layers are moving in the same direction the squalls, though constant in direction, are likely to be harder. The hazy sky is a sign of air stability and the hard, clear horizon a sign of instability.

The circle round the moon is a pretty reliable warning of dirty weather. Here, warm air forced up by an advancing front has formed a steadily thickening layer of high cloud, which gradually gets lower as the front moves in. This accounts for the rider that the bigger the halo the sooner the blow. If this advance cloud is low enough and dense enough to give rain it is a sign that the low is to be of some importance and hence another old couplet, 'Rain before wind, sheets and halyards mind'. Again, 'When stars hide soon rain will betide' is a somewhat vague way of saying the same thing. All in all, it is a reminder to watch the night sky as well as the day sky.

If we could predict wind strength accurately – when will it come and how hard will it blow – ninety per cent of our sailing worries would disappear. Enough wind is the joy of sailing, too much of it means worry and hardship. There is a lot to learn about seagoing in small boats, but learning the winds is perhaps the most vital thing of all.

Wind

Short of cribbing from half a dozen serious works on the science of meteorology, and trying to write a seventh and less valuable book on the subject, the most that can be done in a single chapter is to skim over the basic principles.

By 'weather' the yachtsman is really speaking about wind, and wind is the mass movement of air. It moves from high to low pressure areas like water running down a mountainside and the steeper the slope the stronger the current. The face of the earth is covered by warm and cold belts according to the location from Equator to poles, and like oil and water these warm air and cold air regions are reluctant to mix. Instead of graduated slopes of pressure from poles to Equator, the two warring bands of temperature meet and swirl, causing bulges in the frontiers. Up goes warm air above the cold, forming a low pressure area and the air begins to whirlpool.

Due to the rotation of the earth the air circulates in an anticlockwise direction in the northern hemisphere. The cold air sweeps around forcing the warm air to rise above it (the 'front'). Ahead of the shovel-like cold air goes the warm mass in a wedge, leading the bulge and giving a 'warm front'. Sooner or later the cold air overtakes the warm front and shoves it up above sea or ground level. The depression is then said to be 'occluded' and is beginning to spend itself.

The whole system is on the move. It moves along rather like a spinning top. The hurricane, which is a depression on a grand scale, follows a fairly well defined route – but by no means so clearly defined that it can be dodged with certainty. The depressions which affect the British Isles come whirling down from the North Atlantic. They are mapped and reported by satellite and observer stations, and usually pass to the north of these islands. The average rate of travel seems to be around 25 mph with the winds blowing slightly inwards towards the vortex rather like water going down a plug, and in just the same way the speed of the wind gets higher and higher as it nears the centre.

This whirlpooling is the reason why the yachtsman in his boat may experience in the second part of a gale a possible wind shift from south-east to south-west followed by another shift into the west and a final petering out of the blow from a nor'westerly direction. The centre of the depression would be to the north of him in this case. Should he be right in the line of travel, however, he might experience a vicious southerly which falls to an odd calm before coming in from a northerly direction, or, if he's to the north of the centre, which is the exception in these waters, the wind shift may be from south-east to north-east, finally blowing itself out from north or north-west.

It is plain to see why knowing where the centre lies is very important to any yachtsman faced with staying away from what may turn out to be a lee shore. Lacking a shipping forecast or a positive idea of which way the depression is heading, the rule for locating the centre is to face the wind, when the centre will be on your right hand. Naturally it is important to know that the wind you are experiencing is actually a part of the depression.

All this time the barometer has been reacting to the pressure gradient. It may fall steadily and rise steadily as the depression wheels past leaving the yacht in its fringe; on the other hand it may fall slowly at first and then pitch. It may then rise sharply as the centre passes over and with the rise a sudden, savage blow from the northward which soon falls lighter. 'Sharp rise after low soon foretells a harder blow' runs the old jingle, and how right it is!

The approach of the warm front with its drizzle, the gradual backing of the wind (backing means changing direction anticlockwise, e.g. west to south), and the increase in velocity with that murky yet strangely translucent greyness all around, typify the path of the depression. This is the time to watch the barometer closely. The steady decline over a period of perhaps a day or so will have suggested a large low-pressure system ('long foretold long last, short notice soon past'). The sudden sharp drop, though it may only be a small one, is just as important to the small-boat man, for it hints at a small, though very active, depression moving in quickly – the type of small low which so often slips by the forecasters as an inconspicuous trough and later suddenly deepens.

The occluded front with its unstable warm air shoved skywards over the wedge of cold air can produce a squally type of weather which, while lacking the greater threat of a very active and deepening low, can stand close watching. So too can the sudden shift of wind which follows the passage of a front when a sharply defined 'low' is followed by a steep ridge of high pressure – sudden torrential rain and vicious squalls which may end rapidly and leave a clearing sky and a steady breeze from a totally different quarter.

The appearance of the sky after a low has passed is often quite distinctively 'nor'westerly'. Colours seem to be brighter, the sea shows deep, dark blue wind ruffles, the sky is deep blue and dotted with the tattered white clouds which have replaced the low altitude stratus.

Since most depressions pass to the north of the British Isles with their familiar sequence of the passing fronts, should they pass south of us the weather pattern may be puzzling. There are no such fronts to be experienced, just the wind shifts and change of barometric pressure. They are none the less dangerous for that.

High pressure systems, ridges and anticyclones as opposed to troughs and cyclonic systems, are generally looked upon as the good fairies of the weather world, but the rule that any steep slope means fast running 'rivers' of water or air must not be overlooked. A very steep 'high' can produce strong winds around the outer edges. In a depression the winds blow round the centre and slightly inwards in an anticlockwise direction. This is the exact opposite in the case of the anticyclone.

Anticyclones *usually* mean gentle breezes with the whole system moving along slowly, sometimes remaining stationary for days at a time and gradually declining: settled, hot weather in summer or perhaps hazy, overcast but warm weather. In the early part of the year and in the springtime, an anticyclone can mean bitterly cold winds and grey murk, particularly if settled to the north and bringing down Arctic air as it circulates.

The small steep high, the 'dog-day' which so often appears between lows, the 'weather-breeder' as the old-timers call it, is often the only chance a yachtsman may have of making his quick passage home before the next low hits him. He must not be fooled by it. It may last twenty-four hours, but it may be less. This is the time to watch the weather and not over-strain his luck. The low which follows one of these smiling days is often a big one.

It often happens that the sailing area is between two systems, say a high to the south and a low to the north. One might be forgiven for assuming that being half-way between them, moderate weather would be the result. But very often a 'gear-wheeling' effect occurs. Clockwise winds to the south and anticlockwise winds to the north produce a strong westerly wind between them.

This is a very bare summary of the way the weather works. For the most part it consists of a variety of half-day heat-waves, pocket gales, rain, cloud, shifting winds and a barometer which twitters uncertainly up and down. The troughs, cols, wedges, ridges and so on which drift and swirl around us night and day are impossible to isolate, for the layman at least. The broad understanding of it all is the only thing possible. Just as a seaman can distinguish the tide-rip from the regular movement of wind-driven water, or the ripple over a bank from the ripple of a light breeze, so he must be able to recognise trouble in the air when he sees it.

The barometer

One barometer without any other information can only tell you about half the picture. But it cannot be dispensed with. The ideal form of instrument is the barograph, since the wanderings of the needle are traced upon a dated and time-recorded chart. At a glance you can see how the barometric pressure is behaving. As it is the steepness of a system which causes the winds to be strong, and as an observer is constantly on the watch for a sharp fall or rise, it becomes a matter of luck whether his haphazard tapping of an ordinary glass is rewarded with such a dramatic piece of weather evidence.

Here a point about tappers: strictly speaking one should never tap a barometer, but should set the dummy recording hand at fixed and frequent intervals during the day (and the night!) and graph the rate and extent of movement between times. In practice, the majority of yacht barometers are inexpensive instruments which are by no means as delicate as they might be and can stand a *gentle* tap. A sudden jerk upwards or downwards just *may* be caused by a sticky movement suddenly freed. This is particularly likely when one goes aboard after a week of absence and non-tapping.

Continuity in fair weather and foul is important. One person only should re-set the hand of the barometer. If everybody is fiddling with it (unless there is a written log of its movements), it will be impossible to know what is going on. Morning, mid-day and evening settings are the minimum but on passage the barometric pressure can be logged each watch; this is quite as important on a small craft as on a large one, and moreover it is something for the watch-keepers to do.

In home waters the average sea level pressure is around thirty inches, which means pretty settled weather on the whole. A slight fall is by no means a sign of doom. The glass may fall for the collapse of a small ridge or the arrival of a shallow trough, which in itself may mean no more than a cloudy day. Warm air or moist air (even in the absence of a definite warm front) cause a slight fall and cold, dry air brings a rise. Diurnal rise and fall, a normal daily occurrence of no other significance than the passage of night and day, should be ignored.

The famous generalisation laid down by Admiral Fitzroy is well worth repeating. Barometers rise for northerly winds including winds from north-west through north to north-east. They rise for dry or drier weather, for less wind, or for several of these changes. The exception is when strong winds bring rain or snow from the north. Barometers fall for south winds (south-east through south to west), for wet or strengthening winds or for several of these reasons, save when moderate winds with rain or snow come from the north.

Direction, wind force and humidity affect the barometer, and the greatest falls come when all act together, reading lowest when wind and rain come together with southerly winds and reading highest in cold, dry northerlies.

From this it can be seen that with the barometer should go the thermometer if readings are to be interpreted with any precision. To go further, a hygrometer to record humidity should come into it. Obviously, an owner will need to be making a hobby of the study to go to these lengths. That it is worthwhile goes without saying, but a small yacht makes such demands upon her crew that detailed met. study becomes impractical.

The forecasts

To listen to an area shipping forecast and disregard all areas except the one in which you happen to be sailing is no way to get the best information from the weather picture as a whole. The experienced man can be seen listening to a forecast with both hands – literally so. The general situation may show that there is a low to the west of him and turning north while deepening. He at once begins trying to visualise the overall effect this will have on his own area, how the wind will behave as it passes and changes direction – hence the hands: he uses them as an aid to imagination.

Ashore, the synoptic charts printed in simplified form in some of the more earnest dailies are a splendid follow-up to the shipping forecasts. Better, from the point of view of study, than the television weather maps for they can be saved day by day and watched as the low pressure and high pressure systems advance and retire, grow and diminish.

There is a similarity between a weather map and an ordinary land map which gives contour lines, since the purpose of the contours is to trace the height of the land in one instance and the height of the barometric pressure in the other. On the weather map these lines are called isobars and the general effect is to create an impression of hills and valleys. The closer they are together the steeper the slope and the stronger the wind. But the wind flows roughly along rather than directly across them.

A watch on the Atlantic weather maps reproduced in the newspapers gives a general guide to what may be developing. Sometimes a line of lows can be seen coming in one after the other. Not all may affect the British Isles, since they may be diverted further north, but it does seem that once a run of depressions begins there will be a period of one day fine, two days of foul weather, with the wind shifting constantly between south and west. 'When the wind backs against the sun trust it not for back 'twill run.'

At sea, and denied both television and a morning paper, the alternative is to jot down the area forecasts on a blank chart (tear-off pads are on sale at most big yacht chandlers). The circulatory flow of wind and the strength in each area can be noted, and the degree of visibility, temperature and so on fill in the details of the picture. Thus a yachtsman in area Wight may hear of a low approaching from the Atlantic. He may be in some doubt whether to make a short hop to the

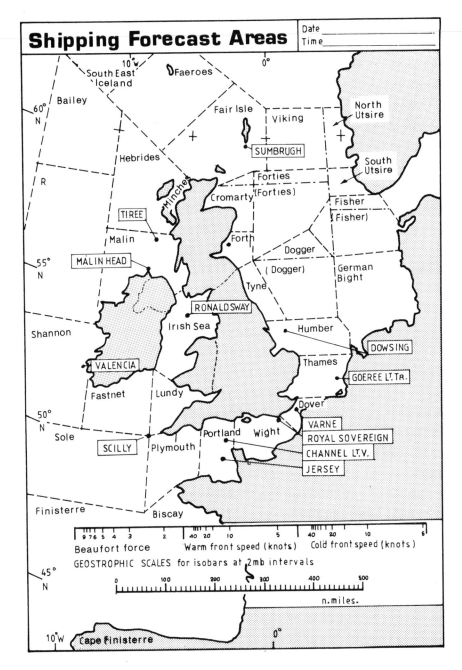

Fig. 50

next port. His barometer is falling slightly, the forecast for Plymouth–Biscay is bad but *his* weather is still fine. Should the Coastal Stations' report give drizzle and low visibility at Start Point he can be fairly sure that he is in for the treatment. This is when he begins to look closely at the sky – sunrise, sunset, height of cloud, hardness of horizon and so on. He will expect the wind to back towards the south and freshen a little, he may even note a long ground swell moving in over an otherwise smooth sea, forerunner of the disturbance. Incidentally, ground swell is not a certain sign of bad weather because the depression causing it may alter course. It can also be caused by moderate winds close at hand rather than a more distant storm, but it is one more shred of evidence.

If he is wise he will either stay where he is in his little cruiser or make the passage a short one. It is a decision which may take a very great deal of courage to make, if the sun is still shining.

The effect of the land on wind

Coastwise sailing puts a yacht within the influence of the land, which affects the course of the general wind direction. Far out at sea a true and steady wind may be blowing, but inshore, direction, strength and general character may be quite changed.

The obvious cases are the land and sea breezes of hot weather. Most people know that as the land masses warm up more quickly than the sea, hot air rises from the coast, flows seaward at a higher altitude, cools and is drawn inshore again in a circular movement – the result is a sea breeze. It may not begin to make itself felt until the day is well advanced. It may not materialise at all and it is rarely felt more than ten miles offshore even in the Mediterranean. The land breeze of late evening is a reversal of the same system, land cooling rapidly, sea temperature cooling slowly and air flowing offshore at sea level and back inshore at a higher altitude. Just now and then the yachtsman meets this lovely offshore breeze, and the fast night passage over calm water and in a warm, fragrant wind is something to rave about. Long before the night is half over he may be left becalmed, of course. It needs to have been a very hot day for the land breeze to be felt in force. In both cases the nature of the land affects the wind behaviour. Fields and built-up areas heat up more rapidly than densely wooded land.

More often than not the true sea or land breeze caused by land-heating becomes diverted by the influence of the existing weather systems. An offshore breeze due to some passing high or low can result in a flat calm as soon as the hot air circulation begins, the onshore breeze which *should* be blowing being stalemated by the opposing force. By the same token, the light *onshore* breeze of early morning which develops into one of those boisterous half-gales that lash the coastline in hot and brilliant sunshine can be no more than the sea-breeze aiding and abetting it. The old cry 'they only forecast force three' is usually inspired by something of this kind. By early evening the wind has steadied down and by dusk, when the offshore wind begins, it meets that same little onshore breeze and a night of flat calm follows. The person who can recognise this sort of weather for what it is and plan accordingly can go to sea and enjoy some spirited sailing.

On the whole, winds are more stable at night. A cold layer forms and permits upper winds in warmer air to slide over the cold base. It is when these conditions are reversed, cold over hot, that unstable conditions develop and the down-blasts of cold air cause squally weather. It is even said that cold air is 'heavier' of impact upon a sail and that waves become steeper in unstable conditions.

Land 'bends' the wind, as anyone who has raced a dinghy will know. If a wind is blowing down the coast and parallel to it, we are likely to find that close inshore it is blowing diagonally *across* the shoreline (Fig. 51)

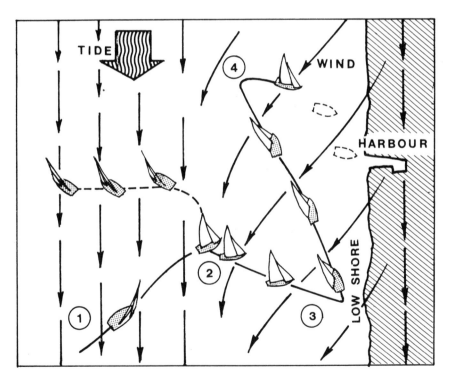

Fig. 51   The wind has bent as it crosses from land to sea. The yacht at (1) has tacked inshore and been headed. (2) She has gambled on finding a steady, freer wind on the next tack and she goes about at (3) to work up the coast over the tide. She sails well above her harbour (4) before going about. If, on the other hand, she had followed the dotted track she would have made little ground as the tide strengthened.

from land to sea. In a river this may be the other way round and at each shore the wind will bend and blow diagonally across it towards the land. If, at the same time, the onshore breeze conditions are in force this bend may be much more acute. The wind may be almost dead onshore along the coast and further out it may be blowing practically at right angles and dead down the coast. It often pays to explore a little. Though knowledge of met. may be too light to predict with certainty that such is the case, a long leg inshore may prove that it is so. Many people, tacking up the coast, stand inshore, and when they begin to meet a heading wind and lose ground, they promptly go about. It may happen that by standing in still further they may be able to carry the next tack right along the shore.

When the wind is blowing from land to sea or sea to land, it almost invariably bends as it crosses. It also divides to blow around each side of a headland or island. High cliffs cause the wind-flow to lift from sea to land, leaving a dead area immediately offshore. An offshore breeze crossing cliffs also leaves a dead area to leeward, which may extend to as much as thirty times the height of the cliff, but in each case a sloping cliff of less than 45 degrees will have little effect on the wind. A cove or river mouth can produce an accelerated force of wind particularly if it is funnelling down from hills. The yacht which is *just* able to cope with the wind force offshore might well have another roll pulled down if she is to be tacked into such a river mouth.

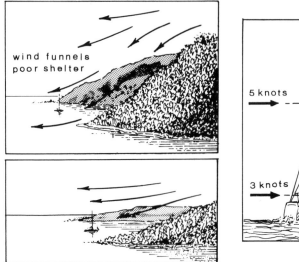
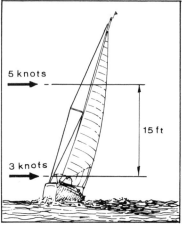

Fig. 52 Wind strength increases with height above sea surface. A high, steep coastline is not always ideal shelter, giving rise to funnel effect and, in mountainous areas, the down-draught of cold air. A lower coastal profile is often better.

Anchoring close under the hoped-for protection of high ground doesn't always provide it, though. In mountainous areas cold, heavy air can plunge seawards with great strength and as any who have sailed charter yachts in the Mediterranean will know, the afternoon blow, although hot and accompanied by sunshine, can cause huge problems of force six to seven calibre, darting from half a dozen directions as luckless yachtsmen try to find an anchorage under the hills.

Wind force

Although this is a particularly gloomy chapter, well studded with dire head-shakings, and perhaps too preoccupied with what one shouldn't do rather than with what one should, the short answer to bad weather in such small boats is that there is only one really relevant 'should': to stay in shelter until the sea smiles again. After all, we go afloat for pleasure. We can take a reasonable amount of teeth-gritting, but saturation point is in every sense soon reached in a small cruiser.

The Beaufort Scale is a constant delight to yachtsmen. We hear of a fourteen-foot cruising dinghy being hove to in a force-8 Channel gale while her crew shelter happily 'below'. We hear of threshing into a force-6 breeze and scudding before force-9 squalls. It is all good fun. Fortunately these tales are almost invariably just wild exaggeration. Small cruisers do come through gales safely, but more often than not the wind forces which blow around the club bar are in reality well down the Beaufort Scale. The fact that gale force winds may be forecast is no proof that the actual wind when it comes attains that velocity.

The problem with this is that a beginner at sea may hear a 'gale imminent' warning for the area, then experience a wet force 6 which is nasty enough but no gale. Thereafter the beginner may think that he knows what gale force is like and have no hesitation about sailing in the face of a gale warning another day. This time it throws the book at him.

In the open sea or in wide estuaries where tidal streams run strongly a full force 5 is all the small boat can handle without great discomfort. Force 5 – the 'fresh breeze' blowing at 17–21 knots – may raise a possible six-foot wave in open water, smaller and steeper inshore, showing many crests and some blown spume. A weather-going tide may produce a bigger and toppling form of sea. Add a low, ominous sky and some rain, and it is easy enough to imagine that the wind is much stronger.

Forecasts giving a possible force 5–6 but with nothing worse in store may be perfectly safe on a passage off the wind, provided the waters are free of ugly tide-rips and easy to navigate, but a beat to windward in these conditions is likely to be so gruelling that only the shortest of port-to-port passages in sheltered waters should be tackled. Force 4 is the favourite and even this will give a lively passage to windward in open waters, while force 3 with a fair tide carrying a beating yacht to windward is a nice working breeze for a little boat.

By all means let the small-boat man look upon force 5 as a gale. By proportion *it is* a gale, but he must get a proper perspective about the true gales of the forecasts and leave them to bigger boats.

CHAPTER FOURTEEN
Rough Water

Waves, with a few exceptions, are wind-driven water. The further they are able to travel without meeting land the higher they become. The depth of the sea and the effect of tidal currents impose restrictions on the wave form which alter its character.

A swell being either the subsiding wave pattern after a blow or the movement of water in advance of wind is of no inconvenience to a yacht at sea, but close inshore in shoal water it tends to shorten and steepen until it plunges and breaks across a bar or shallow patch.

Increasing from catspaws to ripples, then wavelets of glassy appearance followed by larger wavelets of maybe two feet in height with a tendency to break (forces 1, 2 and 3), the waves begin to be built up by the increasing wind in a regular pattern. Through force 4 they become longer, and white horses begin to move among the smaller waves, increasing in number and length through force 5, with spray blowing and larger foam-capped seas appearing at force 6. Thereafter the character changes rapidly. A heaping sea with foam blowing to leeward from breaking crests, and later the true blown spindrift whipping in banners from crests and long, orderly streaks of foam patterning the longer backs of the seas – this is the force 7–8 gale. Above this it is all beyond the scope of the small cruiser; it is all bad and to be out in it will be to lose all academic interest in the exact force of the wind at the time.

Shoal-water waves

Quite apart from the big seas raised by high wind, the question of shallow-water seas must be remembered. In a fresh breeze, or even a moderate breeze if it has shortly been preceded by much wind, shallow water in the entrance to a river in the form of a bar often produces conditions dangerous to small craft.

There is no question of advising how to set about surf-riding in over a shallow bar; you just don't attempt it without the knowledge and the right sort of craft. There are the borderline instances though, the occasions when, having gone in so far, it is no longer possible to turn back.

From inshore, where the height of the seas can be properly judged, a breaking bar always looks worse than it does from seaward, and hence to the small-boat man happily standing in for the river without a care in the world. At a certain point the yacht will suddenly seem to drop bodily into a big trough, then astern of her comes a huge comber, advancing like an express train. It will lift her, and she will begin tobogganing down the forward face of it, bows deeply immersed, stern in the foaming crest. She will either broach to and be overturned, or she can allow it to pass ahead of her without trouble. Alternatively it may fill the cockpit and the following sea will catch her out of control.

The only action to take is to *keep going*. Never, at such a late stage, attempt to turn and make offshore again in panic. Keep absolutely straight, keep the fore-and-aft trim a little by the stern and crew weight low and most of all keep the speed down. Drop the mainsail in a heap and let the jib carry her in if there is time to prepare. There will be a distinct line of breaking, fast-moving crests, and then there will follow an area of white water where the seas have expended their force and it will be over. Better that it should never have begun, perhaps.

Approach all bars with foreknowledge gained from the pilot book. Take stock of the forces of the wind and the recent weather history. Note the presence or otherwise of a distinct swell, check the tide height and state of tide because a fast ebb against an onshore wind is to be avoided. Remember that most bars, most of the time, are passable, otherwise the place would be completely shunned by yachtsmen. Don't be spooked by a white crest or two but sail up and down and examine the situation if there is any cause for doubt.

The small shoal-draught yacht is less likely to hit the bar than a deep-keeled vessel, but the risk may be there and must be considered as it would certainly be the finish of her. The simplest way of checking in advance that a bar carries enough water for safe crossing is to take a there-and-then sounding at some fixed position just offshore, such as a cross-bearing taken when the ship is centred on leading marks or close to some beacon or buoy. If the chart shows a least depth at that known point of, say, two fathoms and the echo sounder reads three and a half, then obviously there is one and a half fathoms to be added to the soundings shown on the bar. Further, it is safer to deduct half the estimated height of the seas (in fact, it is less than half) from the expected figure to allow for sinking in the troughs, but naturally such fine limits are to be avoided as you must have a margin of safety. Such calculations should be in the nature of reassurance.

This only applies to bars which are constant in character; there are also bars which are constantly on the shift and never the same shape or position for two years running. These call for up-to-date knowledge and special care.

The effect of wind upon a fast tidal current has been mentioned time and again in this book, and it cannot be over-stressed that tide races, rips and overfalls are best avoided (and usually very easy to avoid). The seas in such places rise in sharp pyramids and fall flat on their faces only to jump up again a few yards away. Big sleek swirling 'smooths' appear which spin a boat around in defiance of her rudder and troughs seem deeper than usual. There is rarely much need to bother about these horrors in gentle weather. In fact it is educational to shoot a race provided there is enough wind to give normal control, but in anything above force 4 the small cruiser does well to stay clear.

The pocket gale

Although it may seem that the only safe behaviour is to be like the candlestick fisherman who stayed ashore because there was too much wind if the flame blew out, and stayed ashore becalmed if it didn't, the frame of mind which finds alarm in every puff of wind is something to be avoided like the plague. Worry is tiring and it is contagious.

Inevitably the small cruiser will hit patches of rough going which may not have been foreseen. They last a few hours, or just as long as it takes to round a headland, but they can be worrying to the inexperienced. Faith in the cruiser, and trust in good gear, are the essentials for peace of mind. Worry about either takes all the fun out of yachting. The weaknesses may be inadequate staying, or neglected wires, poorly fastened fairleads, worn sheets and old sails. To be watching and fussing over such things for fear they may fail is to be ill-fitted to cope with any outside troubles.

Any normal boat will tell you when she is being pressed too hard. She should have enough sail to go to windward easily without smashing and flinging her bows around, staggering and lurching. A long beat should only be undertaken if the crew is strong enough to do justice to the boat and, for most people who are unused to being offshore, this may mean that by the time each of a three-man crew has done a two-hour trick one at least will have had enough of it. The owner who takes account of this will budget for an outside eight hours of rough going and lay plans to have shelter under his lee at the end of it. In all probability the wind will ease or shift by then, and he can take a second look at his crew before tackling a longer leg.

A few bigger yachts can carry full working sail in force 5–6, but not many. A modern ocean racer may work to windward in force 7–8 and may not need to be hove-to until the wind reaches 40 knots, and it is an odd fact that in an offshore race small yachts often keep going to windward longer than large ones. However, this cannot be carried down the scale to the small cruiser. A fully reefed 18-footer is well pressed in a force 5 wind at sea, but given sail reduction to 'storm' proportions she can keep going in stronger conditions.

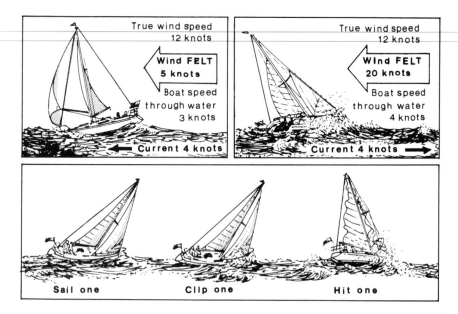

Fig. 53

It seems to be very seldom that one can take a fair tide on a beat to windward without having to roll down a couple of reefs, and the stronger the tide the more necessary this becomes. The reason is quite simply that a 12-knot breeze becomes a 20-knot breeze when you have a 4-knot tide under you sailing to windward (Fig. 53) – a simple fact which accounts for many a 'yachtsman's gale'. More important, though, is that under such conditions (and remember that the breeze is really only a moderate one) the sea will have become broken with white horses possibly four or five feet high and the going will be extremely uncomfortable. With such a tide to help it is sensible to shorten sail right down to a snug rig.

Sailing to windward with a strong fair tide often means that the wave spacing doesn't fit the shorter boat at all well. She sails over one sea, clips the crest from the next and pitches headlong into the third (see Fig. 53), then, almost at a standstill, she gathers way and repeats the whole performance. A bigger yacht is more likely to thunder from crest to crest in a deluge of flung spray but keep going. The only answer for the smaller cruiser is to slow her down just a little.

The slower you sail the more comfortable it is, but one must strike a happy medium and let the boat tell you how hard she should be driven. On the whole it is better (and usually faster in the long run) to come off the wind a shade, ease an inch of sheet and sail a good full-and-by course rather than point up tight and hobby-horse along at a couple of knots. The alternative is to motor-sail. Here again, though, she may only require a low throttle setting to keep her moving over the waves; hammering the engine is wasteful and exhausting because a given size and shape of hull can only be forced through broken water at her proper speed.

Wind strength on a run

It is very easy to miscalculate wind strength when running or with the wind on the quarter and the boat tearing along with dry decks. Some boats run so smoothly that there is not even much struggle to hold them on course and hence no warning. It is only when the boat has to alter course and the wind comes on the beam or ahead that the crew may discover that they are carrying far too much sail. In an emergency, when the boat has to be put hard on the wind they may find that it is impossible to flatten in the jib sheets and that the boat is pressed hard down on her beam ends. On such a run the skipper should watch for those black catspaws of wind on the water and the tendency for wave crests to blow off in spume and other signs, such as nearby yachts beating to windward. The aim should be to carry the right amount of sail for manoeuvring the boat at all times – or ship a racing crew.

In a short-handed small cruiser the classic trouble-fostering situation is the run which gradually becomes faster and rougher until only the skipper (who is also the navigator) can cope with the tiller. The result is that the boat hurtles down-wind, barely under control. The skipper cannot leave the helm either to shorten sail or to navigate. A more experienced crew would be able to round up, reef the boat and maybe heave to while the vital navigation was done, but apart from getting the mainsail down in haste the boat runs on with the motion getting ever wilder. With luck there is only open water ahead, but all too often the only thought of all aboard is to run for shelter down-wind. The risks hardly need stressing.

Bad weather and the crew

Noise and movement are the enemies of endurance. A three-man crew leaves no reserve for lame ducks. Should two men fall low the safety of the cruiser is undermined, since there is a limit to the time that one man can keep going without rest and food.

The food question in heavy weather is critical. Food is warmth and energy, optimism and level-headedness. Without it a man begins to fail. The belief that food must be cooked is open to doubt. There is really no reason to suppose that hot cooked food is more nutritious than raw or cold. The struggle to cook on a very small boat often results in making the cook seasick quite unnecessarily and, while the moral value of a hot meal counts for a lot, it is far more important for all hands to stay well and take nourishment in some other form. In fact, it may not do any harm to go for twenty-four hours without eating; water they must have, but shore living will have left them well nourished. The danger lies in reaching that point when appetite no longer functions as a warning to re-fuel.

A diet of brown bread, raisins, cheese and so on is of far more value than the usual tinned lash-up stew, and water is far less likely to induce seasickness than tea or patent coffee.

Small meals (not snacks) are easier to digest and easier to organise. They also give the queasy a fighting chance to stoke up during his occasional periods of well-being.

It is a sound plan to have a heavy-weather ration kept aboard in one particular place, never to be touched at other times, but ready in the emergency. Self-heating soup is expensive, but one tin can restore the morale of a weak crew. Horlicks produce a variety of scientifically prepared food concentrates specially for hardship conditions such as mountaineering, lifeboat survival and extended trekking. These heat- and energy-producing foods are high in carbohydrate and fat, and low in protein. Curry and meat in brick form for heating with water, stew bars, concentrated oatcake and special non-thirstmaking fudge typify the sort of foods available from them.

Alcohol is a useful food used with discretion. It is an immediate energy and heat producer, but the letdown afterwards is fast. It should be saved for the man who is going off watch when a quick slug of Scotch will help him to make the most of his one- or two-hour stand-easy. Nuts are another quick energy producer, chocolate, of course, and plenty of raisins; sugar in any form, and fruit if you've got it. Plenty to drink is important. Five hours without liquid, and a man is already beginning to experience the first symptoms of dehydration. The often-heard cry 'I'm dying for a cup of tea' has an element of truth.

Seasickness is the arch-enemy, though, and is allied to noise and movement, cold and hunger. All too often a man will go sick simply because he is hungry and morbidly mistakes the hollowness of hunger for *mal-de-mer*. Eat and keep eating as long as you can, night or day.

There is still no cure for seasickness. Marketed drugs help some people more than others, but there is no guaranteed cure. Most of them induce intense drowsiness, which, while being fine for anyone who can die happily in a deck-chair on a steamer, is poor compensation to the man who must struggle to stay awake at the tiller. It is no use being unsympathetic with the sufferers – they are usually beyond shame, anyhow. Now and then a person may be quite seriously ill after constant retching, and it is unwise to treat all horizontal shipmates as malingerers. By the same token many a crew has been bullied back to work, and incidentally back to health, by a skipper who can discriminate.

Warmth and fresh air, the familiar horizontal position and food if it can be taken are the only things which seem to matter. Too much liquid can cause sickness, and tea seems to be particularly bad. Sitting down below instead of lying down can bring it on, or, for that matter, any smell, taste or sight of food at a critical moment.

Keeping warm and dry is a never-ending bother. Loose woollen clothing, long woollen pants and vest, long-tailed shirts and in general all the most unlovely garments you can think of seem to be the best. Certainly it is useless to expect to stay warm with six sweaters on top and a thin, damp pair of jeans on the lower half. Wool socks and loose boots – even half-filled – seem warmer than wet canvas shoes, and a pair of wet-suit gloves kept somewhere on board will one day become valuable.

Oilskin suits should always be bought big. Try the smock on over a sports-coat and imagine trying to struggle it on over wet wool. Trousers should come high but never the elastic-waisted things which leave a bare section of back exposed when you bend. The one-piece boilersuit-type oilskin suits are best of all, perhaps, as they are easy and quick to get on and off – an important matter in conditions which make dressing-up a performance likely to take as much as fifteen minutes each time.

The wet oilskin worn below-decks is an amazing water-carrier. Dry accommodation becomes saturated in a very short while, but to stipulate that the watch below should strip off on deck is a little harsh when conditions are bad and there is very little room to do it anywhere else. An old towel to rub off the worst of it before diving below to strip off properly saves quite a lot of drips.

Bad weather

In a suitable type of craft, well equipped and with the right type of crew we don't *fear* bad weather in summertime, but unless we are racing we avoid it, because it is hard on our sails and gear and because it is highly unpleasant.

Unfortunately, the preliminary to bad weather is often a four- or five-hour spell of magnificent sailing. With shelter ahead this may be splendid, but on a passage outwards it is a bait to lure the yacht further and further from shelter. The question of seeking shelter is one of the oldest of all seafaring problems. The land is a deadly enemy unless the vessel is under full command and able to be beaten offshore again if anchoring is not a safe policy.

Very few yachts are powerful enough for their crews to beat off a lee shore in an onshore gale once they are close in and among confused water. A crack ocean racer could do it, perhaps, but a tiny cruiser might not.

In theory any lee shore which has a convenient river mouth leading to shelter ceases to be a danger to the yacht scudding in with a gale astern. The problem is to be sure of finding it. Such a hell-for-leather race for shelter might begin in clear visibility, but there is no assurance that driving murk will not close it to a few hundred yards long before she gets close – and if she misses she is in bad trouble.

The average seagoing yacht offers a choice. She can stay out, well offshore, in reasonable safety (save for the risk from steamers), or if she is turned down-wind on a run for shelter. The better facilities for navigating and the fact that she is better able to beat back out of trouble give her a good margin of safety.

It follows, then, that any run for safety must have an easily attained goal, a wide estuary with deep water, a bay or a headland. In the English Channel, for instance, there is a natural abundance of shelter from westerly weather all along the English coast, mainly in the form of headlands, but the easterly blow is a different matter, and so is a southerly. This type of open-sided shelter, however, is not particularly safe for very small craft if there is a chance of the wind backing and cornering her, blocking her escape.

If she is going to run for a difficult mouth she should do so long before the bad weather is on her. Remember that a 'low' will be moving at about 25 knots, the yacht may make six or seven. If she has forty miles to go and the weather is already thickening she just won't make it.

This doesn't preclude her owner from having a shot at it if the shelter he is making for can be reached obliquely – if it is not a dead lee shore, in fact, or if the wind is not likely to back southerly and make it into a lee shore by the time he gets there. He can run for it while running is safe under normal sailing conditions, scud under a small jib or bare mast for a little longer than that, perhaps, but once the seas begin to break and wave-planing begins it is time to take stock. If shelter is still beyond reach, the temptation to keep running wildly, to hang on and hope, has to be put well aside. Lack of bad-weather experience is a great nuisance

Fig. 54 A small yacht running down-wind parallel to the coast must make a 90-degree course alteration to enter the shelter of the river; this brings her beam-on to wind and sea and if the tidal stream is also on her weather side, any hazards to leeward may mean having to bring her on the wind in order to keep clear. Good reason for her crew to have snugged her right down well in advance.

here. It may be possible to run safely for several more hours, but one dollop of water in the cockpit and the frightened owner thinks he has been pooped. Knowing no better he very wisely rounds up.

Such a run, with wind and tide under her, perhaps, very often leaves an owner unprepared for the real weight of wind when he does at last think of rounding up. Very few small cruisers are ever reefed down to the tiny scrap of sail which is all they may carry in even a moderate gale – some will be unable to carry any sail whatsoever. Running under four or five rolls plus working jib may seem exhilarating, but on the wind in a real blow she may take no more than six feet of main plus a jib no larger than a shirt. Not one small cruiser in fifty carries real hardweather sails in her lockers, and certainly no proper sheets and fairleads for them.

Heaving to in a gale means lying often almost beam-on under a tiny scrap of sail or no sail at all and letting the ship lurch away to leeward as she will. She may well have to be handled the whole time since lashing the helm of such lightweight craft liable to be spun and chucked in all directions is hardly as practicable as it is in a displacement hull. Under a storm trysail, it should be possible to keep a small cruiser more or less heading the seas with one bow and sailing slowly. The aim is to see that she takes them under her shoulder, climbs and rolls down the other side. In no circumstances should a helmsman luff full into a sudden big breaking sea for fear of the cruiser being stood on her tail and pitchpoled backwards.

Lacking a storm jib, a good terylene mainsail rolled right down, or provided with a deep enough reef, will certainly keep her head up, and by adjusting the tiller and lashing it she may lie to under it, but the sail must not be allowed to flog. The deafening crackle of a flogging sail in a gale rarely continues for long without loss of the sail.

If such small boats are to come safely through a bad gale at sea without the proper sails they must be allowed to exploit the buoyancy which is their redeeming feature. To drive them is impossible, to maintain them at an angle to the seas which allows them to ride up and over means keeping headway on them by carrying sail, and to run means that their empty-paper-bag characteristic must be offset by towing some bulky object astern on a long line. Settee mattresses roped together have been recommended as they quickly absorb water, become submerged and cause a great deal of drag, but it rather depends upon whether the foam stuffing is absorbent or of the closed cell type which doesn't absorb water. The mattresses would need to be slit so that water can get through the plastic exterior case. Other recommendations include an anchor lashed to a couple of fenders or a big sail bag stuffed with cushions and weighted with chain and streamed on a warp long enough for the bulky object to lie in the trough between two waves. This is only an indication of scope, however, because the waves will be advancing faster than the yacht is drifting. In truth and in such wild conditions rigging or improvising even the most basic things is incredibly difficult.

What is perhaps more important is to ensure that should a small yacht be rolled right over, such heavy objects below as the cooker and the battery, or batteries, are firmly fixed so that they cannot bombard the saloon, also to have a strong bolt fixed on the inside of the top washboard so that these could not fall out and leave the saloon open to a rush of water. Keeping the water out of the hull and the crew inside it is probably all that can be done in extremes of weather and by a small crew of perhaps not very experienced, wet and frightened people. It is some comfort to remember that with the exception of some extreme wide-beam racing designs, more conservative designs can be rolled right over and survive with their crews – provided people were either battened below or hooked on by their harnesses.

An along-shore gale, although seemingly safer by far than the deadly onshore gale, may still mean that a small cruiser sailing under bare pole or a scrap of mainsail and using her engine may find it impossible to turn at right angles to the wind for the purpose of entering a narrow harbour entrance or sheltering river. As soon as she brings the wind on her beam she is laid flat and she cannot be headed up for the entrance.

Scudding downwind parallel to the land it may not occur to anybody that the shelter now in sight may prove to be the real danger. It is wise to try turning the boat across and half into wind well before reaching the entrance just to see how she behaves. In any event, it will probably be necessary to turn in well before the entrance has opened up. It is also vital to note whether the ebb is running out of the haven, because the cross sea created may be dangerous to a small craft. It is considerations such as these that mark the wise and careful seaman.

Heaving to under bare mast with helm lashed a-lee or scudding under a bare mast while towing a mattress bundled up on the end of a warp (warps alone are too light) are both possibilities which must be proved. The important aim is to do anything to keep the boat sailing slowly, to let the sea overtake her or pass harmlessly under her. At such times the passage is of secondary importance. Shelter may be no more than a few miles distant but the ship must be handled as though it were a hundred miles away.

CHAPTER FIFTEEN
Distress

It seems a little unfair to follow up so dismal a chapter with an even more depressing subject, but while the reader is in sober mood the matter of dealing with real trouble may be received with deeper attention.

Of all the yachts which use distress-signals it is some comfort to know that only a small proportion of them are in genuine trouble, beyond their own ability to cope. Moreover, the reasons for their predicament are in most cases due to carelessness rather than the dangerous nature of the sport. Figures of lifeboat rescues are a bit frightening until the assistance rendered to rowing dinghies, Lilos and motor boats out of petrol are deducted. The instances of yachts in dire distress due to extremes of weather are less common. More often than not it is a case of frightened, cold and seasick people who have run out of seamanship and enthusiasm. In the light of this, maybe it can be seen why this book nags so much about combining seaworthiness of boat with sea-fitness of crew, and staying within the limits of skills and endurance whenever there is a choice.

Troubles seldom come singly. A block jams, the cruiser luffs, hits a buoy, holes her bow, etc., etc. Usually some quite small failure can bring about a state of disorder, and this leads to faulty decisions and poor handling. Good gear, forethought and a clear appreciation of how serious or otherwise the situation may be will avoid at least fifty per cent of trouble. Good sails above all are trouble savers, a blown-out mainsail could mean a down-wind course and heaven only knows where that may end.

Ultimately, practically all trouble at sea dates from a wrong decision somewhere back along the line (and this excludes the decision to buy a boat). Somewhere there was a choice of doing one thing or the other. There is only one way in which an owner can shuffle his ideas into correct focus at the time of making that decision. It is to range his facts in order of importance rather as though he was sitting in judgement upon his own actions: whether to gamble on a tricky river entrance or sail twenty wet and weary miles further on, whether to go to sea in face of a bad forecast to be back in time for work on Monday. A weighing up of consequences and penalties leaves no doubt of the wise choice.

There is one great fallacy of the coasting yachtsman that needs knocking on the head right away. It is that no matter how hard it may be blowing, a coasting passage, down wind with plenty of rolls in the mainsail, is safe enough so long as you can 'nip in' to shelter if it gets too bad. Under a bare mast or scrap of jib the small cruiser may be able to scud safely enough for hours on end provided the following sea is not breaking dangerously, *but* should the crew try to put her on a reach in order to fetch into a river-mouth, she will need some mainsail and, scrap though it may be, it may put her down flat on her ear, so flat that she cannot stagger the short distance into shelter. This has happened over and over again, not always disastrously, perhaps, but usually it has been a lucky lull which has brought the boat through it. With a following tide sweeping along the shore it may be even more difficult to claw inshore.

Another risky delusion is that you can always run her ashore in the event of bad weather. In a fresh breeze and on a suitable sheltered shore this may be so, but it takes a very experienced man to decide when and where. Obviously, a rocky or cliff-bound shore is a suicidal place to beach a boat in onshore weather. The 'soft' shoreline can be equally dangerous. A beach which is steep-to will be fringed by plunging surf which will dump the boat, draw her back, dump her again and so on. It is often quite impossible for a man to haul himself out of the water due to the under-tow of receding surf even though the distance may be a matter of yards, unless of course there is a shore-party of rescuers waiting who know their stuff backwards.

A beach of normal slope may mean the boat striking or being overwhelmed at some distance from the shore. She may broach to in the surf well before she has reached easy swimming or wading distance. Perhaps the safest way to get ashore would be to let go the anchor and hope that she drags it steadily into the shallows; this way she should stay bow-on to the advancing breakers and move very slowly astern, which is almost the proper manner of tackling surf in an unsuitable craft.

The long, shallow shoreline offers the only reasonable chance of beaching in safety, but it is a gamble unless the shore is known. As the boat comes into shallow water, and it may take her a mile or more, the seas grow correspondingly smaller until she finally grounds in little more than wavelets. The crux of the matter lies in the state of tide and whether there are any offlying banks. At high water, the long, shallow shore may be fringed by a steep seawall or groynes which could be highly dangerous to hit. The offlying bank may result in a smashed hull. The intervening stretch of deeper water remains to be crossed somehow – this, incidentally, is where the boat with built-in buoyancy offers a reserve of safety.

Beaching is something to be undertaken only as a very last resort. That it must be considered is only part of the business of being a seaman, but it should only be considered judiciously.

In the final outcome, the decision to signal distress must be made boldly. Either the owner considers his ship in danger or he isn't sure, just worried. He must make a definite signal while there is a chance of being seen and while there is time for rescue forces to get into action. He may lose his mainsail with shoal water to leeward. He can motor while fuel lasts and just hope to claw off, but if failure to do so may mean stranding with darkness ahead and danger of breaking up it is foolish to gamble on a small anchor holding him off. It may take some hours for a rescuer to reach him, so the decision to signal is plain. On the other hand, with a tide about to turn and carry him clear it is a fair gamble to take.

The increasing use of VHF radio has greatly increased small yacht safety. With pyrotechnic signals there is always a strong doubt about them being noticed in the murk of typical bad weather and the distressed don't always know whether the signals have been seen, although coastguards will fire a white rocket in acknowledgement. Having fired their rockets and held a good reserve for use later as may be needed, the waiting period begins, with all its worry and uncertainty. It may in some circumstances take perhaps several hours before help arrives.

With VHF radio voice contact is made, the situation can be explained and discussed and advice given and thereafter in accordance with international MAYDAY procedure every ship in the area is on the lookout. When rescue arrives the lifeboat or helicopter crew can give their orders directly and clearly instead of having to shout and gesture; moreover, lifeboats and helicopters may carry position fixing radio equipment which can pinpoint the casualty. Not least of all this is the reassurance communication gives. Without this reassurance, and believing that their distress signals have not been seen, a small yacht crew might attempt some desperate alternative and worsen their chances. Finally, although there shouldn't be any priority of importance about it, a yacht with VHF remains constantly tuned to the distress channel 16 and ready to give help or relay signals from anybody else in distress. Having radio aboard is in a sense a surrender of self-sufficiency and the idiot chatter of other (illegal) users can be trying at times, but today's conditions offshore have altered and perhaps we must alter a little as well.

At least six red distress-flares and at least one daylight smoke-canister should be carried by any small yacht going offshore, preferably many more including six hand-held starshell pyrotechnics. It may take many fireworks to attract attention and several more to guide rescuers to the spot at night. A really powerful torch should also be at hand.

Once a flare is sent up, the yacht is at once acknowledged to be considered by her owner as in distress and in need of assistance – a point to be remembered before pooping off for any superficial reason. This brings up the question of salvage, which is discussed later on in the chapter. By daylight the hoisting of clothing in the rigging or the flying of the ensign upside down are both hailed as signals of distress, and anything in the nature of frantic waving with both arms by one or more people amounts to the same thing. Lacking proper flares, yachtsmen have often attempted to summon assistance by setting light to petrol-soaked rags, and in a large number of cases they have managed to set fire to the ship as well. If the need is so pressing that this risk seems worthwhile, the 'cresset' should consist of rags bound round a boathook; the whole thing can be held aloft and dunked over the side if necessary.

Perhaps one of the sanest plans for the small-boat man is to keep a friend ashore notified of his movements when long passages are involved – it must be a sailing friend, though, who understands the chances of delay and can hunch when delay seems ominous. Coastguards and RYA urge that all small craft should have the name of the yacht painted in large letters somewhere on the hull or coachroof so that in the event of an alarm, wild-goose chases can be eliminated and time saved. At all events, any small craft which is unduly delayed at sea should be reported to the local harbour office on arrival just in case a search has been called. The number of yachtsmen who go in ignorance of their supposed loss seems to increase by the year.

The organisation behind sea rescue services is a tight one. A yacht in distress off the coast may be reported by coastguard, police, other shipping unable to get close, or the holidaymaker on the beach. The message is passed on to the controllers who decide whether rescue by helicopter is possible. In winds exceeding 45 knots, during darkness or fog or at a distance of more than sixty miles, air rescue is not practicable. Likewise if the assistance of a lifeboat is needed to tow a vessel clear of danger towards which she may be drifting, either it or both services may be brought to bear.

There is a great deal which the yachtsman can do to help, above and beyond waving his trousers about and setting off rockets. In daylight, a smoke-signal either of the Wessex type or some improvised cresset can be made ready for when the helicopter is sighted. If the yacht is in the sort of trouble which is not likely to be obvious from the air, such as leaking fast beyond the ability of her crew to cope, any deliberate disorder of gear on deck – lowering the mast, streaming sails over the side and so on – will help. If other yachts are anywhere in the same area, although perhaps not visible from the water, this is more than ever important.

For the actual rescue, if the yacht can be kept head to wind so much the better. Helicopter crews have one great fear – that the lifting wire they lower may get tangled in the rigging of the yacht or, for that matter, be made fast there by the yachtsmen in their ignorance. Such a thing could easily wreck the aircraft. To this end, any backstays, topping lifts and so forth should be cleared away, to leave the after part of the yacht bare of snags. If sails are still set these must be lowered because the slipstream could capsize a small yacht.

Ideally the yacht survivors will be able to stream their dinghy astern from which, one at a time, a helicopter crewman will be able to lift them safely, but a small inflatable dinghy is not suitable for this because the down-draught of the rotors will make it scud all over the place and possibly even capsize it. A plastic or solid dinghy is less vulnerable. Lacking this the survivors, wearing properly fastened life-jackets, might even have to enter the water and get clear of the yacht by the few yards necessary, but this must only be done on instructions from the rescuers. Lifting gear consists of a belt which loops under the armpits with a toggle to slide down to the chest, but a pick-up net may be used in the case of children or people incapable of helping themselves. The readiness of helicopter crews to go out on a rescue operation is something to be thankful for – they may even welcome the chance of getting some live practice, but this in no way detracts from the gratitude we owe them.

If helicopters are concerned with saving our necks for us, the Royal National Lifeboat Institute is concerned with saving both our necks and our boats. Life comes first, though, and a coxswain is under no obligation to risk his crew or the lifeboat if conditions make towing unnecessarily hazardous. Or it might be that the yacht has an uncontrollable leak which makes her progressively harder to control on tow, or a rudder may be jammed hard over necessitating a tow alongside which conditions prohibit. A lifeboat's return from a service must not be unduly delayed because there is always the real possibility that she may have to go out on another call immediately. It is hard for an owner to see his boat left to her fate but a coxswain knows his trade or he wouldn't be a coxswain.

Many yachtsmen also fear that rescue of their yacht may incur a salvage claim by lifeboatmen, but while this is their right in law, of an average 3,000 rescue launches annually there are only one or two claims a year. A lifeboat is never launched with salvage as its purpose.

In the case of rescue by lifeboat, either a large lifeboat or an ILB (inflatable lifeboat), there is often quite a lot that yachts' crews can do to make things go more smoothly. Every lifeboat service is different according to the nature of the emergency and so no fixed rules can be laid down, but some of the following will be possible.

If the lifeboat is going to come alongside or close by, make sure that no loose ropes are over the side which could foul propellers, and clear up any loose gear on deck because a lifeboatman may have to make a flying leap, which is hazardous enough without slipping or tripping on wet sails. Try to keep warm; even if wet through, wrap up in sleeping bags to conserve stamina which may already be undermined by tension. Lacking VHF, have flares handy to guide the lifeboat because you may see them before they see you. Keep everybody together, all wearing life-jackets.

If it seems likely that a tow will be needed try to decide whether the yacht's foredeck cleat or post will be strong enough to take the mighty snatches and tugs that a rough sea will cause. The lifeboat coxswain will probably want to put his own towrope to use; don't argue about this because the coxswain is in charge of operations. It will be a bigger rope than any aboard the yacht, so decide whether the cleat is big enough. If in doubt pass all (or several) of your warps in a big loop from forward right aft around the sheet winches or stern cleats. This will transfer some of the strain from the foredeck cleat. If the mast is stepped right through the deck this can be used as a towing point, but *not* if it is stepped on deck.

Get some sail bags ready for use as chafe preventers where the towrope passes over the bow, and if the bow fairlead is a small one, get a length of rope ready for bowsing the towrope down. The tow may involve a lot of sheering around and it is important that the tow should be from the centre of the bows.

It may be wise to inflate the dinghy and let it lie astern as a precaution – the life raft if you have one – and the boat is in danger of sinking. The dinghy might be useful later during the rescue. If anchored, can you be sure that the anchor can be slipped if necessary?

At night, the yacht's lights can be left on, but if there is any chance that the engine may be needed don't run the batteries down. Leaving the sails set, or the mainsail at least, can sometimes steady the boat and it makes her easier to see, but all sail should be taken down when the lifeboat approaches. One reason is that if a rocket line is used to provide a means of pulling a towrope aboard, a sail could deflect it.

If the yacht has been dismasted it may not be possible to get the broken spar back on board. Work will be made hellishly difficult by the rapid jerking roll of a dismasted boat, but try to get loose ropes out of the water and if possible disconnect all stays' except the forestay so that the boat will lie to the wreckage as if it were a sea anchor. It is worth investing in heavy duty wire and bolt cutters because dismasting is not so uncommon and the few tools aboard will be hopelessly inadequate if the wreckage has to be got rid of quickly – as might be the case with the yacht close off a lee shore.

Above all, *stay with the yacht as long as she is afloat.* It may be that nobody is capable of doing any of the things listed above, but you can still try to keep warm and keep up your morale.

Salvage

The essential matter is that salvors must be able to show that without their efforts the vessel would stand to be a total loss. The firing of rockets is proof that the owner is worried, but he can still bargain for 'assistance' rather than admit complete loss of control. One must use sense over this. A truculent attitude in a tight spot is not the right line at all. If he is in serious trouble let him leave the job of rescue in more experienced hands and not impede the rescuers, but by the same token he must be ready for the unscrupulous who paint a lurid picture of fictional perils when all that is required is a simple tow from A to B.

Whenever possible a price for assistance rendered should be agreed on the spot, and the owner should keep dark about whether or not he is insured; witnesses should be present at such deals. The owner must remain in command of the whole works too, so that the tow-boat becomes no more than a form of power. He should pass his own towrope and remain at his own tiller. In the case of a lifeboat service the coxswain is in charge; he has to be. His prime object, remember, is to save life and if the boat can be saved as well, or used as an instrument in saving your lives, so much the better.

A salvage award will depend upon a Court's decision, and this will be based upon the dangers and difficulties of the job, risks involved, and time and trouble expended. If the owner is able to arrange a private sum instead of allowing the salvage claim to materialise he should pay up on the spot and be content. Nevertheless, the salvage award, which may amount to half the value of the yacht, is still a cheaper way out for the insurance company than footing the bill for complete replacement.

A sense of proportion is needed throughout. An owner should recognise genuine kindness with gratitude and reward it with a proportionate sum.

The danger lies in innocently accepting assistance without arrangement. Even the loan of a big anchor can mean the boat becomes salvage if the case can be proved. Keep the insurance company informed, for their interests and the owner's are closely linked. But at all costs don't jeopardise the safety of your crew in an attempt to be smart.

A great deal more damage may often be done to a boat in the course of an ill-planned rescue than she may suffer as a result of the emergency. Towlines made fast to forestays or shrouds, the arrival alongside of a rough fishing-boat hull, towing at high speed and berthing afterwards in some commercial dock, all can result in damage to topsides and deck or even holing of the hull and loss of mast. The same holds true for the rescued crew. Attempts to leap for safety should be strictly avoided. Dangers, from the screw of the rescuer to yachtsmen unwise enough to attempt to swim for it and even superficial injuries following an unnecessary scramble, are usually avoidable if all keep their heads. The exception to the rule is if a lifeboat coxswain told survivors to jump in, one at a time, for easier and safer recovery than risking going alongside the yacht.

The old truth that yachtsmen should never, never attempt to swim for the shore can bear repetition. For as long as the yacht remains afloat – and this may be indefinitely – the safest place is aboard her, whatever else may be going on. There will obviously be the exceptions, but the rule is the thing to remember. That life-jackets should be aboard for each man of the crew is basic common sense.

Fire

There was an instance of a yachtsman who filled a kettle with petrol in the dark and burnt out the yacht; he was lucky to get away with a whole skin. The fault lay in using identically shaped jerry-cans for water and fuel. There are innumerable cases of explosions and fires great and small, but not one single case which was unavoidable.

Gas-bottles, as everybody knows, can be allowed to leak, and the leakage being heavier than air trickles down into the bilge. Paraffin stoves can be allowed to flare up, methylated spirits can be spilled and cause a blaze, and so on, *ad infinitum*. Wooden boats have been potential bonfires for hundreds of years and plastic hulls are no better, burning fiercely once a fire gets a hold. Perhaps even worse is the amount of black and toxic fumes given off by burning plastics, particularly foam-filled mattresses. Diesel engines are far less of a fire risk than petrol types but although diesel fuel is not as explosive, it burns and spreads fire throughout the boat. Most boats in any case carry some petrol aboard for an outboard motor.

Half a cup of neat petrol in the bilge can blow a boat apart; the vapour can lie undetected for days. Fill cans and tanks over the side, and keep empty cans stoppered if they are stowed in lockers. Mop up even the smallest spillage; and, should any petrol go below, pump out the bilge at once and open up the cabin sole, lockers and hatches to ventilate the bilges. Even a tank which is filled carefully without drips is dangerous if the breather pipe is *inside* the cockpit, as the filling process drives out vapour which immediately goes below. Don't fill the outboard in the cockpit or even on the stern in a light following breeze and certainly douse all naked lights.

Bottled-gas stoves are quite safe as long as they are efficiently used. Trust your nose and suspect everybody else of carelessness. Make 'turning off at the bottle' an instinctive reaction, and don't regulate the burner heat by turning the flame low or it will blow out.

If there are paraffin, petrol and water aboard, see that each liquid has a distinctive and differently shaped container and label each one.

Fire extinguishers are usually far too small in capacity. Nowadays conscience is placated by installing just one small aerosol extinguisher on the bulkhead. This is fine if there are three or four more in a handy locker. Most yacht dealers supply approved types of extinguisher, but some are to be avoided whatever their efficiency, since they produce dangerous fumes. CO_2 extinguishers are safe and effective, but methyl bromide and chloro-bromomethane extinguishers are bad, while water, though adequate for simple fires, should never be used on fuel blazes.

In the event of a fire at sea, draught must be kept down to the minimum, and usually this will mean putting the yacht on a run at once and closing the forehatch once everybody is abaft the fire and out of the cabin. If the fire is right aft, naturally this will not be practicable as the flames will be blown forward and spread.

Anyone who has tended a garden bonfire will know that once you have a really hot core to it anything will burn, no matter how green or damp. While chemical fire extinguishers will smother and exclude oxygen from a fire, nothing cools down a hot core like water, and plenty of it.

Serious leaks

No bilge-pump which cannot be worked constantly without undue fatigue should be installed. A big pump in a small boat may look disproportionate, but it is an important extravagance. On the modern glass-fibre boat there is very little chance of serious leakage unless it results from a collision or stranding on a rock or underwater wreckage. The only possible action to take is to rip out the interior carpentry until the damage can be reached and the hole or crack stuffed with a towel. This is often easier said than done because the interior GRP moulding of the hulls in most modern boats makes ripping out impossible.

The vital decision must be made in the first moments after the damage has occurred. There may have been an almighty crash and the boat may have lurched as she hit some heavy floating object, perhaps in the dark. There will be a natural tendency towards panic and perhaps the sound of rushing water; in the shallow bilges of many of today's boats water may already be seen sloshing around.

If the yacht has a life raft the sensible thing is to get it ready for use or, if it is an inflatable dinghy, to set crew to work pumping it up; meanwhile life-jackets must be put on while the skipper tries to assess the true damage. If the yacht is plainly sinking too quickly for further action and there is VHF radio aboard a MAYDAY call must be made without further debate.

It may be possible to buy time by pumping and bailing into the cockpit with a bucket and the time should be spent in gathering blankets, waterproofs (hypothermia is the greatest danger to survival in raft or dinghy), distress flares, fresh water and any loose or untinned food. Much depends upon where the incident takes place and food may not be a problem, but warmth will, even in mid-summer in European and UK waters. Once again, having made ready to abandon, *stay with the yacht as long as possible.*

It may also be that damage is slighter than thought early on and when the boat doesn't appear to be sinking after all, some further attempt to save her may be made. Water entering a hull sounds far noisier initially than later on. It may be possible for a swimmer attached by a safety line to find the leak, perhaps just under the bilges, and stuff, say, a face flannel or rags into it, just enough to staunch the inward flow of water, enough at least to make pumping and bucketing worth trying again. Even a handkerchief may help as it will tend to be sucked into the hole. However, the swimmer must not keep at it too long and become deeply chilled because this could be fatal if the crew had to take to the raft after all.

Insurance

It is an extravagance to sail without insurance cover. *Your* actions may not cause damage but those of some unknown person might.

The company takes the condition of your boat on trust, quoting after assessing your case, taking experience, age of boat and engine, etc., into consideration. Cover applies to a specified cruising area and some companies are reluctant to cover the small cruiser for longer passages, a fact to be ascertained at the beginning. Loss or damage by fire or accident – collision, wreck, heavy weather, etc. – and also theft, are covered; but masts and sails when racing or sails when set are not usually covered, and neither is damage to an engine unless part of a larger claim. If sails are damaged while stowed, or damaged as a result of a collision, we'll say, compensation is usually given. Risk of loss overboard of an outboard may have to be covered by a separate arrangement.

It is possible to cover for total loss only, but this is a doubtful saving, especially as damage may entail virtually rebuilding the whole cruiser. Some people undertake to stand the first fifty pounds of any claim as a means of getting a lower premium, but in a bad season, or for a beginner, this may add up to more money in the end than the loss of a no-claims bonus.

Marine insurance companies are very fair and very human. They hate to be served a fast deal and react as one might expect. They like notification of any shift of boat while laid up at the lower laying-up rates, and the yard that slaps in a big bill for 'handling' a yacht during a blow should be referred to the company at once. Never leave a stranded boat to her fate simply because she is insured, the underwriters just may not wear this one. They will be very sympathetic, on the other hand, to an owner who does all he can to save his boat even if she ends as a write-off. In any fracas with another yacht, just as in motor insurance, an owner should find out the other company involved.

Third party insurance is vitally important. An adequate cover makes only a slight increase in the premium, but the number of cases which have recently arisen, and which involve owners in huge sums of compensation for injury, make third party cover an urgent necessity.

It is worth shopping around for insurance, but it is also wise to have your choice vetted by an expert, such as a broker, because there can be exclusions which make a premium look very attractive if the small print isn't understood. One typical loophole is the clause which says that the insured must notify the insurers of any change of circumstance likely to affect a claim. *Any* circumstance could include an owner's temporary disability, such as having an arm in a sling or a patch over one eye when, say, a collision occurred.

CHAPTER SIXTEEN
Single-handed Sailing

There is a temptation to think of the single-hander as being a person of great stoicism crossing oceans, alone for weeks at a time and given to other eccentricities. In truth, a person is single-handing every time he or she lets go of the tiller and allows the boat to sail herself for a moment or two while another job is attended to.

Having the helm under your hand is a delight most of the time – one of the reasons for sailing at all is that controlling a sailing boat is a satisfying thing to do. There are times, though, when it becomes not merely tedious but exhausting and there are other times when being *unable* to let go of the tiller means the neglect or the skimping of something else more vital, perhaps safety. A typical example might be the skipper who badly needs five minutes in which to study the chart very carefully, but cannot do so because there is nobody to trust (especially on a dead run) or because crew or companion is seasick. If the skipper could become a single-hander in the full sense of the word a great deal of worry and trouble could be averted.

How does she behave?

Before any considerations of wind vane or other automatic steering gear comes the basic consideration of boat behaviour. What will she do at any particular moment if you simply let go of the tiller and stand aside? Cruisers vary a lot. Some will proceed, slowly changing course as they luff up into the wind. If closehauled some will continue to steer as good a course (or better) than when under the helmsman's hand. Yet other cruisers will swerve violently into the wind within seconds of the helm being released and either lie head-to-wind a'shake or fling themselves round on to the other tack and lie hove-to. Still others may carry lee helm in lighter winds and they will bear right away until they gybe themselves all-standing. Under engine yet other characteristics emerge. A big propeller and its paddle-wheel effect will drive some craft round in a steady curve, others, and many modern boats, will curve off slowly at first and then fling themselves into a full helm attitude, turning so rapidly that a man can be flung overboard by it. In every weight of wind the characteristics will change.

Not only is it very interesting to know the characteristics of your own boat and fun to find out, but it is *essential* to know before we can begin to single-hand. For instance: a cruiser may be sailing along on a broad reach in a steady force 3–4 breeze and the helmsman wishes to make a quick trip forward to check the anchor lashings. If he doesn't know his ship he will lash the tiller amidships and then dash at great speed up the deck and back again hoping to get back to his helm before she does . . . what? To begin with, one should *never* make quick dashes along small and lively decks, it is far too risky. Next, how much does it really matter if she does stray off course a bit?

Lashing a tiller to hold an exact course is only practicable in a cruiser of such steady directional character that she barely needs it lashed. Usually, one spends minutes deciding on the exact angle at which it should be held and then by shifting one's weight from aft to forward, the trim is sufficiently upset to alter her sailing balance and the carefully selected helm position becomes useless. In the case mentioned, slacking off the mainsheet *and* the headsail sheet together and allowing the boat to slow right down, sails shaking and lying beam to wind, would be more sensible. It is no great effort to sheet in again and the helmsman would have time to *walk* and time to carry out a proper inspection forward.

Practically all yachts will lie beam-on (1) if they are slowed down by freeing the sails before letting go of the helm, and (2) if the helm is held a little to leeward; we are talking now of a tiller, of course. In my own boat I have two lengths of rubber cord, one from each side of the cockpit, and each has an eye seized in the end to slip over the tiller. We might call these helm a'lee holders our first piece of single-handing equipment.

Ordinary single-handing equipment

Ordinary, because it is simply everyday stuff modifying existing ship's equipment. Whether the purpose is to facilitate single-handing or not, anything that makes the working of the ship easier, simpler, has a place aboard a family cruiser. There may be plenty of willing hands to handle the sails and gear in fine weather but all too often and like it or not, the skipper, like the Mate of the *Nancy Brig* (remember Bab's Ballards?) may be cabin boy, navigator, cook and foredeck hand rolled into one when the seas begin to roll.

Working from bow to stern the single-hander's additions may be as follows: a stopper such as a split cotton reel seized around the forestay to prevent the lower jib hank from jamming on the splice of the forestay (if spliced); a length of rubber cord seized at its middle to the foot of a pulpit stanchion, which has an eye in one end and a toggle in the other. This provides a rapid lashing for a sail which is lowered in haste. The single-hander can lower, lash and be at the main halyard inside seconds. Failure to lash the headsail means that it will blow half-way up its stay again, fill, and handicap the manoeuvre. The halyards too have their bitter ends secured to the deck so that they don't escape and there are toggle lines to hold the coiled rope safely. Hitching over the top of a cleat is fine but sooner or later off comes a coil.

If the headsail sheets tend to snarl up on a mast winch now and then something must be done because there may be nobody to send forward to free them while tacking up a crowded anchorage. Another (thick) rubber cord rigged when under way, running from about four feet up the mast down to the foredeck cleat, will act as a deflector. If rope is used it also makes a good handhold. The single-hander will have pockets for winch and reefing handles and a place for a knife with spike or a shackler right at the foot of the mast. The loss or the lack of any of these may mean precious time lost on a trip aft.

Nowadays, slab reefing is finding much favour over roller reefing, especially for single-handing. I can haul down a deep reef in 60 seconds quite unaided and I can recommend it. With reefing comes the allied task of stowing the mainsail. When single-handing this is a job which takes precious seconds at a time when time is pressing. The ship may be shaking sail off preparatory to a mooring pick-up or she may be bringing up at anchor; either way there is much to attend to and all that is needed is a quick stow good enough to hold the sail down and tidy up loose and trouble-fraught bits of line. Canvas sail tyers are as quick as the man who uses them but if used, they, or a couple anyway, should always be hitched to the cabin top grabrail at sea, using a slip hitch. A better idea in some ways is to run parallel lengths of rubber cord along and below the boom, if the sail is to be slab reefed, each seized to the other at 2-foot intervals with a plastic hook strung on one side in each section. To use this method one simply grabs the cord from each side, up over boom and sail, and engages the hook.

The mainsail luff has slides. A luff groove attachment to a mast means that the whole sail spills out of the track at every lowering, blowing everywhere and prohibiting a quick re-hoist should it be needed. A luff fitting sail can be converted by fitting toggles and any sail maker will do the job.

On the coachroof top a small car-type compass can be mounted instantly when required; this obviates the need for the proper compass on short coastal passages and gives a rough heading. Much of a single-hander's navigation is by eye and he glances from chart to land constantly, gauging angles and offings as he goes. The car compass aids his visualisation although it is *not* trusted for important bearings.

The cockpit has a couple of open pockets fixed to the forward bulkhead for the purpose of stowing safely any small object that might be in his hand at a moment when something urgent needs doing – a gin glass in particular. There may be some quick method of closing the open companion against a sudden shower, such as a canvas flap on Velcro fasteners, and there will be a good deal of non-slip material laid on locker lids, side decks and steps – as elsewhere on deck, because falling, let alone falling overboard, is a grave risk for anybody who is quite alone.

In addition to the rubber cord helm a'lee lashings there is the tiller lashing. This can be rubber cord or terylene line- either way it spans the cockpit, it is instantly detachable and the tiller is engaged and held by means of a jam cleat or a complete turn of the cord around the tiller. The aim is that it should be possible to ease the tiller fractionally one way or the other until the exact position is found which holds the ship on course – with the proviso mentioned earlier that a shift of weight can play hell with the setting.

The boathook lies along the deck held by instant release rubber cord lashings; fenders, a warp, a heaving line and a collection of useful short ends of rope live in one place in one locker, instantly available.

The great value of having a roller headsail doesn't need to be pointed out. A single-hander with a roller headsail may not have to leave the cockpit at all during a short passage, and only to reef the mainsail in any case, which adds enormously to overall safety and to avoiding fatigue. The same might be said of a simple anchor windlass in any boat over, say, 26 feet in length. It will not be used much but when it is needed badly it will save the lone crew from the sort of desperate over-exertion that can lead to injury.

Self-tailing sheet winches are another godsend to the single-handed; there are a variety of types available, including a double ratchet form which means briefly that the struggle to pull the handle over top-dead-centre when it is furthest away from you is obviated simply by reversing the rotation into a second lower gear. These are of course very expensive bits of equipment, but there is a very simple device which can be rigged up for the cost of a bit of rubber shock cord and a couple of jamming cleats (Clamcleat serrated jammers are ideal). On either side of the cockpit abaft the winches there is a length (found by experiment) of 10 mm shock cord secured at its after end to the inside of the coaming or some other convenient place. On the other end of the cord is seized a jamming cleat that nicely fits the sheet. The sail is sheeted in until the winching reaches the point where a second pair of hands are needed to tail the sheet; it is then simply a matter of reaching for the jam cleat, stretching the cord a couple of feet, jamming it onto the tail and then leaving it to apply tension. Sometimes it is possible to make one cord and cleat serve both winches.

The above is the basis of it and it varies from boat to boat. There is nothing specialist about it; many hundreds of ordinarily crewed cruisers carry it or something like it. The individual boat and the ingenuity of her owner dictate what you'll find but the aim is always the same – to save seconds.

Stopping the boat

We have reviewed one method of stopping her – by freeing sheets on a reach. One can achieve the same by backing the headsail and lightly freeing the main, with helm lashed a'lee, or by lowering the headsail and freeing the main or indeed by lowering the main or perhaps *half* lowering to destroy its shape and drive. In all these cases we are left with a ship which is still under control by sail, which is not the case if we simply drop the sails completely.

Knowing the behaviour of a boat under bare pole is important, though. One can be moored or anchored in wind-against-tide conditions and know that anchor can be raised or mooring let go, usually with perfect safety under bare mast alone (she pays her bows off down wind with enough steerage to be held against or steered across the current), or again, failure of the engine while motoring with sails stowed can lead to a critical situation if you don't know what the boat is likely to do. Almost always, she will turn her stern into the wind and drift half-beam-on down wind and slightly ahead; *almost* always. This is something to find out about because it may make all the difference between knowing that the ship can be controlled for long enough to investigate the cause of engine stoppage and knowing that you have no control and only a limited time to do *something*.

It is a mark of the good single-hander that he does know what his boat is liable to do and, to the second, just how long he has to do this or that job before the helm needs his attention. Stopping a boat is an everyday requirement for the coastal single-hander. Where another skipper may sail flat out into an unknown river, steering with his backside while trying to digest pilot book and chart and to con his way past unfamiliar marks and buoys, the single-hander will round up, lie to and sort himself out before proceeding. Not bad procedure for anybody.

There is nothing antisocial about single-handing, indeed most of the ocean-crossing breed are very extrovert people who love a party; they have an aptitude for self-sufficiency and loneliness, and although it may bother them at times, it is just a price they pay for their complete and utter independence. Their *self* dependence is something else. They cannot talk over a problem and if they come and go at their own whims, the mental and moral exercise of having to keep their own counsel is something which makes for a better and indeed more considerate skipper in a crewed boat. The family cruising yachtsman or woman who occasionally sails alone knows how to give a reasonable order to others, not issuing a stream of them, some countermanding others. He also learns to plan a few steps ahead in every move he makes.

Forward planning

A good case in point would be the laying alongside of a cruiser by a single-handed yachtsman as compared to the same operation performed by a somewhat tardily crewed family boat. In the former case the lone crew must lay out the fenders and warps, have ready a heaving line and boathook, perhaps clear away his anchor ready to drop if his engine is at all temperamental and, for the same reason, see that his sails are ready for hoisting and held by a couple of tyers with slip knots. The latter outfit make for the berth with, perhaps, fenders out and trailing and a bunch of people obscuring the view by standing on the foredeck. The heaving line will be got out hurriedly and not re-coiled ready to throw, warps will be in a similar state, there will be much shouting of orders and should the engine stop the circus will be coming to town. Exaggerated a bit, perhaps, but it happens. The moral is readiness and the single-hander *has* to be ready.

At other times he applies the same forward thinking. He pagemarks his almanac and pilot book, rings round inconspicuous dangers on the chart, fills the kettle whenever a spare moment arises, stacks his sails in the best order for use and sees that they will come out of their (correct) bags tack first. He takes his meals when he can be sure of enjoying them in peace, he leaves his oilskins in easy reach, thinks out alternative options for making for shelter, lays out his sleeping bag ready for use, hauls up anchor chain and restows it prior to reaching the anchorage (to ensure that it will run freely) and he may even inflate his dinghy and ready a kedge and warp if entering a shoal river on a falling tide. It adds up to old-fashioned seamanship. He *has* to do these things to stay out of trouble and it becomes second nature to think ahead. The ordinary skipper can only benefit by single-handing for a couple of days now and again.

Vane and autopilot steering

Many cruisers can be left to sail themselves closehauled but virtually none will do so on a reach or a run without special arrangements or equipment. There is a simple arrangement of lines and cords (Fig. 55) which utilises a spare headsail and which will suit many but not all craft; otherwise a self-steering gear of some type is needed.

In broad terms there are three main types. There is the automatic helmsman which is based upon a special compass which, once set to the course required, signals an off-course port or starboard and cuts in an electric motor to apply rudder as required. There is adjustment for the width of the on course band and provision to overcome the tendency to 'hunt'. Such auto helmsmen are designed to limit the motor use and so

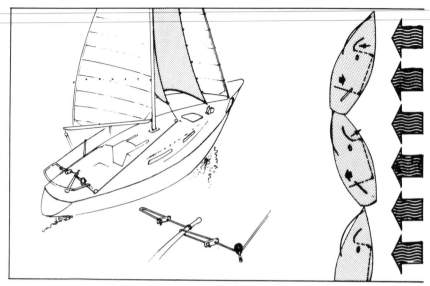

Fig. 55 Tiller lashing to port is of rubber cord. Surgical tubing or bicycle inner tube cut into strips is ideal.

conserve electric power but naturally the cutting in and out of an electric motor is the guts of the operation and it will be more or less according to whether the yacht is lying to an easily held course in a smooth sea or a wild, yawing course in a tumble of following waves. The other two types are both wind vane arrangements.

The more basic is the vane which is mounted on a horizontal axis and which is set up edge-to-wind. Any deviation from course causes the vane to present one of its surfaces to the wind and in so doing flop over under the wind pressure. A system of lines conveys the wind power to the tiller, which is moved accordingly, and the necessary amount of rudder is applied. The essential weakness of this type lies in the fact that while a strong wind provides plenty of power, a light wind offers very little power. This might seem to be acceptable on the assumption that the wilder the weather the harder the work and the more power needed, but it is *apparent* wind that we are concerned with. A boat making five knots to windward against a 20-knot wind could be expected to produce an apparent wind of around 25 knots and the same boat, running before the same wind at 5 knots, would experience a *15-knot* wind. It often happens that a sailing cruiser may need to be steered down wind in a tumble of a following sea and in a relatively light following breeze; the horizontal axis type of vane then lacks the power to cope with the amount of rudder work required.

The third main type of gear is the wind/water powered mechanism. A wind vane again senses any deviation from course and moves as it is deflected but this time instead of being linked directly to the tiller it is

Plate 22 The Autohelm 2000. One of a range of auto pilots of great sophistication. An auto control locks the pilot onto the heading being steered; it also features an off-course alarm, auto-trim and seastate compensation. A wind vane option exists. (*Photo: Walter Gardiner*)

linked to a blade or 'paddle' which is hinged in such a way that it projects downwards into the water at the stern of the boat. As the boat sails, this paddle trails edge-on to the wake but if the vane is deflected by a deviation from course, it *twists* the paddle which instantly swings out sideways under the pressure of water against its inclined surface. The power generated thus is substantial and a clever linkage transmits it to the helm. Even a slight deflection of the vane in a light breeze therefore is enough to twist the paddle and release its powerful action. There are a great number of vane steering gears, all related in some form to these basic ideas. They vary from 'sticks-and-string' arrangements to very sophisticated pieces of engineering.

Yet another variety combines both the automatic helmsman with its electrics and the wind vane. In this case the vane is tiny, no bigger than the palm of a man's hand, and its deflection sets in motion an electric motor which operates a push-pull arm linked to the tiller. At least one such (Autohelm 2000) also combines a compass unit, thus giving a choice of compass or vane control at the flick of a switch and a quick resetting of the control column. A big advantage here is that the boat which may have made a passage under vane, getting the best out of a closehauled course perhaps, can, upon entering the river, be switched to compass for a course dead down the middle. Vane steering, in the tricky puffs and slants of a river wind, would send the boat swerving all over the river obedient to the shifting wind direction. Current consumption is not greater than that of, say, a navigation light and for single-handed coasting, creek crawling and ordinary passage making this type of gear has about everything. There remains the sole snag that, *should* it go wrong, there isn't much that one can do about it whereas the 'Meccano' construction of the pure vane leaves the handy man some scope for improvisation.

No gear is instantly usable. It has to be fitted, adjusted and understood. One man may curse the same equipment that another man lauds. Properly adjusted, a vane steering gear will steer a far better course to windward than a human helmsman because it is more sparing with the helm movements. Such gears are really tiller *holders*; the boat shifts off course, the device finds a new position in which to *hold* the tiller and when found it doesn't move again until a new hold is needed; the human tends to move the tiller constantly.

Self-steering gear set up to maintain a course which may last for days on end is one thing but gear which is used off and on during the busy hours of a short coastal passage, among traffic, around obstructions and in and out of rivers, is very different in application. If it takes ten minutes to set up for a long haul it doesn't matter; if it can't be set up within seconds for the short term stuff it is more nuisance than help. This ease of use is something to examine in the light of the sort of sailing envisaged, and something to be taken into consideration when buying.

Self-steering gear of any kind or design shares one great weakness; *it can't see where it is going.* There is also an uncanny tendency for such gear to single out the other boat, the solitary buoy, beacon or rock in sight and make straight for it. I have watched my own gear at work and marvelled at this particular aptitude.

A single-handed coastal passage

We'll assume that the owner of a 30-foot auxiliary cruiser is about to make a short passage between rivers. He makes his assessment of wind, tide and weather in the ordinary way and bends on an appropriate headsail. He may, if the wind promises to freshen, bend on a smaller headsail *below* the first, hanking it to the stay by leaving off the bottom sail hank of the sail in use and lashing it in a tight, neat bundle clear of the deck along the pulpit. To change sails he will merely have to (1) lower, (2) transfer halyard, tack and sheets, (3) unhank the first sail, and (4) hoist.

He will have looked up his tides to see how they affect his passage, made notes of rise and fall times at the place she is making for and pre-read pilot book instructions; he will read them again as he makes the approach but, having read them earlier, they will be familiar and more easily digested. If the passage is to be a busy one or a rough one he will have prepared a few sandwiches, filled his kettle, put a teabag in a mug and other such domestic jobs. His oilskins will be laid out on a bunk and everything below will be stowed as if for gale conditions.

Under way, he heads down river. If he has one, he may cut in his self-steering gear on the straight reaches but it is more likely that he will enjoy sailing his boat; later, when he gets busy and a bit tired, is the time when he will look to it for help. Under self-steering gear there is a big temptation to wander around catching up with small maintenance jobs – none too wise in a river crowded with moorings. To this end it is an advantage to have a forward facing port light so that when below he can take an occasional peep forward without having to keep popping up on deck.

At sea, course laid, he sets up his self-steering and relaxes. It is now that he can take time and care in his coastal pilotage, wander around looking at the set of his sails and generally relax himself, but he will still be keenly aware of the real danger of self-steering gear, namely the risk of falling overboard and being left astern as the ship sails on placidly. He may or may not wear safety harness the whole time. There is much argument about this. My own theory is that it should always be worn.

With self-steering there is time to move slowly and carefully. He cultivates (or should) an instinctive catch-and-grab mode of walking the deck; one hand never lets go before the next clamps on, even at the mooring. To work, there is always an arm around a stay, a spine wedged for balance, a knee locked against a mast – or he sits down, instinctively. An almost bigger risk than falling overboard is in falling back into the cockpit, down the main hatch or against some sharp projection with an ensuing injury that for a single-hander can be a grave danger.

As he approaches the destination he decides whether he is going to make for the marina or dock or whether to anchor. He may be able to make a decision but if he can't, he prepares for both. He hauls out warps and fenders, recoils and lays handy in the locker. He hauls out a few fathoms of anchor cable and runs it back into the locker, ensuring that when needed it will come out in a clean run. He may stow his anchor at the stemhead. He may also give his engine a short run to warm it up (if it responds to that sort of treatment) and he has a last good look at the chart – henceforth he will be having to take hasty glances at it.

His approach to the chosen anchorage is typical. He may well decide to find his spot under engine. He positions his boat in that part of the fairway that gives him the greatest available time for sail handling and slows her right down on the reach, lets fly sheets completely and lashes the helm a'lee. If he had been beating up the fairway this manoeuvre would have been started well over to one side of the channel or on the windward side if one favoured more than the other. He can now lower and stow headsail and mainsail, securing both with temporary, easily slipped lashings. He makes all ready for letting go anchor and puts the engine, which was at tickover, into ahead.

He may circle the chosen anchorage several times, sizing up swinging scope and distances, depths and the consequences of future wind shifts once anchored. This circling is well worth while because the aspect alters constantly as seen from different angles and the single-hander above all doesn't want to make extra (3 am) work for himself.

Such is the typical single-handed coastal passage. It *should* be little different to any crewed passage – except that it may well be a great deal more seamanlike.

If single-handing makes you scrupulously careful it is because there is an underlying danger to it. Falling overboard could be fatal, even if some clever device was rigged involving a trailing line which threw the self-steerer out of action and luffed the boat. The boat would almost certainly continue to move and it would take a very strong fit person to haul back to the boat and *then* somehow climb back aboard. This is not the only danger. A fall due to a lurch of the boat could mean a broken ankle, concussion or perhaps a broken wrist or finger, any of which could incapacitate the person.

This is why slow, careful movement about the boat is so important and it is also a very good argument for fitting a VHF radio.

CHAPTER SEVENTEEN
How to Test-sail a Small Cruiser

Most yachting magazines carry sail test reports on new boats, but these vary a great deal. Some magazines are purely interested in flattering the products of their advertisers and any defects will be either skimmed over, hinted at mildly or ignored. Other magazines make a genuine attempt to be candid, mentioning defects in design and handling quite objectively – and then effusing over some other feature in an attempt to keep the advertiser happy; it never does, and you can be sure that in trying to be honest with the reader the editor will be in trouble, possibly even threatened with a law suit.

These reports are based upon a brief sail, although one British magazine at least always tries to spread the test over two days, including a night on board. These short sails cannot be expected to represent the boat in all kinds of wind, sea and weather and the reports describe what the writer found on a particular day. Apart from these magazine reports there may be no other source of information, although currently *Yachting Monthly* runs a service called Second Opinion which puts readers in touch by phone with existing owners of some hundreds of different classes of sailing cruiser.

An owner-to-be will have narrowed his search to two or three boats if he is buying new and perhaps to only one if on the second-hand market, since he is dependent upon what is available at the same time. Almost all builders offer test-sail facilities (or should) but a trial sail in a second-hand boat is not always possible as the transaction may be taking place during the winter.

Most boats are chosen and bought jointly by a married couple who will have discussed what they want and what they can afford and since they have narrowed their search they go for their test sail slightly biased in favour of the boat; later they will debate the boat in detail, accommodation versus performance, having weighed up the all-in cost after adding certain optional extras. These vary from boat to boat and the builder's main aim will be to present an attractive package at an attractive price. Take a pocket calculator on a test sail. Something like a spray hood may be essential and taken for granted on the test boat, but it may well cost another £100. Although many married couples are equal partners in experience as sailors, the majority of boat buyers are men, either in their own right or having had the final decision landed in their laps. Henceforth (and apologies where needed) I shall refer to the buyer as 'he'.

He must be fair to the boat and to the salesman. If she is a true *pocket* cruiser of less than 24 feet overall length, he should resist the temptation to take a crowd of friends with him because his party plus salesman, and maybe one other, will overload the little craft and distort her true qualities. For this reason it is as well to ask in advance whether he will be having to share a sail trial with another buyer.

The salesman may be an employee or he may be the actual builder; he may be a yard boatman. The extent of the trial sail is a bit affected by this. A builder or designer will have no objection to a very thorough trial, but there may be a shade of resistance from the boatman, who wants to get home by knock-off time. The weather must be considered and the restrictions imposed by having to catch tides and so on. On the other hand, the prospective buyer is perhaps about to lay out a great deal of money. There are nuisances who go around taking sailing demonstrations and who have no real intention of buying – the builder or his man will have suffered them in the past. The aim is to be considerate regarding the length of the sail, but adamant about the things to be done during it.

If time permits, or maybe between making or taking in sail, try her under jib alone and main alone. In light airs she may not handle very well, particularly if she is a twin-keeler, but if she will handle well enough to tack and gybe smartly in a moderate breeze, she has a great advantage to the single-handed man or do-it-all-myself owner.

While sailing, notice the course sailed when closehauled on each tack (by compass) and from this calculate how high she points *and still sails*. Don't expect her to point up within 45 degrees and still tramp along, but be critical of a boat which 'points but doesn't go'. Notice too how lively her helm is. A boat which flies around on the other tack the second the tiller is released is an annoying creature for the cruising man, but if she is so insensitive that the tiller feels sluggish she won't be much fun either.

Safety when going forward, ease of handling jib sheets, ease of starting engine and so on are all points to note, as also is the accommodation layout when actually sailing. Locker doors which fly open, mattresses which slide off, etc., should be checked. Consider chart work below, cooking and sleeping at sea, access below in wet weather and so on.

An engine trial is worth having if time allows. Stop her and let her drift to a standstill, then try backing and filling ahead and astern to make a tight turn. If there is a smart breeze try turning down-wind and then completing the full circle by heading into the wind to see whether her bow windage is excessive for the power available.

Make notes about everything you do for future reference. Measure wind speed if possible and speed of boat for sail area, also roughly the

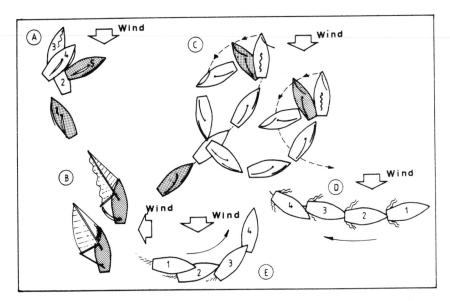

Fig. 56 A: slow-tacking with minimal steerageway will reveal any tendency towards a sluggish helm. B: slow the boat by letting fly both sheets, see whether she will lie quietly beam-on, also try sailing her under mainsail only, then jib only. C: with sheets home tack her and keep the tiller where it is. A handy boat will make a complete bearing off and gybing circle, then tack again and continue to circle. D: test her under engine only in a straight sternboard across the wind and E in tight into-wind turns.

angle of heel. Failing this and while moored alongside get everybody amidships and then put your full weight out by the shrouds on one side. Note the amount of freeboard remaining. When testing the next boat on the list repeat this dodge – a tender boat will be obvious to detect although bear in mind that according to hull form some have more initial stability than others. A cruiser that sails on her ear is a curse in any case. See how far you can steer her dead astern in a straight line.

If conditions, such as a narrow river, preclude much in the way of manoeuvre you will have to be content to note angle of heel for given wind, weather helm, etc. Tacking at normal speed teaches very little but after a couple of normal tacks slow her right up by pinching her until she is barely moving and then see if she'll still go about. If she gets in stays so much the better. See how quickly you can recover control. On a reach let all sheets go and see if she lies quietly. Try bearing away with a tight mainsheet and anything else which is plainly unfair. A normal boat can't be blamed for misbehaving, but if she's unusually good it will be apparent.

The weather dictates the general programme. On a light air day one can only go through the basic drill of tacking and gybing, heaving to and manoeuvring under power, but the appropriate sails (biggest genoa) should be worn. Many small twin-keel cruisers are sluggish in light airs and give a poor impression of their qualities below force 2. By the same token there is no hint concerning weather helm and in a stronger breeze they may gripe up hard as soon as they are heeled; they may also be tender. In such cases, it is better to try for a second trial at a later date if this is possible.

With anything of a working breeze general manoeuvrability may be tested by putting the boat about, leaving the jib sheets untouched and keeping the helm hard over so that she tacks, bears away, gybes, comes on the wind, tacks again and so on. A handy boat will often keep up this catch-my-tail routine indefinitely – she may be reluctant to bear away with the mainsail hardened in, though. These tricks do more than give a *feel* of the boat. She may still be hard of the helm on the wind. The important thing is to avoid a sail test which consists of a straight sail out and back again, as this reveals very little.

In a fresher breeze weather helm can be assessed. No small cruiser should be so hard mouthed that the tiller needs to be hugged hard up against the chest. A pocket spring balance hooked over the tiller might show between 5 and 10 lb of pull required, which isn't *too* bad. Some need an 18 lb pull and this is bad. Notice the stiffness of her, too. In a force 4 breeze she should have plenty of freeboard out of water under normal sail, and depending on size, of course, a small cruiser may be better for a couple of rolls in the mainsail in winds approaching force 5; she should still not be burying her rail.

Reefing is a sore defect in many new boats. The alloy boom of equal thickness for its whole length sags at the clew after 4–5 rolls have been taken in. The cure for this is to glue (Araldite) battens or 'whelps' to the outer end for about $\frac{1}{3}$ to $\frac{1}{2}$ its length, tapering forward to nothing; this causes the leech to build up a slightly larger roll than the luff and consequently lifts the boom end. On a sail test, and if time permits, try reefing her 5–6 rolls. Let the mainsheet fly, put her on a reach under the jib and let go of the tiller; she should sail herself. Keep the halyard taut and let the boom climb up the gooseneck track as it turns, paying out halyard as required. If a boat is hard to reef and a major defect is the cause this is a very serious disadvantage. Finally, be fair; you can't have everything and the perfect cruiser has yet to be designed. A good compromise for the size and the price is what you are looking for.

Additional Notes

Sail handling

While the value of a roller headsail in cruising is beyond question it is not unknown for the sail to jam so that it will neither roll up nor unroll. In worsening conditions this could pose serious problems. Sometimes turns of line jam each other in the drum and all that is needed is a little extra power, perhaps by taking the line to a sheet winch. Plainly, though, undue force must not be used if the cause of the jam is not known. In some cases also a jam can be caused by the halyard of the sail rolling up with it; this depends upon the type.

Yachting Monthly carried out experiments in a rising force 6 to find out how best to cope. Being unable to unroll and then lower the sail the experimenters tried removing the sheets and simply unwrapping or wrapping (according to what is needed) the sail around the stay. This might be possible in light airs but it was not practicable in force 6. Use of the spinnaker halyard as a wrap-round was not practical either, as the turns were forced upwards by the flogging sail. The best approach, they found, is to sheet the mainsail hard in and motor in tight circles. One sheet was removed and other taken bodily forward so that a crew member could retain control while passing the coil around the rolling sail. In this particular case it required a dizzy twenty-two circles.

Motoring in a circle is also the best way to deal with a large genoa which has 'hour-glassed' (the head of the sail on one side of the stay, the foot on the other, plus several turns). This can happen on a run in a following sea and as the sail cannot be lowered the boat is out of control until the mess has been cleared.

Avoiding collision

Read and understand the International Regulations for Preventing Collision at Sea. Rule 17, dealing with two sailing vessels meeting, has been altered of recent years and beginners under instruction by experienced but out of touch old-timers may be wrongly informed. The present rule is that the vessel with the *wind on her starboard side*, whether running or beating, has right of way. If both vessels each have the wind on the same side (whether both on the port side or both on the starboard side), the vessel which is to *leeward* has right of way. Thus a vessel beating on port tack gives way to one running with the wind on her starboard (her boom to port) and a boat beating on, say, starboard tack has right of way over one running on starboard. *Note*: under the *old rule* a closehauled vessel had rights over a running vessel in all cases.

It is assumed that the basic rules are known. Remember that starting an auxiliary engine is to assume the role of a power vessel, and thus the rules of behaviour for power in relation to sail or other power craft will apply. Yachts racing are by courtesy given right of way by other yachts not racing except where this is unreasonable or likely to create a confusing situation. Remember that, no matter what actual rights a vessel may have, avoiding collision is the aim. A rigid adherence to a right of way may have to go by the board as a last resort if the giving way vessel is under difficulty in complying. Right of sail over power is limited by common sense. Furthermore, and this is very important, in confined waters or buoyed channels a large powered vessel may have sovereign right of way according to area rulings.

Unfortunately the rule that power gives way to sail is one of the few things which the beginner seems to remember and many seek to enforce it without realising their danger. A large ship cannot stop suddenly even with her engine going full astern, nor can she alter course as quickly as a small yacht. She is forced to keep up a speed which gives her proper steerageway and this alone carries her onward at a rate which makes it impossible to pin-wheel in and out of a fleet of small craft. At close quarters vision is very limited ahead from a position on the bridge of a big ship, particularly in the case of many container ships, and the last-minute alteration of course of a yacht tacking across the bows may not be seen.

Alterations of course should be definite ones and made in good time, particularly at night. Confusion over intentions is dangerous and needless and it is usually safer to shape a course to pass astern of any ship rather

Fig. 57 A: Starboard tack (black) has right of way. B: Black on port has ROW over white, to windward, on port. C: Black on starboard has ROW over white on port tack. D: Black on starboard has ROW over white on port. E: Both on starboard but white is windward boat and must give way. F: White is the windward boat and must give way. G: White is the overtaking vessel and must give way. H: White is on starboard but because she has her engine running (driving) she becomes a powered vessel and must give way. I: Yacht must give way to a vessel restricted by her draught in a dredged channel. J: Both alter course to starboard. K: Black is under sail and has ROW over white which is under power. L: White has the other vessel on *her* own starboard bow and must give way. M: Separation lanes; yacht must cross at right angles or as nearly so as possible, and give way to big ship traffic.

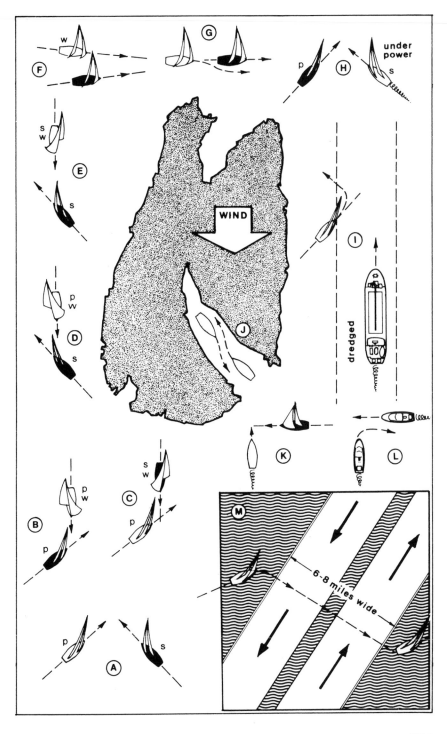

than try to force a right-of-way which, in many waterways and all separation zones, *does not exist.*

Traffic separation lanes

In areas of concentrated shipping, 'lanes' have been established which (should) channel heavy shipping along eastbound or westbound (north or southbound) lanes, thus minimising the risk of head-on collisions. Strict rules forbid transverse crossing and where this is unavoidable craft must cross as nearly at right angles to the traffic stream as possible and at the best speed. Small yachts shall NOT impede big ships in such waters.

Having regard to the difficulties of slow moving small craft in strong tides, the problem may exist at times in which a course to cross at, say, 45 degrees, is faster than one at 90 degrees. The yachtsman must do his best to hasten his crossing time, using his engine to this end but, as stated elsewhere in this book, heading up too much to allow for tide may confuse approaching shipping as to the real course.

Keep an orderly ship

No matter how easy-going one may be at home, a boat at sea is different and the ability to act quickly in an emergency largely depends upon being able to get at various items of gear quickly. Sails should be free in their tracks, halyards ready to run, anchor cable free to run by virtue of having checked it prior to anchoring, perhaps by hauling up a little chain and letting it run back into the locker.

Cockpit lockers are notorious hotbeds of disorder and warps should be hung up, secured with a slip-hitch, the kedge free to be got at and the essential boarding ladder (if not kept on deck) given a priority stowage. Coil, coil and coil sheets again and again by force of habit so that they will always run, keep engine and other spares in a known and handy place, carry the right tools to cope with any normal shipboard job and don't allow the chart table drawer to become a free-for-all stowage for suntan oil and camera accessories. Think out every move in advance, tell the crew what is to be attempted and don't handle the boat faster than the crew can handle the sheets.

The dinghy

Ferrying shorewards and back in the dinghy can be the most difficult and even dangerous operation concerned with cruising. Life-jackets should be worn if there is any chance of a rough ride, and always at night. If you go ashore in daylight expecting to return at night always take an anchor and line, a torch and something to act as a bailer. Even inflatables need this sort of gear aboard them.

There are several key dangers. Transferring from yacht to dinghy and back again, changing places at the paddles when the rower becomes tired, and overloading, perhaps as a consequence of going ashore when conditions were a windless calm and finding that conditions for the return trip are very different. The rule for boarding the dinghy is bowman first, who holds on to keep the dinghy steady, stern passenger next, and centre-sitting rower last. If there is a strong tidal current running past the yacht it is better for the rower on the centre thwart to enter first so that the bows are not depressed, then the stern, and last the bow passenger. On returning, board the yacht in reverse order, but remember that first to climb on board must take and secure the dinghy painter.

Changing places in a loaded dinghy of any kind is bad news and if the rower needs help it is better for the person sitting aft to help by pushing the oars while the rower pulls. *Never* overload. A rigid dinghy can be swamped as she pitches, taking water in over the stern. Make two trips or don't go at all. Even with an outboard motor the risk remains, and perhaps it is even greater because an overloaded dinghy motored too fast takes even more water aboard.

Anchoring

Chain versus rope

Best tested short link galvanised chain costs more than double the price of equivalent nylon rope. For example $\frac{1}{4}$ in (6.3 mm) chain with a breaking strain of 4400 lb versus $\frac{7}{16}$ in (10 mm) nylon breaking at 5500 lb. Breaking strain in this case is about double the working load. Another example would be chain $\frac{5}{16}$ in (8 mm), breaking strain 880 lb, versus $\frac{5}{8}$ in (16 mm) nylon, breaking strain 9500 lb. Chain is heavy but compact and easy to self-stow by reason of its weight; rope is bulky, lighter, but not easy to stow unless special provision is made for it. Chain usually run out cleanly but rope has to be paid out by hand to avoid tangles. Rope bought from a reputable maker is a known quantity and condition can be gauged by simply looking at it; chain on the other hand, and especially bought with a second-hand boat, has been known to have faults due to auto-welding during manufacture.

Against the above arguments it must be said that chain, by reason of its weight and catenary curve in use, offers over double the holding power for a given scope and drag; more scope of rope is needed, and therefore the cost advantage of rope versus chain is reduced somewhat. The usual compromise is a two-fathom length of chain (usually quoted as 5 m) attached to the anchor and a nylon warp for the rest. Compared to an all-chain scope this rope/chain arrangement is improved over plain rope to between half and three-quarters the holding of all-chain.

The holding power of an anchor varies from 2–7 times its own weight for a Fisherman to 30–100 times the weight for a Danforth or CQR. The load which a boat can put on her anchor in a gale, but not plunging or sheering, is roughly her overall length × 2, × 10 (thus a 20-footer is 20 × 2 × 10 = 400 lb load), and much less under normal conditions; the effect of jerking and sheering in a seaway can double and treble the overall loads.

Paint the chain or rope at leadline intervals in similar markings as a guide to the amount of chain you have let go or have still to haul in.

Never throw an anchor over the side – it might catch in your clothing and take you with it. A 'shackle' of chain is 15 fathoms. Anchors used with rope instead of chain should be one size heavier. When mooring alongside with *nylon* lines in average heights of tide, make the lines fast at half-tide and they'll stretch enough to be right at low water.

Always mark your mooring-buoy with the displacement or TM tonnage of your yacht.

Drift lead

If dragging at anchor is suspected, lower the hand-lead to the sea-bed and allow it enough slack line so that the normal swing and surge of the boat will not disturb the lead. If the yacht begins to drag, the line will be found stretching taut.

Chain collar

A fouled stockless anchor (CQR, Meon, or Danforth) can often be cleared by the following method. Take a short length of chain and join the ends to make a 'collar' of about 12 inches diameter. Lowered down the taut up-and-down cable on a line, the collar will slide over the upright anchor shank, the cable is then slackened, simultaneously jerking upwards on the collar line. With a little luck the anchor will be tripped clear of the obstruction.

Emergency anchoring

Unless the anchorage is known to be excellent holding ground, such as firm mud/sand, and there is good shelter from rough water, strong or gale force winds call for mounting an anchor watch. Objects in line ashore can be watched as a warning of the boat beginning to drag. Should she drag, and if letting out more scope of cable doesn't stop her, you should be prepared to consider moving somewhere else under engine. If there is no other proper anchorage and the weather forecast is serious it may be possible to find a mud shore under the shelter of the land and anchor where the boat will take the ground – uncomfortable, but provided a violent wind shift is not expected which would make it a lee shore later on it is preferable to losing the boat or sustaining heavy damage.

If there is room astern it is sometimes possible to let go a second anchor while dragging so that the boat comes up on both in due course. Alternatively, motor out to one side a little way and let go the second anchor so that the boat rides to a 'V'. The second anchor must be at least 75 per cent of the weight of the main one if this is to be worth while.

The use of an anchor weight (guardian or angel) is highly recommended. What is needed is an outsize shackle which can be lowered down the cable on a light line and attached to which is a weight such as a lead pig or scale weight of around 20–30 lb. The pin of the shackle must be seized so that it cannot roll itself undone and the weight should be lowered one-third to half the way down the cable. The effect will be to dampen any snatching and keep the pull in a more horizontal line.

Navigation

A chart table and a bookshelf are essential for ordinary basic navigation. Either a permanent table big enough to accommodate an Admiralty chart folded once, or a removable table capable of being fixed firmly and positioned where the navigator can sit at it out of the way of random foot traffic, should be built. It needs a drawer underneath, folded chart size, a pencil rack and space off the chart surface to put the various instruments. The bookshelf within arm's reach takes the almanac, tidal atlas, pilot books, logbook and so forth. A proper chart table has a psychological effect on the navigator, inviting more careful work. It isn't only a place to work, though, it is a place for pondering.

Passing headlands

Even when passing safely outside a headland it is helpful to know distance off, especially if on watch alone and the helm can't be left for a proper fix to be taken. If the log is read when the headland is bearing $26\frac{1}{2}$ degrees *forward of the beam* and then read again when it is bearing $26\frac{1}{2}$ degrees *abaft the beam* the run between is equal to the distance off when abeam of the headland (this assumes little or no tidal current).

Passing at a safe distance

Based on the 1 in 60 rule, i.e. in a distance of 60 miles a 1-degree deviation from course will total 1 mile at the end of the passage, if a light (for instance) is seen ahead at a distance of 15 miles (one-quarter of 60) and it is desired to give it a 4-mile offing, bring it 16 degrees on the bow – or 8 degrees for a 2-mile offing.

Logbook

Rule vertically as follows: time, log, course to steer, barometer, notes (i.e. headlands abeam, fixes, weather, etc.). It is important that all courses steered, positions estimated or checked, leeway and any information relevant to the plotting should be noted. Chart plots should be marked on the chart with time and log-reading. Thus, the workings can be gone over from the beginning of the passage in case of later uncertainty.

Compass deviation

An outboard motor stowed close can cause 40 degrees of deviation. Simple check: mount a second, accurate, borrowed compass on the coachroof or in any place where is no possibility of deviation from metalwork. Align it with the lubber-line exactly fore and aft. When the boat is just afloat on the mooring have two people watching ship's and coachroof compasses and one man wading overboard to swing the cruiser right round her mooring, heading on each point of the compass. Note readings as in the following example. Coachroof compass N, Ship's compass 005; Coachroof NE, Ship's 046; Coachroof E, Ship's 93, etc., etc. The deviation card would then read:

For N   . . . steer 005
NE . . . steer 046
E   . . . steer 093
etc. around the compass and . . .
W   . . . steer 264 etc.

Get under way with the engine running and check by steering on each heading; also under sail steeply heeled (sitting to leeward maybe). If there is much extra heeling error, a tip suggested by Robert Tucker is to make an inclinometer (small pendulum) marked with heeling error on each degree of heel.

A simple alternative way by which a steering compass can be checked by accuracy on all headings is to tow a man astern in the inflatable dinghy with a bucket towing astern to steady it. By means of a carefully sighted hand-bearing compass he can align mast and backstay and call out when he is 'ON' for each heading. The yacht, meanwhile, is motored absolutely straight on each heading, the helmsman noting actual ship's head at the time of each 'ON' call.

A more sophisticated method is to take a dummy compass or pelorus. Cut out the compass rose from an old chart and glue it to stiff card, then contrive some sort of sighting arm which can revolve about a centre drawing pin. This card must be mounted on the top of the coachroof with its N/S line exactly fore-and-aft. You need quiet water and a prominent object five or more miles away. On the chart plot the bearing from your manoeuvring point (just off a navigation buoy perhaps) accurately as a *magnetic* bearing. Under engine, and very slowly, make a series of runs across the line of the bearing. Each time the line is 'ON', note the dummy compass bearing. If your steering compass is accurate its heading will match the heading shown by the dummy, but it will probably be plus or minus a few degrees on some headings. Work right round the compass from N through E, S, etc., either as above or in increments of 20 degrees.

Calibrating the log

It can't be assumed that all that is needed is a couple of runs over a measured mile, one with and one against the current, and an average taken. In an ideal world a period of slack water with no current at all would be found, but this is unlikely unless a lake or a land-locked tideless area can be used. It is better, then, to choose a period when any tidal rate is likely to be fairly constant in one direction. Make two runs at constant engine revs, turning the boat at the end of each without altering revs and noting the exact time and log-reading for each run. Divide the distance of each leg by the time taken on each run, add the results, then halve them – this cancels out tide effect. For example:

1 nautical mile in 10 minutes
Speed = $1/10 \times 60 = 6.0$ knots downstream
1 nautical mile in 15 minutes
Speed = $1/5 \times 60 = 4.0$ knots upstream
Hence $\dfrac{6.0 + 4.0}{2} = 5.0$ knots average speed

To find the tidal rate, subtract the lower figure from the higher and divide by 2 to produce the average tidal rate
$\dfrac{6.0 - 4.0}{2} = 1$ knot tidal rate

Knowing that there is a 1-knot tidal rate means that we can find the distance the log *should* have registered instead of what it *actually* registered, e.g. with a 1-knot current with us on our 10-minute downstream run we will have gained one-sixth of a nautical mile (0.17) and so the log should read 1 mile minus 0.17 = 0.83 naut. m. Any difference between this figure and what the log actually reads will be the error. Find the error in the same way for the upstream leg and then find the average.

A much easier way to go about determining log accuracy is to check it whenever possible on buoy-to-buoy runs, making minor allowances for current and building up an overall picture of whether it tends to over-read or under-read and whether the error is great or insignificant. Of the two, slight over-reading is preferable.

Timing drift, Dutchman's log

One knot equals roughly 100 feet per minute. Measure a handy length along the deck such as edge of forehatch to other end of cockpit – a distance of perhaps 16 feet. Throw overboard, ahead of the cruiser, a tightly rolled ball of paper (if wind is practically non-existent) or an empty bottle on a length of fine fishline for recovery. Start the stop-watch as it passes the first position and stop it as a watcher shouts 'NOW' at the aft position. If the time taken was, say, 3 seconds, the sum is resolved quite simply:

$$\frac{16 \times 60}{3 \times 100} \text{ or } 3\frac{1}{5} \text{ knots.}$$

Dry-swim navigation

For the purpose of getting to know the chart and finding tidal information quickly, fireside navigation on winter evenings is the next best thing to actual practice.

The 'dry-swimming' rules outlined here are not unlike some aspects of wartime instruction, save that the inclusion of dice and so forth makes more a game of it.

You will need small-scale passage-charts (one chart is enough so long as it deals with waters which are sufficiently littered with navigational hazards to make it interesting), a copy of a nautical almanac, a pair of dice, navigator's dividers and parallel rules, plus a couple of coloured-head pins to represent the yachts.

Starting from an agreed port or river, the first player glances at his watch and looks up tidal information for that very moment. Whatever it may be he must start at once – and it may mean a foul tide out of the river, for instance. The dice are then thrown, both together, and the combined reading taken as the 'log-reading' and since it may be as much as twelve, this is reckoned as being the total of three hours sailing (a low number then simulates a lessening wind). He then checks tidal set for three hours from starting and plots his position. The second player may now start, plotting his tides as they would be three hours after the first player set out. Thus the two yachts sail on, making good three-hour runs and poor ones, being set into all manner of troubles by the tides, having to cross shoal water and checking tide-height for that hour, etc.

The introduction of 'changes of wind direction', forfeits and extra throws can be engineered around the throwing of doubles as in an ordinary dice game. If all relevant information is looked up with each move (allowing 30 seconds to find a light characteristic in the almanac for instance), the value of this game is extremely high and it is also a fine way for a couple (or more) of sailing people to pass a winter evening. By using the charts of next year's proposed cruise there is even more advantage to be had.

Practice at plotting bearings can also be had without going to sea by making a winter weekend trip to the coast armed with a chart, a drawing-board for a chart-table and bearing-compass, rules, etc. Bearings taken of buoys, harbour lights, lightships, and so on, plotted from the land, will give a fix which is easy to check for accuracy. Using an Ordnance Survey map in the same manner, only inland, gives the same opportunity of pin-pointing mistakes but, of course, lacks the added benefit of working with sea-marks.

Chart and compass

(1) *True north* is a geographer's line taken from pole to pole. Broadly speaking, the top of a chart is north and the bottom is south and the chart is laid out to True north.

(2) *Magnetic north* is the ever-altering point, slightly off-centre, to which a magnetic compass points.

(3) *Variation* is the difference in angle between True and Magnetic.

(4) *Deviation* is the angle by which a magnetic compass is pulled out of line by ironwork, etc., placed too near to it.

(5) If, for example, the chart is printed with its Magnetic compass-rose showing the exact variation and the compass is exactly accurate, courses steered and courses plotted using Magnetic north bearings would be identical.

(6) If all courses steered and bearings taken are to be plotted on the chart using True north they must be adjusted for variation. This might involve adding or subtracting large amounts (perhaps 9 degrees).

(7) By using the Magnetic rose on an up-to-date chart, figures dealt with will probably be no more than 2 degrees out and mistakes less likely to be drastic.

Just for the record: converting Magnetic to True, etc.: When applying Magnetic variation and compass deviation, whether working from chart to compass or compass to chart the rule is: if it is west, the compass is 'best', if it is east the compass is 'least'. In other words, to convert a Magnetic bearing to True when the local Magnetic variation is, say, 8 degrees westerly, west being compass best, the 8 degrees would be subtracted. If there was also a 4-degree easterly compass deviation, to allow for east being least, the 4 degrees would be added. The resultant figure would be a True bearing, all the inaccuracies of the magnet having been ironed out. The crux of the matter lies in the references to the compass being 'best' and 'least'. If this is understood then working in reverse, i.e. converting True to Magnetic or compass, follows the same rule. A True bearing on the chart might be 130, and magnetic variation 9 degrees west, 'west compass best'. In other words the True figure must be made 'better' if it is to become magnetic or compass and so the 9 degrees will be added to the True figure, giving 139 degrees magnetic which will be steered. If there is a deviation figure this too must be applied.

With westerly variation common to the British Isles the word MUTS (magnet-unto-true-subtract) is a memory aid.

(8) Working on the chart Magnetic rose only the small differences of

variation and deviation have to be accounted for: compass-card pulled east or west of its source of attraction and chart rose showing variation as it was several years ago instead of at the present. Westerly variation which has 'decreased' or grown less is called 'easterly' error. Compass deviation when the card is pulled to the right (clockwise) by local interference is also easterly error. If the chart has 2 degrees E error and the compass has 3 degrees E error the total of 5 degrees east is applied. Again: 'To the east compass least'. Add working from chart to compass.

If chart variation has decreased during the age of the chart by, say, 3 degrees, giving a chart error of 3 degrees E, and there is a deviation of, say, 5 degrees W on a particular course, the error to plot would be the difference, or 2 degrees W.

Passage plan (before starting)

Study chart and tidal atlas, and tide-table for the standard port upon which the atlas is based (i.e. Dover, Cardiff, etc.). Study local tide-table for suitable time to leave river or harbour. Estimate distance to the next stage on passage, estimate average speed needed in order to carry a fair tide, estimate the effect of light head winds and foul-turning tide, is there alternative shelter *en route*? Study entry to ports or rivers in case of tidal difficulties. Listen to shipping forecasts to the latest possible hour before departure.

On passage

Keep an up-to-date track. Avoid tide rips and overfalls, follow all shipping forecasts, watch the barometer, plot tidal streams even when it is possible to navigate visually (against those times when you will need your skill at working out an off-set). Plan to arrive up-tide of your destination whenever possible. Before entering but not too long before, work out the depth of water likely to be found in the charted anchorages. Check pilotage instructions for port entering signals likely to be displayed on signal masts, etc. If there is doubt about the weather don't hesitate to use the engine in order to maintain average speed according to conditions. Know where you are all the time.

Night-sailing

Lights just seen or dipping

Find a position where the eye is either five or ten-feet above sea level, look up the lighthouse or lightship in the Lights List (in your almanac) and find the height of the light (see table).

The heights of lights are given as height above *high* water. Thus any discrepancy in range or distance off due to applying the table at a time other than high water will have the effect of putting the navigator 'nearer' than he actually is – a safety factor.

Lights seen dipping

Height of light in feet	*Height of eye* 5 feet	10 feet	*Height of light in feet*	*Height of eye* 5 feet	10 feet
	Distance off in miles				
40	9¾	11	210	19¼	20¼
50	10¾	11¾	220	19½	20¾
60	11½	12½	230	20	21
70	12¼	13¼	240	20½	21½
80	13	14	250	20¾	21¾
90	13½	14½	260	21	22¼
100	14	15	270	21½	22½
110	14½	15¾	280	21¾	23
120	15¼	16¼	290	22	23¼
130	15¾	16¾	300	22½	23½
140	16¼	17¼	310	22¾	24
150	16¾	17¾	320	23	24¼
160	17	18¼	330	23½	24½
170	17½	18½	340	23¾	24¾
180	18	19	350	24	25
190	18½	19½	400	25½	26½
200	18¾	20	450	27	28

In the event of the light being relatively low in height while the range of tide is unusually great, the range of tide (if at a time other than HW) should be *added* to the height of the light if greater accuracy is needed.

Light abbreviations (new revised)

F. (fixed) continuous light
Oc. (single occulting) steady light, regular short periods of dark
Oc.(2) (group occulting) in this case groups of two eclipses
Iso. (isophase) periods of light and dark of equal length
Fl. (single flash) not less than 50 per minute
L.Fl. (long flashing) regular flashes of 2 or more seconds
Fl.(3) (group flash) in this case in groups of three
Q. (continuous quick) 50–60 per minute
Q.(3) (group quick) in this case groups of three
IQ. (interrupted quick) rapid flashing interrupted by regular eclipses
VQ. (very quick) continuous flashing at 100 or 120 per minute in bursts regularly repeated

VQ.(3) (group very quick) groups at regularly repeated intervals
IVQ (interrupted very quick) groups with total eclipse at regular intervals
UQ. (ultra quick) 240 to 300 flashes per minute, regularly repeated
IUQ (interrupted ultra quick) groups with eclipse at intervals of long
    duration
Mo.(K) (morse code) repeated signal letter(s)
F.Fl (fixed and flashing) steady with brilliant flash at regular intervals
AL.WR. (alternating) in this case white/red in successive flashes

Lights

In vessels of less than 12 metres length, sidelights must have a minimum
range of 1 mile, masthead lights and stern lights 2 miles. Vessels of less
than 12 metres may carry a combined masthead light. Oil-lamps with
proper cone glasses may meet the above requirements although the
dioptric lens usually accompanying them concentrates the light beam
along a horizontal band which, when heeled, may be shining into the
water on one side and upwards on the other. The biggest problem is to
know whether your lights have been seen; very often they have not. The
safest assumption is that they have not been seen and it is wise to behave
as if this were so. Yacht batteries are another problem. Few yachts cruise
with their batteries better than in a state of half-charge and by the early
hours of the morning they are frequently so weak as to be useless.

Flares

White and green hand-held pyrotechnics are used to draw attention to
position and presence, blue flares are for summoning a pilot, red flares
signal distress. White flares can be ordered from any chandler. A fire-arm
certificate is needed for a Very light pistol.

Life buoy lights

Usually operate by capsizing into float position, thus tripping switch to
dry battery. Bright flash. Should be tested regularly.

Rule of the road

Vessels meeting head on: When red and green you see ahead, steer to
starboard, show your red. Converging: Green to green or red to red,
perfect safety go ahead. (*Note*: maintain a close watch for any change of
course.) White lights are four times brighter than red and five times
brighter than green. All lights on the chart are white unless otherwise
stated. Range of lightship rarely more than 11 miles. Compass lighting:
Do not use a single wire and an earthed bulb, run the wires in a pair close
together or the compass magnet will be deviated.

Fog

Foghorns

Clarion compressed-gas type give 100-decibel volume (300 two-second blasts per container); hand-operated or mouth-horns give less volume. Compressed-gas horns may 'freeze' at the reed in dense fog and in doing so become almost useless.

Visibility

Mist and fog are low cloud, haze is formed by solid particles suspended in moisture. Range is as follows. Thick fog, visibility limited to 1 cable (200 yards). Fog, limited to 2 cables. Moderate fog, less than ½ mile. Poor visibility, under 2 miles. Moderate visibility, under 5 miles. Good visibility, under 10 miles. Very good visibility, under 30 miles. Excellent visibility, over 30 miles.

Check the range of visibility in thick fog by dropping a crumpled newspaper overboard and timing its disappearance against the speed of the yacht. At night a ball of paper soaked in paraffin and set alight can be timed.

It is easy to be overtaken by fog conditions without at first realising it, but in hazy weather once the horizon disappears be wary because unless there is shipping or land in view to give a guide to distance, the horizon becomes a woolly emptiness which could as easily be a few hundred yards away as a mile or more distant.

Foggy conditions are usually synonymous with calm, but occasionally (particularly off west Brittany) a fresh breeze combines with dense fog, and in those waters, fast tidal currents. This dreadful combination means that the boat is sailing fast and making too much noise for a listening watch to be kept; it also imposes a great strain on the navigator if land is in the offing. If possible, seek open water clear of major shipping, or slow the boat right down until you have good steerageway in case avoiding action is needed. Be sure that your radar reflector is displayed to the best possible advantage.

Weather

Clouds as warning of advancing depression

Cirrus, high, delicate-looking tufted or feathery white cloud spreading in from the west to become cirro-stratus or a thin veil which haloes the sun or moon, and later forming lower alto-stratus which is grey and fibrous-looking. When the sky is covered to seven-eighths, bad weather is imminent. In general the steady descent of the cloud base is a sign of bad weather. Haloes can occur with fine settled summer weather, but a check of the general situation is wise. Isolated patches of blue sky in a clouded bad weather sky are a sign of improvement. Damp winds may often be observed by feeling the ropes and sails as a guide. They tend to swell and feel clammy. This may be a sign of an advancing front.

Barometer (generalisations only)

Rapid rise: unsettled weather.

Gradual rise: settled weather.

Rise with dry air and becoming colder (summer): wind from north. After rain an improvement.

Rise with moist air and cold: wind and rain from north.

Rise with southerly wind: fine weather.

Steady glass with normal temperature for the season and dry air: good weather continuing.

Rapid fall: stormy weather.

Rapid fall, wind westerly: stormy weather from the north.

Fall with northerly wind: storm with rain or hail, snow in winter.

Fall with increasing dampness in the air and humidity: southerly wind and rain.

Fall with dry air: becoming colder (snow in winter).

Fall after settled warm weather: rainy squalls.

The Beaufort Scale

(0) Below 1 knot. Calm. Sea mirror-like.

(1) Up to 3. Light air ripples like dimples. Steerageway.

(2) 4 to 6. Light Breeze. Wavelets but no crests. Good handling breeze, gives maybe 3 knots.

(3) 7 to 10. Gentle Breeze. Large wavelets and small crests, waves 2 ft high. Cruisers heel and sail well 4 knots.

(4) 11 to 16. Moderate Breeze. Small waves getting longer with white crests up to $3\frac{1}{2}$ ft. May need one reef at sea, excellent sailing.

(5) 17 to 21. Fresh Breeze. Moderate waves, white horses and some spray. Two or three reefs and smaller jibs. Heavy going to windward at sea.

(6) 22 to 27. Strong Breeze. Large waves forming and white horses everywhere with spray. Fully reefed and storm jib. Bad conditions in a fast weather-going tide.

(7) 28 to 33. Near Gale. Heaped sea with foam in streaks. Small cruisers should be in shelter or making for shelter with care if running. Main down to 5 ft or stowed. Storm jib.

(8) 34 to 40. Gale. Moderately high waves, spindrift and foam blowing down-wind in long banners. Small cruisers may have hove-to or

scudded with fenders, coils of rope, etc., towed astern long before this but in the open sea they must now do so if the sea is big.

Above force 8 the scale continues Strong Gale, Storm, Violent Storm, and Hurricane (9, 10, 11 and 12). In the open sea, force 8 can raise an 18-ft sea, but if there is land to windward it will be far less. Height of sea increases rapidly as fetch or distance offshore increases. Tide and nature of sea-bed also affect the size and type of sea. In any wind force above 3 to 4 the small cruiser must stay well clear of tidal rips and overfalls.

Local forecasts

Most regional radio stations around the coast offer good local forecasts and the value of these and the local forecasts obtainable by dialling a regional number should not be underestimated. The shipping forecast areas cover great tracts of sea and while a forecast may be very accurate over the major part of the area, local coastal regions within it may be experiencing very different conditions.

Tape recordings

The speed at which shipping forecasts are read is often too fast for the untrained yachtsman to write or record on a Met. chart. The use of a battery powered tape recorder is recommended. Thus the listener can note down as much as he is able and then play back at his own speed later on.

Bad weather

Breakers may begin in 2 fathoms with an onshore wind and ebb tide. Wave height is reckoned as two per cent of the square of the wind velocity in knots, thus a 10-knot breeze gives a 2-foot wave. Estimate by sighting as the crests come into line with the yacht in the trough. Calculate eye-level above water line.

Open sea waves average 50 : 1 length : height. When shoaling water equals half the wave length in depth the waves begin to alter form. By the time the depth is ten per cent the wave breaks. Breakers can be reckoned to form in water which is as deep as the wave is high.

A yacht running before a sea must be overtaken. If she tends to dwell on the crests she is in danger of being broached.

Heavy Weather Sailing by K. Adlard Coles (published by Adlard Coles Ltd) is a classic work on yachts in bad weather. It relates mostly to slightly larger craft and it is quite frightening in parts. However, for the conscientious owner of a small boat it is essential reading.

Motor sailing

It is not always advantageous to use the engine and sails together in order to punch to windward in a blow. Unless the propeller is deeply immersed in solid water and relatively slow turning, large and of coarse pitch, the heeling and pitching of the yacht combine to keep the propeller racing in light water near the surface. Better to motor dead to windward, albeit very slowly. Motor sailing, with a minimum of sail tightly sheeted, may however be more comfortable. The use of the engine with sails to help the yacht to point up and make ground in short, steep seas is another matter. In this case the engine is run at half revs (or less) and it serves merely to help her carry her momentum.

Index